BEING A PHILOSOPHER

BEING A PHILOSOPHER

The History of a Practice

D.W. Hamlyn

London and New York

First published 1992
by Routledge
11 New Fetter Lane, London EC4P 4EE

Simultaneously published in the USA and Canada
by Routledge
a division of Routledge, Chapman and Hall, Inc.
29 West 35th Street, New York, NY 10001

© 1992 D.W. Hamlyn

Typeset in 10 on 12 point Bembo by
Falcon Typographic Art Ltd, Fife, Scotland
Printed in Great Britain by
TJ Press (Padstow) Ltd, Padstow, Cornwall

All rights reserved. No part of this book may be reprinted or reproduced or utilized in any form or by any electronic, mechanical, or other means, now known or hereafter invented, including photocopying and recording, or in any information storage or retrieval system, without permission in writing from the publishers.

British Library Cataloguing in Publication Data
Hamlyn, D.W. (David Walter)
Being a philosopher: the history of a practice.
I. Title
190

Library of Congress Cataloging in Publication Data
Hamlyn, D.W.
Being a philosopher: the history of a practice / D.W. Hamlyn.
p. cm.
Includes bibliographical references and index.
1. Philosophy – Study and teaching – History. 2. Philosophers.
I. Title.
B52.H25 1992
100 – dc20   91-40390

ISBN 0-415-02968-6

To Eileen

CONTENTS

Preface	ix
Introduction	1
1 THE ANCIENT GREEKS	**7**
The Presocratics	7
The Sophists	11
Socrates	15
Plato and the Academy	17
Aristotle and the Lyceum	23
The later schools	29
2 THE MIDDLE AGES AND RENAISSANCE	**35**
The early Middle Ages	35
Abelard and dialectic	37
The mediaeval universities and the curriculum	39
The rediscovery of Aristotle: St Thomas Aquinas	43
Duns Scotus and Ockham	46
The Renaissance	50
3 THE SIXTEENTH AND SEVENTEENTH CENTURIES	**52**
The late Renaissance: Bacon and Hobbes	52
Descartes and Cartesianism	55
Spinoza	60
Leibniz	61
Locke	65
The intellectual milieu and the limitations of the universities	69
4 THE EIGHTEENTH CENTURY	**73**
The Enlightenment	73

CONTENTS

Berkeley	76
Hume	79
Scottish universities and the Scottish Enlightenment	83
The German universities: Kant	87

5 THE NINETEENTH CENTURY — 92
- *The general situation in England* — 92
- *J.S. Mill and nineteenth-century English philosophy* — 93
- *Journals and philosophical societies* — 98
- *The new University of Berlin: Fichte* — 101
- *Hegel and the Hegelians* — 103
- *The critics of Hegel: Schopenhauer and Marx* — 108
- *Romanticism: Kierkegaard and Nietzsche* — 114
- *Late nineteenth-century German philosophy* — 119
- *The situation in France* — 121
- *The rise of philosophy in the USA* — 123

6 THE TWENTIETH CENTURY — 127
- *The professionalism of twentieth-century philosophy* — 127
- *Institutional arrangements: the significance of teaching* — 128
- *The exceptions in Britain: Russell and Wittgenstein* — 137
- *Other institutional factors in Britain and the USA* — 146
- *The situation in Europe: Germany and elsewhere* — 151
- *France* — 156

7 CONCLUSION — 161

Notes — 174
Index — 181

PREFACE

When, in 1987, I produced my *A History of Western Philosophy* (London: Viking), later to be published as *The Penguin History of Western Philosophy*, I adopted the policy of confining myself, by and large, to the philosophical views and arguments of the philosophers discussed. Not all histories of philosophy have taken that form and those that have not have usually tried to put the philosophers in their social and historical context. As far as I know, there has been no previous attempt, certainly no recent attempt, to write a history of philosophical practice. Yet it is probable that what philosophers do is as much a puzzle to the average person, even the average educated person, as what they think. It seemed to me, therefore, that the writing of a history of philosophical practice, even, as I admit, a highly selective or summary history, was both something that I could usefully do when I retired (somewhat early) from my chair at Birkbeck College, University of London and something that might help to put present-day philosophy, as it is carried out, in an illuminating context. This seems particularly relevant when, as now, philosophy and philosophy teaching are under restraints and attacks from the authorities.

It is of course impossible to dissociate philosophical practice entirely from philosophical thinking and theory. What philosophers do is intimately related to what they believe. Hence, in what follows I have from time to time had to say something about the philosophical theories put forward. In some cases, some readers may find these remarks too brief to be illuminating. In that event, I can do no more than refer such readers to other writings in the history of philosophy, including my own *History*, referred to above. Nevertheless, what I shall primarily be concerned with is philosophical practice. I would have described the book as a history of philosophy as an institution were it not for the fact that, given the point that philosophers have sometimes had no direct institutional backing, this might be misleading. In a wider sense, however, this is what the book is – a history of philosophy as an institution, not a set of beliefs.

Most of those to whom I have mentioned the project have either been slightly puzzled by it or (and these are, I think, the majority) have thought it a fascinating idea. Whether the way in which I have given substance to that idea is what they have had in mind I leave it to them to decide. Nevertheless, I am grateful to Professor Ted Honderich for being, as I believe, a member of the latter class, and for urging me to go ahead with the writing of the book, as well as securing its publication. My wife, Eileen, who is an excellent critic of my writing as well as one who has a good sense of the philosophical, has read the typescript and made a number of very useful comments. I am grateful to her for that and for putting up with the circumstances of the book's composition.

I would like, finally, to acknowledge yet again what I have derived from many years of philosophical practice at Birkbeck College, from my colleagues there and, above all, from the many generations of students who have made sure that my enthusiasm for the continuance of the practice of philosophy has been maintained.

INTRODUCTION

Philosophers do not, in my opinion, stand in the highest repute at the moment, at least not in Britain. There is more than one reason for this, and it may be worthwhile to spell out some of them. In due course I shall go into the changing history which lies behind the present situation, from which it may be possible to draw certain morals, apart from its own intrinsic interest.

In Britain, philosophy is now pursued for the most part in universities. There are some philosophical amateurs, in some cases talented amateurs; courses on certain aspects of philosophy are given in other parts of the higher education system apart from universities and polytechnics; and philosophy is now taught in some way and to some degree in certain schools. It remains true that most philosophy is taught in universities, and the subject is mainly pursued and taken forward in universities. The same is probably true in most other countries. It has not always been so, but is so quite generally now. In the course of recent financial cut-backs in universities in Britain, and to a certain extent elsewhere, philosophy has certainly suffered, and there is no doubt that many university administrators see little value in it. The criteria for success in philosophy are obscure; its methods are hard to understand, and it has no obvious connection with hard and tangible objects. There is, finally, the point that philosophers are professionally much involved in criticism and argument. Since Socrates set himself up as the 'gadfly of Athens', philosophers have often functioned as pin-pricks for, and sometimes have been the bane of, authorities.

It is not just that. It might indeed be argued that it is the institutionalization of philosophy that has worked to its disadvantage. Is it not the case that the two greatest philosophers in Britain this century – Bertrand Russell and Ludwig Wittgenstein –

had at most a somewhat tangential relation with universities? May not real philosophical progress depend on a relative freedom from such an institutionalized framework? These are questions which I must consider and try to answer in due course.

A point of a quite different kind is that Anglo-Saxon philosophy (that is to say, philosophy carried on in the medium of English, or as an echo of this) has become quite technical. There are some philosophers in Britain (and it is a phenomenon which is perhaps less acute in continental Europe and in philosophy of a non-Anglo-Saxon kind) who deplore this. They might claim that it is a product of the domination of natural science and the consequent urge to look as scientific as possible. However that may be, the increasing technicality of philosophy makes it increasingly difficult for it to be assimilated within general culture. This is much less of a problem in, for example, the USA, where the general culture is much more scientifically orientated, and where the very scale of intellectual engagement – the great numbers of those involved – makes it possible for a whole host of different things to co-exist. But England (and I say England, meaning not to include Scotland and Wales) is a country where the dominant ethos, at least at present, is anti-intellectual. Most philosophers have experienced the horrifying and possibly horrified silence that follows the admission that that is what one is. Many people cannot tolerate what they cannot understand and what they think is beyond them.

But, it might be said, there is nothing new in all this. Have I not already made reference to Socrates' role as the 'gadfly of Athens', and did not Athens put him to death at least in part because he pursued that role? No recent philosopher has experienced that fate. The Logical Positivist, Moritz Schlick, was shot by a deranged pupil, but that is not even the exception which proves the rule. Nevertheless, if philosophers insist on being hypercritical, ought they not to expect what they get? There is, however, more to it than that. The Athens of the time of Socrates was, by modern standards, a very small and restricted society. Everyone knew about Socrates. Whatever one believes about the authenticity of the 'Socrates' who appears in Aristophanes' comedy, *The Clouds*, what is there represented as at least a caricature of Socrates would be a pretty poor joke if the average Athenian could not see its relevance, and something of its point. A similar situation is not likely to hold good today, when society is so much larger and so much more complex in nature. Whether Socrates entered into the political affairs of his time is a moot point, though what he had to say no doubt had political relevance. The kind of political activities which Bertrand Russell, in this century, engaged in, and was so well-known for, is exceptional for a contemporary philosopher in Britain (though perhaps less so elsewhere), and some philosophers would regard that part of Russell's life as a kind of philosophical irrelevance. Such attitudes may not add to the popularity of philosophers since they suggest a certain cultural isolationism.

Whatever the proper diagnosis of the reasons why, it cannot be denied that in general philosophy in Britain has come to have less and less of a major role in, at any rate, general or popular culture. One sign of this is that, while thirty years ago it was quite common for philosophical books to be reviewed in the 'quality' Sunday newspapers, this is very rare now, unless the book is by someone who is a 'name' for other reasons. Books on history are still regularly reviewed in this way (though there are some signs of revolt against technicality, even scholarship, here too); but this is not the case with philosophy. Let me repeat – I am speaking only of Britain; I know very much less of what is the case elsewhere. It might be said that philosophers in Britain have only themselves to blame for this state of affairs. They have not cultivated those responsible for whatever goes on in the name of popular culture. I believe this to be at best a half-truth. The element of truth in this accusation derives from a desire on the part of philosophers to be seen as practitioners of a 'respectable academic subject' with its own proper standards. Such a desire is, of course, praiseworthy in itself, but its consequences have to be noted. The question remains about why the disadvantages of those consequences have become more acute in recent years. The answer to that question is probably quite complex, but in providing part of the answer it would not be altogether inappropriate to refer to a certain philistinism which is prevalent – some of which has undoubtedly had to do with governmental 'philosophy'.

A possible response to all this is that it does not really account for the unpopularity of philosophy in comparison with other academic subjects. Of course, some other such subjects – classics, for example – have also come to be regarded in a lesser light than previously; this is often on the grounds of their contemporary 'irrelevance', a judgment which is, at any rate in the case of classics, both false and irrelevant itself. But the unpopularity of philosophy (a state of affairs which, incidentally, is not reflected in those who have had a taste of it, many of whom respond with enthusiasm) derives also from the fear which seems to be a natural product of a lack of understanding of what philosophy is all about. To acquire that understanding it is of course possible to read introductions to the subject, but the difficulties inherent in producing an 'Introduction to Philosophy' which is true to the subject in a way which gives a good sense of it without being condescending to the reader are well-known. There are also available histories of the subject in varying degrees of comprehensiveness, intelligibility, reliability and interest. But such accounts of the thought of philosophers do not always manage to make clear what philosophers do, as distinct from the thoughts and arguments that they produce. (And that I have to mention both thoughts and arguments is itself one small indication that there is a question about what philosophers do; for the relation between the thoughts and the ideas that philosophers have and how they argue in connection with them is one of crucial importance.)

There is also the question of how what philosophers do is received and regarded by those with whom they have to live. When I have tried to explain to those who have asked about the project involved in this book, I have of course made reference to the present standing of philosophy, how it is regarded by contemporary society, and to its institutional character. At the other end of the historical scale, I have made reference to something that took place near the beginnings of philosophy among the Greeks, about which I shall have more to say later. One of the earliest Greek philosophers was Heraclitus of Ephesus. He produced a series of philosophical remarks of an epigrammatic kind. Argument still goes on as to whether he wrote a book, but the epigrams were certainly recorded in some way and passed into the subsequent history of philosophy. Even in the ancient world he was known as 'the riddler' or 'the obscure', and various stories about the oddities of his conduct have been handed down to us. What those oddities amounted to and how much truth there is in the stories are also a matter for argument.

But there is a question to be asked about it all that is not generally asked. This is: What is one to suppose that Heraclitus meant to do with his epigrams, and how did people regard them and what he did with them? Take one example, the remark which is one of two which T.S. Eliot prefixed to his *Four Quartets* – in its more traditional translation 'The way upward is the way downwards.' Is one to suppose that he wrote this down in some way, and for whose benefit and to what point? Or, did he come down into the market-place of Ephesus, as Socrates later did in Athens, and say this either to those standing around or to his friends and associates? And how did they receive it? Did those standing around say or whisper to themselves something like 'There he is, at it again'? But Heraclitus came from an old aristocratic family; Diogenes Laertius says in his life of the philosopher (whatever value can be attached to that) that he 'resigned the kingship to his brother' (IX.6).[1] This may not mean quite what it seems at first sight to say about the political organization of Ephesus at that time. The descendants of the founder of Ephesus were called 'kings', and Heraclitus was probably in the direct line of descent from the founder. So can one expect others to have treated him with a certain respect? If so, such giggling at his remarks as may have taken place must have been behind hands or from some other place of concealment.

But perhaps nothing surprised those present. There is a story, reported again by Diogenes Laertius in his *Lives of Eminent Philosophers* (IX.3), that when Heraclitus was found playing dice with children he said to those who asked him why he so spent his time, 'Why are you surprised, you wretches? Isn't it better to do this than playing politics with you?' His attitudes to his fellow-Ephesians appear to have been always thus. None of that, however, answers the question of what they thought he was up to. They were no doubt puzzled. Were they also interested, intrigued or just bored? What was he doing? These questions may be unanswerable now by us, but perhaps I have said enough to indicate that there is a problem here. It is not quite a philosophical problem, although its solution is not altogether irrelevant to the interpretation of Heraclitus' philosophy. It is in part a sociological and historical problem, and it is one which belongs to the same family as all the questions which I have been raising about the standing of philosophers today. For a philistine populus of Ephesus (if it existed, as it most probably did) would have been no different in this respect from modern philistines.

But as things went on, the position and practice of philosophers changed in very many ways, though not in every way. There is Socrates the gadfly, and Plato the founder of the first philosophical school, but also the man who attempted, no doubt idealistically, to put his political theories to practice in Syracuse, with disastrous results. There is Aristotle, encyclopaedist of philosophy with a rival school and rival organization, but a foreigner in a sometimes antipathetical Athenian society. And so on, through the history of the ancient world. With the coming of the mediaeval world things are very different. Philosophy and its practice become in some ways an offshoot of the activities of the Church, but one in which in due course whole philosophical systems are taught and handed down. The Renaissance, which is in most ways a fallow field philosophically speaking, in turn initiated a new humanism, so that by the late seventeenth century philosophy became for the most part secularized. Some universities had by then been in existence for centuries, but by and large they do not figure to a great extent in the history of philosophy. In different ways the same is true of the seventeenth and eighteenth centuries. The main philosophers of this period were individual scholars who relied on the patronage of a variety of persons and institutions. The rise of the modern university system, particularly in Germany, led to a different situation, and the early stages of this can be seen with the great German philosopher, Kant.

Thereafter, with some important exceptions, it is the universities which determine the course of philosophy, so that today, as I have already pointed out, it is rare to find a leading philosopher who is not also a university teacher. That situation has become quite general. It has inevitably affected the practice of philosophy and perhaps also the character of philosophy. There are, no doubt, morals to be drawn from it all. I hope at any rate to show that if the lay person is to appreciate philosophy he or she must have some sense of the context of its practice. And that is neither obvious nor something simply to be taken for granted.

Let me emphasize, however, that what I shall be concerned with is the practice of philosophy under whatever conditions have made progress in philosophy possible. From time to time I shall indicate that things have gone on in the name of philosophy with which the leading philosophers have had nothing to do, for example, what went on in the universities in the seventeenth and early eighteenth centuries. If someone objects that I underemphasize such things I can reply only that my concern is with the practice of a living philosophy, something that really deserves the name of 'philosophy' and which makes consideration of its practice philosophically worthwhile. Hence my account presupposes a judgment about what has been philosophically worthwhile, and that I freely admit.

1
THE ANCIENT GREEKS

THE PRESOCRATICS

The example of Heraclitus which I mentioned in the Introduction is not a peculiar or isolated one. Nor are the questions which I raised about it in any way artificial. It would be good to know about the exact context in which philosophy was born in ancient Greece, but the circumstances are in any event puzzling. Philosophy, we are usually told, began towards the end of the seventh century BC with Thales of Miletus, was carried on by his disciples Anaximander and Anaximenes, and then moved to Ephesus with Heraclitus. Pythagoras also originated in Ionia, in Samos; but he then moved to southern Italy at Croton, where, as Aristotle would have it, a number of branches of philosophy grew up under the 'Italians'. Only later, in the fifth century BC, did philosophy come to mainland Greece, and then initially in the person of Anaxagoras, who came again from Asia Minor.

I am not concerned here to speculate, as many others have done, about why philosophy was born in Greek colonies in Asia Minor, and thereafter in Italy, rather than in mainland Greece. Nor shall I attempt to trace in detail the themes that such philosophy followed. These can be read about elsewhere.[1] Suffice it to say that the general trend of the thought of these ancient philosophers involved speculation and to some extent argument about nature, about the possibility of change, of generation and destruction, and how all these are to be explained if they are possible. Parmenides of Elea in southern Italy argued in very abstract, though poetical, terms that these things are not really possible, and the later Presocratics tried to show in various ways that they were possible after all, though they showed no signs of understanding his arguments.

One thing, however, that ought to strike anyone reading about these people is that they were nearly all leading men in their cities. This is true of all the earliest philosophers up to and including Parmenides of Elea. Of the later Presocratics Empedocles was certainly a leading political figure in Acragas in Sicily, while Anaxagoras, who spent most of his philosophical life in Athens rather than his birthplace Clazomenae, was a friend and associate of Pericles, the great Athenian general and statesman in the middle of the fifth century BC. He was eventually prosecuted for impiety, which may have been a way of getting at Pericles on the part of Pericles' opponents. Only in the case of Leucippus and Democritus, the founders of Atomism, are we quite ignorant of their status in their societies, although Democritus is reported to have travelled extensively and consulted various wise men.

Similar travels, to Egypt, for example, are attributed to Thales, who began it all. They are not impossible; Miletus did have a colony in North Africa at Naucratis (one, incidentally, of at least forty-five). But visits to Egypt were a commonplace attribution to various philosophers by later authorities, especially when they wanted to explain mathematical knowledge. It was the conventional wisdom that the Egyptians, who certainly exhibited technological skills, invented mathematics. If Thales was well up in his society he could certainly have found the means to go to Egypt. Miletus is generally said to have been a flourishing trading and commercial port, with contacts not only with countries elsewhere in the Mediterranean but also with the great powers in the hinterland of Asia Minor, Lydia, and behind that, Babylon and Persia. How big was it, though, and how did that affect Thales' standing in society? The trouble is that we do not know the answer to that question, and most of those concerned with the history of philosophy do not even ask about it. Later, a decent-sized Greek city might have a population approaching 20,000 citizens. Miletus might well have been much smaller, but certainly not negligible in size. Unless a philosopher had other claims to fame he might go relatively unnoticed in a city of that population.

But Thales did have other claims to fame, and although the same cannot be said to the same extent of his immediate disciples, who may have depended on his social standing, it does hold good of most of the later Presocratics, as we have already noted. Some of them wrote books, and the way that, and extent to which, these could have become known elsewhere depend on the details of ancient book production and dissemination. Books were generally written initially on wax-tablets which were then transcribed on to papyrus rolls. How many copies of any one book were available is difficult to say. We are told that Anaxagoras' book was to be purchased in Athens for one drachma – which is the equivalent of a day's wage for anyone working on the Acropolis at the time. How many would pay a day's wage for a book these days, and how many did then? Libraries did not exist at this time, although some great libraries existed in the Greek world in the post-Aristotelian period. Nevertheless, one can assume that a book written by a philosopher would eventually become accessible in some way to those who were interested, and that word of new philosophical thoughts would eventually become known through travellers of one kind or another. But with what degree of reliability?

How much did the philosophers themselves travel so as to make contact with fellow-philosophers? At the beginning one hears little of this sort of thing, and presumably there were no other philosophers for the Milesians to contact. The same applies to Heraclitus, for that matter. Pythagoras, as already indicated, migrated from Samos in the Aegean to Croton in Southern Italy, where he established a cult. One comes to hear of other Pythagorean cities in that part of the world, and tradition has it, for whatever it is worth, that Parmenides of Elea, which is nearby, was influenced by the Pythagoreans. But they themselves were secretive, especially perhaps after the discovery of incommensurability, which may well have been very upsetting for the initial Pythagorean belief in an ordered, measured world. They espoused a way of life governed by cult rules, as well as a set of philosophical doctrines, but this was, as might be expected of a cult, very much an in-group matter. Eventually some of the philosophical doctrines were written down, although our sources to these today are very uncertain, even if Pythagorean thinking was certainly known to Plato and Aristotle.

Of Parmenides, Diogenes Laertius, writing probably in the third century AD, reports (IX.21-3) that Sotion of Alexandria, who may well have orginated the practice of compiling the views of previous philosophers arranged in schools,[2] said that Parmenides was a rich man. Diogenes Laertius also reports that according to Speusippus, Plato's nephew, he acted as a legislator for Elea. So it would appear that he too was a leading man in his city. His writings, in hexameter verse, were clearly known to, although very imperfectly understood by, his Presocratic successors. Plato represents Parmenides, in his dialogue, the *Parmenides*, as having come to Athens when Socrates was a young man, accompanied by his main disciple, Zeno, also of Elea. Plato was not greatly interested in the actual history of these things, and the dating may well have been adjusted to allow Socrates to meet these philosophers. Plato is thus able to record the influence of Parmenides and Zeno on himself through the dramatic device of a conversation with Socrates. The source of the report is in any case set out in a curiously indirect way. Antiphon, who was a half-brother of Plato, is said to have heard it from one Pythodorus, and he is made to describe the events to Cephalus of Clazomenae, who is the official narrator in the dialogue. Plato, of course, was far too young to have witnessed the events, but the distancing of himself from them may have relevance to the historicity of the account. It is not impossible that Parmenides and Zeno visited Athens at some time, and it is clear that Plato's readers would not have found this form of direct contact between one philosopher and another improbable. But beyond that, we know little or nothing about Parmenides' doings.

Empedocles of Acragas in Sicily seems to have been a picturesque character, if even half of what is attributed to him is true. One story which has captured the popular imagination is that he died by throwing himself into the craters of Mount Etna, his intention being, Diogenes Laertius reports (VIII.9), 'to confirm the report about him that he had become a god'. But it is a story which was not exactly uniformly accepted even in the ancient world. It is clear, however, that he was, once again, a wealthy man, although he was also a leading democrat in his city and a distinguished orator. Aristotle indeed reports both these things and says that Empedocles was the founder of rhetoric. He was also later given credit for being a doctor, and, even if that is not correct, his poems, said by some to be written after the style of Parmenides, show a considerable interest in physiology. Once again we have the picture of a wealthy and locally distinguished man. The two poems, *On Nature* and *Purifications*, were written in hexameter verse again and were clearly published in some form, so as to be accessible to later philosophers.

The main facts about Anaxagoras have been mentioned already. He came from Clazomenae in Asia Minor but spent most of his life in Athens, where he was the friend of Pericles and was eventually impeached for impiety, no doubt because he *was* a friend of Pericles. So one can imagine him hob-nobbing with the cream of Athenian society, even if at the end he had to leave the city and take up residence in Lampsacus. His book was, according to the *Phaedo* of Plato, read by Socrates, who found his views initially interesting because of his appeal to mind or intelligence in explaining the nature and course of things, but ultimately disappointing because it turned out to be yet another appeal to what Gilbert Ryle in this century has called a 'para-mechanical cause'. Still, it looks as if reading Anaxagoras' book was *de rigueur* among mid-fifth-century Athenian intellectuals. He appears to have been another wealthy man who gave himself up to philosophy and what then went by the name of science.

Of the Atomists, as already indicated, we really know next to nothing, as far as concerns their personal circumstances. There are, in any case, other Presocratics whom I have not mentioned, so that my survey has no pretensions to completeness. Nevertheless, the general picture is of wealthy and at least potentially influential men, who devoted a good proportion of their time to intellectual inquiry and writing. How much they communicated with each other remains unclear, but their activities seem to have been quite public, and their writings became well known. They clearly found the abstract questions with which they were concerned fascinating. Whether or not they were understood by their fellow-citizens, they had standing. Indeed some of them seem to have had the status of prophets, and their public performances, whatever their nature, were events. It is probable, however, that whatever respect was given to them by their fellow-citizens, came to them in part because of their wealth and the position and standing that resulted from that. The situation may have been slightly different in fifth-century Athens, which was something of a cultural and artistic centre. Anaxagoras who, as we have seen, was a friend of Pericles may have influenced the tragedian, Euripides, who was interested in contemporary intellectual movements and thought. If so, and perhaps anyway, one might see Anaxagoras as having the same kind of status as that possessed by a leading French philosopher in modern-day Paris – part of a general intellectual ferment. If this is less true of his predecessors among the Presocratics, it is because they were more isolated figures and did not live in the same kind of intellectual milieu.

THE SOPHISTS

The rise of the Sophistic movement in mid-fifth-century Greece introduced another element. The Sophists have had a bad press through the pages of Plato, because of the opposition to them and criticism of them expressed so forcefully by Socrates. That is no doubt unfair. Philosophically, they stood in opposition to the main trend of Presocratic philosophy because of their emphasis on man, on human judgment and the relativity of that. But they were opposed to them in other ways too, particularly in their evident wish to be thought professionals.[3] Protagoras, one of the greatest of the Sophists, was, like Anaxagoras, a member of Pericles' circle, and is reported by Plutarch to have spent a whole day with Pericles discussing where the blame was to be put for an accidental death from a javelin at an athletic festival. He is also reported, however, as being the first to have charged fees for his teaching, and this was clearly part of the professionalism.

This has seemed to some equally the source of the disapproval epitomized in the attitude of Socrates. It is doubtful, however, whether the Greek world in general would have disapproved of them just for asking for money for their teaching – provided that they really had something to teach. It is clear that the up and coming young men (the 'yuppies' perhaps) of Greek society (and not just Athenian society) thought that the Sophists did have something of use to teach, and so did their fathers. The Sophists claimed to be able to teach a variety of things – rhetoric, memory training, the use of language, to mention just some examples – which were summed up under the heading of *aretē* or excellence. It was the idea that such excellence could be construed as moral excellence or virtue that Socrates objected to. But in truth what they offered was what might make the learner a 'top person' in the society to which he belonged (and it was inevitably a 'he', given the nature of that society). Rhetoric, for example, was of evident use where power lay in the ability to influence the assembly by making speeches. The other skills that they offered to teach were no doubt thought to have a similar utility.

Hippias boasted of the amount which he earned in this way in a single season in Sicily, but this was probably by no means untypical. Socrates is represented by Plato in the *Cratylus* (384b) as making a joke about not being able to afford the long course given by Producus, which cost half a mina, and having to put up with a one drachma lecture, which cost a fiftieth of that. It will be remembered that a drachma, which was the reported price of Anaxagoras' book also, was the standard day's wage for anyone working on the Acropolis in Athens in the mid-fifth century BC.

I have often asked students, but received little in the way of an answer, how many of them would pay a day's wage for a philosophy book, and the same question can be asked about the cost of a lecture. What about a seventh of a year's income for a course on the different senses or uses of words, which was what Prodicus seemed to specialize in? However that may be, it is clear that the courses were well-attended.

Plato, in his *Protagoras*, gives a brilliant description of the teaching practices of the Sophists in his account of Socrates' visit to the house at which Protagoras was staying in Athens. Plato's account of the Sophists must be treated with at least some circumspection because of the evident disapproving attitude of Socrates, his mentor, to them. In some of the things which Plato has to say in the *Protagoras* he may have had his tongue somewhat in his cheek. The dialogue, in which the course of events is reported by Socrates himself, begins with Socrates being woken before dawn by Hippocrates who comes with vast enthusiasm to tell him that Protagoras is in Athens. Socrates, it might be noted, knew this already! While it is getting light the two walk around the courtyard and Socrates expresses his usual scepticism about Sophists, asking Hippocrates what he expects to get from Protagoras in return for his fee. Eventually they set out for the house of Callias, where Protagoras is staying, and when they knock on the door the porter, a eunuch, opens it, exclaims 'Ha, Sophists! He's busy', and slams it shut again. So, the other side of the coin to Hippocrates' enthusiasm is the exasperation of the person who has to deal with the practical consequences.

However, they are eventually let in when they explain that they are not Sophists and have come to see Protagoras, not Callias. Inside, Protagoras is walking up and down in the portico, conversing with a number of people, some of whom seem to have been eminent Athenians, although most of them, Plato is careful to note, were foreigners. Socrates says,

> As I looked at the party, I was delighted to notice what special care they took never to get in front or to be in Protagoras' way. When he and those with him turned round, the listeners divided this way and that in perfect order, and executing a circular movement took their places each time in the rear. It was beautiful.
>
> (*Protagoras* (315b2); W.K.C. Guthrie's translation)

There is a touch of irony in this description, as there is in the general account, but the procedure is no doubt accurately depicted. Socrates next mentions Hippias as sitting on a throne. (The word *thronos* is the same as that used much later in describing the institution of 'Chairs of Philosophy' in Athens by Marcus Aurelius.) He is answering questions put by others, mostly, it seems, foreigners, who were sitting on benches around him. Finally, there was Prodicus who was still in bed wrapped up in rugs and blankets in a room that had been a storeroom, but which had been cleared and made into a guestroom. Those with him were sitting on other beds or couches. 'What they were talking about', says Socrates, 'I couldn't discover from outside, although I was very keen to hear Prodicus, whom I regard as a man of inspired genius. You see, he has such a deep voice that there was a kind of booming noise in the room which drowned the words.' There is no doubt irony here too. Prodicus is depicted later in the dialogue as intervening in a heated exchange between Protagoras and Socrates in terms which involve the making of 'nice distinctions'. Prodicus sounds from Plato's presentation to be the original 'linguistic philosopher', and others might regard it as a good exhibition of pedantry.

There is nothing quite like the formal lecture here, although Hippias' answers are from the throne and thus *ex cathedra*. I believe it to be a quite general assumption in the ancient Greek world that teaching and learning, and *a fortiori* all inquiry, should proceed through some form of discussion. Dialogues, as Plato presents them, are merely artistic versions of what would be expected of any attempt to provide information and understanding. Plato's dialogues, at the beginning notable for their sense of drama, especially in their setting, become more and more formal and dramatically bare. This shows something, I suspect, about Plato's increasing didacticism and perhaps his increasing sense of the impossibility of gaining the conviction of others on what he wanted to say.

It would be wrong to depict the Sophists simply as teachers of the skills that were necessary to get on in contemporary society, although it was no doubt this that young men and their fathers paid to obtain – and paid well. But that does not make them philosophers; the word 'sophist' itself merely suggests cleverness at this and that. (It is indeed one of Socrates' perennial criticisms in Plato's dialogues that the Sophists have no special expertise and certainly not an expertise in *aretē*.) But they were also philosophers in their own right, mostly concerned to promote a scepticism about the claims of the Presocratics about nature, mainly in the interest of an emphasis on what is human, social and man-made. Little of their writings has survived, so that we tend to rely on sources such as Plato and the later Sceptics for our knowledge of their views; and Plato was generally hostile, while the Sceptics saw their views as grist to their particular mill. If Aristophanes in his comic play *The Clouds* was, in his depiction of Socrates, relying on a popular conception of these matters which his audience could react to, the average Athenian must have seen little difference between them and Socrates. For him they were all intellectual radicals, up with the latest intellectual fashion. They were all, even more than Anaxagoras was, like fashionable Parisian philosophical intellectuals, as Anglo-Saxon philosophers tend to regard them. But to get a better view of this it is necessary to go on to a consideration of Socrates himself.

SOCRATES

Socrates (470–399 BC) lives almost entirely in the pages of Plato and Xenophon, and the latter was not a philosopher and may be a secondary source in any case. Apart from these two, there is, as I have already mentioned, Aristophanes' play, *The Clouds*. The portrait of Socrates presented there is almost scurrilous, depicting Socrates in his 'thinking-shop' in a basket hanging from the ceiling where the air is thinner, and concerned with such things as the length of a flea's jump. Scurrilous perhaps, but it was no doubt all good clean fun to the average Athenian. And if a joke is to be really funny, it must have some foundation at least. Plato in his *Apology* makes Socrates call the jury to witness whether they have ever seen or heard him engage in such things. Plato also saw him as one of the greatest of Athenians and that is an opinion that has stuck, despite occasional scepticism. Socrates was eventually put on trial, on the conventional charge for one whom people wished to discredit (as with Anaxagoras) – impiety. But in the course of the trial the charge was changed to that of corrupting the young, and of that Socrates was found guilty. He was also condemned to death, having annoyed everyone by proposing as his penalty a free dinner each day; and the death sentence was eventually carried out.

This is described, along with an account of the philosophical discussion carried out during his last day, by Plato in his *Phaedo*. Whether that account is accurate is doubtful. Certainly it is very unlikely that Socrates could have held all the philosophical views put into his mouth by Plato; many of them seem incorrigibly Platonic. The whole event or series of events has, however, the smell of politics. The charge of impiety is in effect a political charge, and the charge of corrupting the young suggests that Socrates was being made a scapegoat. The young, those on whom the Athenian democracy was based, were held by some, probably conservatives, to have let Athens down in its misfortunes at the end of the Peloponnesian War, and Socrates was being made responsible for their supposed defects of character.

Conservatives of a certain kind have been ever thus, seeing a challenge to their views, particularly political views, as a form of corruption. The persistent criticisms that philosophers go in for are, and always have been, liable to be seen as that sort of challenge. What sort of man was Socrates, however, in reality? Since our view of him is gained mainly from sources that may be prejudiced in one way or another, it is difficult to be sure, but some things seem reasonably clear. In the first place, Socrates was not a rich man, and unlike the Sophists did not make money by his practices. His mother was a midwife and his wife a vegetable seller. It is not evident that he ever did anything to earn a living himself, although some of his hearers found it puzzling that he constantly made reference to those involved in some form of skilled occupation, such as potters and seamen. On the other hand, he did his military service as a hoplite, and for this he would have had to have bought his own suit of armour.[4] So he was by no means a pauper.

Plato presents him as having a fairly constant interest in the latest young men in Athens, and some of these, for example Meno in the dialogue of that name and Alcibiades in the *Symposium*, are made to assert in very definite terms the kind of fascination that he exerted for them. His influence over them, particularly over leading but problematic figures such as Alcibiades (who was the man whom Athens could not do without but equally could not cope with at the end of the Peloponnesian War), may well have been what his accusers had in mind in bringing him to trial. Many of Plato's dialogues begin with Socrates' confrontation of one or more of these young men, and subsequent discussion tends to undermine their claims to knowledge on this and that, while bringing out on the way certain characteristic Socratic doctrines, such as that virtue is knowledge, that the virtues form a unity, and in general that what is supremely desirable is the care of the soul. Kierkegaard saw that last claim as the central feature of Socrates' philosophy, and there is some plausibility in that view. Nevertheless, Plato in many ways presents Socrates as having a somewhat negative function in his argument with others, even if some positive beliefs underlie the criticisms. Certainly, Socrates was a very different sort of man and of a very different character from Plato himself; he may have been a different sort of philosopher.

However, it is likely (and Aristophanes' caricature seems to confirm this) that many Athenians saw no difference between Socrates and the Sophists. He was after all predominantly critical, and he too set great importance on *aretē*, even if he did not interpret the concept as they did. Those who were close to him no doubt saw that underneath all this was an intense seriousness of mind, and this is one of the things that, for the sharp-eyed reader, comes over from the pages of Plato, for whom, despite the differences, Socrates was the dear but revered master. How close Plato was to Socrates in point of fact is a matter for argument. He was not present at the discussion in the prison during Socrates' last day; he is said to have been ill. It is not unreasonable to wonder, however, whether Plato was as close to Socrates as his writings might otherwise suggest. He was in any case a much younger man and would have been among all those young men in whom Socrates was physically interested (for Athenian conventions about homosexuality as a social practice must not be ignored) and who no doubt sat at his feet in return. Given that background, it is difficult to draw any inferences about the practice of philosophy in general from Socrates' own practice. He was, as he himself said, in the *Apology* (30e), the gadfly of Athens. He had a passionate concern for truth and singleness of mind, combined with a no doubt irritating tendency to insist on his own ignorance.[5] In a larger and different society he might have been treated differently – as irritating perhaps, but not a case for prosecution, let alone death. Nevertheless, because of his method of argument and the seriousness of his aims in using it (to follow, as he said, the argument, where it leads – something that presupposes the supremacy of reason), not to speak of his moral convictions, he has been seen by many as a prototype of the true philosopher.

PLATO AND THE ACADEMY

Apart from differences of age, Plato (c.427–c.347 BC) was a very different sort of man from Socrates. Also, while Socrates wrote nothing, Plato wrote a whole series of dialogues, although, as he himself said in the *Seventh Letter*, if that is genuine,[6] he never wrote a treatise on philosophy. He insisted that knowledge of philosophy is to be best acquired only through instruction and a life in a fellowship which may lead to the generation in the soul of something like a 'blaze kindled by a leaping spark', which may then become self-sustaining. Perhaps that was the aim of the Academy, the school which Plato founded in the part of Athens, outside the walls to the north-west, which bore that name.

The dialogues, or at any rate the earlier ones, give the impression of being records of actual Socratic discussions. But they cannot really be exactly that. My saying that raises what has become known as the 'Socratic question' – to what extent is the Socrates of the dialogues the real Socrates? I do not wish to become involved in that question to any extent here, although it is fair to say that I believe it incredible that Socrates can have accepted all the beliefs that are put into his mouth; some of them, particularly the references to the Platonic 'Theory of Ideas', which Aristotle, for one, said could not be attributed to Socrates, seem peculiarly Platonic. The dialogues are in any case very much dramatic works, particularly the early ones, and Plato's retention of the form in his later writings, though with less respect for drama and more concern for didacticism, looks like the persistence of a habit. I believe that, again for dramatic reasons, Plato used historical persons, including Socrates, in those dialogues in order to say, roughly, 'This is what I have learnt from this person.' Hence, the way in which Socrates is presented in the dialogues amounts to Plato's acknowledgement of what he thought he owed to him, and when Socrates is not a participant it is because the views expressed are too far away from those of the actual Socrates to be put into his mouth.

Other views have been held on the function of the dialogues, including that put forward by Gilbert Ryle[7] that the dialogues were meant for some kind of public or private performance, perhaps on the analogy of the dramatic festivals. But if, as is more likely, they were published in order to be read, it was surely to give some sense of participation in a philosophical discussion of the kind that Socrates engaged in. They were thus a kind of second-best version of what Plato, as expressed in the *Seventh Letter*, saw as the way to acquire philosophical wisdom, knowledge and insight. It is a fair assumption, therefore, that the true way of acquiring these things was, in Plato's view, to be found only in the Academy itself.

Plato was a wealthy man, and came from a wealthy family. In the ordinary way of things he might have been destined for a life in politics in Athens. But the contemporary political situation was not favourable to that, and it is possible that the treatment of Socrates changed his ambitions. Diogenes Laertius (III.6) reports a contemporary claim that at 28 Plato left Athens and went to join Eucleides, of the Megarian school of philosophy (a kind of offshoot of the Eleatics) in Megara. Of what happened next we have little idea, though the tradition speaks of travels. The one certain thing is that he ended up in Syracuse, where Dionysius I, the father of the Dionysius already mentioned (see note 6), was then tyrant. Diogenes Laertius (III.18–21) even tells a story of his offending the tyrant and of his being ordered to be sold as a slave at Aegina. He was then, according to the story, ransomed by an acquaintance, Anniceris of Cyrene, and when friends in Athens tried to repay the money it was refused. 'Others assert', Diogenes adds, 'that Dion sent the money and that Anniceris would not take it, but bought for Plato the little garden which is the Academy.'

However all this may be, Plato was about 40 when this took place. It was not until he was about 60 in 367 BC that, on the death of the older Dionysius and his succession by his son, Dion invited Plato to come to Syracuse to undertake the education of his brother-in-law. Of what happened in the interval we really know nothing. For the rest of his life, another twenty years, Plato was very much involved in the affairs of Syracuse, giving support to Dion, and he visited the city twice with almost disastrous results. His motivation in all this is not entirely clear, but it has little to do with philosophy as such, however much Plato may originally have wanted to try the experiment of setting up a 'philosopher king', as the *Republic* puts it. Subsequent events are likely to have more to do with his personal relationship with Dion. More important from the point of view of philosophy is what went on in the Academy, and on that subject we know only too little.

It has indeed been claimed by Harold Cherniss[8] that Plato gave no teaching in philosophy there, apart from one public lecture, of which we have some evidence. All Plato's philosophy on this view is in the dialogues, in spite of apparent references by Aristotle, who was a member of the Academy for nearly twenty years, to Plato's 'unwritten doctrines'. This is not the place in which to get involved in the vexed question of these 'unwritten doctrines', though many scholars have found the views of Cherniss on this matter quite incredible. The public lecture, which may be recorded in the fragmentary work of Aristotle 'On the Good', is said by Aristoxenus, a follower of Aristotle who wrote on music, to have been habitually reported by Aristotle in terms which suggest that it was not a complete success, to say the least. For he says, if he is to be believed, that people came expecting it to be about 'some of the accepted human goods such as wealth, health, or strength, in sum, some extraordinary blessing'. But they found that it was about mathematics, numbers, geometry, astronomy, and finally about the good being one (if that is the right translation of the last few words of what is said). Aristoxenus goes on to say that they found it completely surprising, and some despised it, while others condemned it. Is this just an exemplification of public attitudes to philosophers in general or is it that Plato misjudged his audience? It may very well be the latter.

There are perhaps some indications that this was not untypical of Plato when he became involved in more technical issues – and it is not unusual among later philosophers either. Plato, the great communicator of the earlier dialogues, becomes very obscure in some of the later ones, and the second part of the *Parmenides* in particular has almost defeated a whole host of commentators. Moreover, Aristotle once or twice expresses doubt as to what Plato may have meant, on issues that might have been sorted out simply by asking Plato. What were Plato's relations to other members of the Academy? Was he perhaps a rather august and distant figure whom one did not approach easily, at any rate in his later years. (He was, it should be remembered, about 80 when he died.) On the other hand, if the *Seventh Letter* is genuine, the passage which I mentioned earlier about instruction and a life lived together producing a spark which kindles a blaze in the soul, may sum up Plato's conception of life in the Academy. One of Cherniss's reasons for rejecting the idea of philosophy being taught there is the evident emphasis on mathematics, as witnessed perhaps by the fact that there is a tradition to the effect that over the door of the Academy were the words 'Let no one who is unskilled in geometry enter here.' Distinguished mathematicians, such as Eudoxus, were either members of or associated with the Academy. Moreover, the programme of studies set out for the guardians in the *Republic* puts great weight on mathematics, which in one form or another is to be studied for ten years until the age of 30. When would further study in philosophy have taken place?

That is in some ways a rhetorical question, since, in spite of the length of the course, there was still plenty of time for other things. The Academy clearly attracted young men for whatever programme of studies it provided. (There is even a very late tradition that there were some women among them.) How those studies were taught is another matter. It would be a mistake to underestimate the role which the Greeks gave to discussion and argument. Isocrates, who was head of a rival school which maintained that rhetoric was the key element in education (though no doubt, as with the Sophists whom he criticized, an education which had political ends), attacked the Academy for teaching young men 'eristic'. That term tends to mean 'logic-chopping'; so the criticism amounts to one of those accusations against philosophers of being concerned only with 'argument for argument's sake'. Aristotle's *Protrepticus* was a manifesto put out by the Academy, while he was still a member of it, in support of the educational programme of the Academy against that of Isocrates. It seeks to justify the pursuit of abstract studies both for their theoretical and for their practical importance. One instance of practical utility is, we are told, that the Academy was asked for advice on the drafting of constitutions for more than one Greek city.

Plato's word for his philosophical method was 'dialectic', although the accounts that he gives of this in different dialogues vary and are in any case never totally clear in all their detail. In the late dialogues dialectic becomes associated with the method of logical classification and division. Much of this sounds like conceptual analysis, although the ontological implications of it are different from those of twentieth-century conceptual analysis. This is because of Plato's belief that terms pick out Forms, abstract but real entities amounting to universals but which are also paradigms, standards or perfect models for the things that share in them ('share' being Plato's term for the relationship between particulars and Forms). But Plato's conception of Forms seems to have been by no means uniformly accepted even within the Academy. Aristotle was a great disbeliever, referring to the Forms at one point as 'mere twitterings', and the *Protrepticus* seems to make no reference to the Forms, its argument being couched in terms which, to judge from what remains of the work, seem characteristic to a large extent of the later Aristotle. Speusippus, Plato's nephew, who inherited the Academy on Plato's death (it was, of course, a piece of private property), seems to have thought the Theory of Forms incompatible with the doctrine of logical division and classification, and he preferred the latter (so, presumably, attaching no great weight to Plato's *Sophist*, in which Forms and logical division go hand in hand through appeal to a doctrine of the 'blending' or 'communion' of Forms). There is a fragment from a comic poet, Epicrates, in which members of the Academy are shown engaged in the classification of a pumpkin, along the lines of 'animal, vegetable or mineral' – all good, one supposes, for a laugh.

Clearly, therefore, the Academy set itself up in terms of an educational programme, while members, such as Aristotle and Speusippus, carried on philosophical argument, and published philosophical works. Thus began the tradition of the philosophical schools, which continued in one form or another, and with varying success and degrees of activity, for something like 800 years, until the Roman Emperor Justinian ordered their closure in AD 529 in the interests of Christianity. (Whether that ended all philosophical activity is another matter.) It is easy to see the Academy as the first university, and many have so regarded it. It was not quite that, and one should not read into it all the formal components and activities of a modern university. The Academy was initially a garden where there was gymnasium. Whatever else came to exist there, it provided a centre for philosophical discussion and therefore for philosophical inquiry, for the pursuit of studies in mathematics, and perhaps for argument concerning politics. No doubt the general public thought it a bit mysterious, as they often think today of modern universities; hence the jokes. Moreover, there were rival philosophers such as the Cynics and Cyrenaics, and there were rival and antagonistic educational theories such as that of Isocrates. But the Academy became a constituent and permanent part of Athenian life, attracting to it men from all over the Greek world. With it philosophy became firmly institutionalized.

It is nevertheless a curious fact that, apart from Plato's involvement in the affairs of Syracuse, through the agency of his friend Dion, during the last twenty years of his life, we know very little of that life or of Plato's standing in Athens. The report of the public lecture does not speak very well of his attempt to communicate his thoughts to the general public – but that is counterbalanced by the nature of the great majority of his dialogues. In spite of the difficulty of some of the late dialogues, most of the dialogues are sublime literary works and sublime attempts to convey the spirit of Socrates, even if that is filtered through the mesh of Plato's own, and in some ways rather different, cast of thought. It is customary to speak of him as the first president of the Academy. It was certainly his institution, his property, and his conception. No school of philosophy of this kind had existed before as a place to which people could come to learn and take part in the development of a system of philosophy. Here the system was Platonism, a term which in this context involves more than a reference to a certain philosophical approach and a certain set of philosophical ideas, but covers also a great concern for mathematics and all that then went on under the name of science. When Plato died the school was carried on, although with differences in the philosophical views put forward, by Speusippus, Xenocrates, and others. It went through many vicissitudes in the next 800 years, and when Cicero visited Athens in 79–78 BC he found the Academy as such deserted. It is indeed likely that it ceased to exist as the site of the school after the fall of Athens in 88 BC. But the school went on in some form or other and in one place or another.

ARISTOTLE AND THE LYCEUM

Aristotle (384–322 BC) was, as we have seen, a member of the Academy for about twenty years, and when he came to found his own rival school, the Lyceum (so-called again from its site outside the walls of Athens, probably on the north-east side at a place frequented by Socrates), he no doubt did so in conscious imitation of Plato. When Plato died, Aristotle left Athens (for reasons about which one can only speculate), went to Assos in Asia Minor, then to Lesbos, where it is generally held he carried on biological researches, and was then summoned to his native Macedon to undertake the education of the future Alexander the Great. He was the son of a doctor in Stagira, but his connection with the great and the good has to be noted. There is little point in speculation over what he taught Alexander. In the catalogue of the titles of Aristotelian works that has been handed down to us by Diogenes Laertius there is mention of a book entitled 'Alexander, or on colonies', which may provoke speculation about Aristotle's connection with Alexander's policy of setting up Greek colonies in his expeditions to the east. But to pursue that idea would undoubtedly be a wild goose chase.

At all events, when Alexander took over the throne of Macedon in 335 BC, Aristotle returned to Athens and set up the Lyceum, the site and its buildings being, presumably, rented, since Aristotle, as a non-Athenian, was not allowed to own land under Athenian law at that time. When Alexander invaded the rest of Greece he treated Athens relatively generously, and it has been suggested that Aristotle used his influence with Alexander. This did not obviate the necessity of his fleeing Athens and going to Chalcis in 323 BC, when Alexander died and there was a renewal of anti-Macedonian feeling in Athens. He left, as he is reported to have said, lest the Athenians should 'sin twice against philosophy', the first sin being the death of Socrates. Felix Grayeff, in his book *Aristotle and his School*,[9] gives a glowing account of Aristotle's arrival in Athens in 335 BC, emphasizing his wealth and his liking for luxury, as evidenced by the number of his slaves and the number of rings on his fingers. There may be something in this account of Aristotle's character and circumstances, although the concrete evidence for it is somewhat slender. He was, certainly, a very different kind of man from Plato. He had hob-nobbed with the great, and the great in question, Alexander and his court, were much more eminent than the young tyrant of Syracuse and his brother-in-law had been. Given all that, one can imagine that the Athenians had a somewhat ambivalent attitude to this friend of Alexander, even if he had previously been amongst them for twenty years while a member of the Academy. They might even have thought of him as rather 'jumped-up'.

All this, however, is largely a matter for speculation, and much the same is the case with regard to the Lyceum. A school of this kind, like the Academy, would have had the character of a guild – a grouping of men who were more or less professionals under the head and owner of the institution. It would have been centred on a temple to the Muses – a *museion*, or, in the Latin transliteration, a museum – and is likely to have included a library. Theophrastus, Aristotle's pupil and successor as head of the Lyceum, wrote a history of previous views on certain aspects of philosophy, of which some parts of his work on sense-perception survive. He was, in effect, the first real historian of philosophy, and for these purposes he would have needed access to the writings of previous philosophers; he clearly had that access. The same is true, perhaps to a lesser extent, of Aristotle himself. There is, again, the fact that Aristotle is reported to have collected details of the constitutions of 158 Greek states, of which only that of Athens survives in any detail. So, in effect, the materials for the activities of a research institute must have been there. That must have entailed the employment of scribes (slaves no doubt) for secretarial and publishing purposes. It must have been a highly organized institution, but the details of this are a matter of inference only.

Much the same is true of the teaching activities of the Lyceum. Aristotle is known as the 'Peripatetic', and the word suggests something about walking around. Hence there is a tradition, noted, although not without some doubt, by Diogenes Laertius (V.2) that Aristotle carried on his teaching by walking around the site with his pupils. That is not impossible, given what we have noted already about Plato's account of the practice of Protagoras, but it is by no means certain, and the idea raises some problems about the status of the Aristotelian works. These were edited extensively in the ancient world so that they do not in any case survive as they were written. Moreover, their style of writing, which is far from the discursive and flowing style of Plato's dialogues, has suggested to many that they were lecture notes or possibly in some cases notes taken by students. The latter suggestion provokes some questions, which in fact continue to arise for centuries, until the invention of modern-style paper or other materials suitable for note-taking. The phenomenal memories of many in the ancient world are legendary, but the only plausible material for note-taking would be slates. (Papyrus would be too clumsy, even if it were available. Wax-tablets and stylus are even less plausible because of the laborious nature of writing with them and the small amount which can be written on such a tablet, although the use of wax-tablets for initial book-composition is well-known. Students in the Middle Ages are known from pictures to have used slates.) Even so, not much can be written on a slate, and it is implausible to suppose that much of the Aristotelian works can have been recorded in that way. Moreover, the dramatic openings to many Aristotelian works seem to me more suited to books than to lectures (although others may disagree on that point).

Aristotle's philosophical style is certainly more didactic than that of Plato; one tends to think in his case of doctrines, although it would be a complete mistake to suppose that the theses presented are not backed up by argument. That lectures took place in the Lyceum seems very likely therefore, whatever the style of such lecturing. How big was a typical class, though? Diogenes Laertius (V.37) says that when Theophrastus was head of the Lyceum about 2,000 students attended his *diatribē* (which should mean 'discourse', but might mean 'school'). That cannot mean that the size of the class was of that magnitude, or even that that was the number of students present in the Lyceum at any one time. Theophrastus was head of the Lyceum for about thirty-five years, and probably became its owner when the Athenian law forbidding ownership of land by foreigners changed. It is more plausible to suppose that the 2,000 students were the total during that thirty-five-year period, which gives an average annual intake of something approaching sixty. Whether as many as that came during Aristotle's time is unclear, as is the total number of students who were there at any one time; one has the impression that the school was bigger than the Academy, but that is only an impression. Zeno the Stoic is reported as admitting that there were more students in the Lyceum than in his own school. Even so, it was no university by modern standards, but of a size which made a peripatetic style of teaching just possible, if by no means certain.

Nevertheless, the comprehensiveness of what the Lyceum had to offer, as is evident too from the breadth of the Aristotelian works, was famous. Cicero (*De Finibus*, V.3) spoke eloquently on this, although he could find no evidence of the school's existence in Athens, any more than that of the Academy, when he visited Athens in 79-78 BC. It has indeed been suggested that with effect from the death of Lyco (the fourth head of the Lyceum, after Theophrastus and Strato of Lampsacus, known as the physicist and who, to judge from Cicero's account, may have been a kind of atomist) the school no longer existed in a physical sense. But the tradition of the Lyceum certainly went on, and when Marcus Aurelius endowed four chairs of philosophy in AD 176 he allocated one to Aristotelianism, along with Platonism, Stoicism and Epicureanism.

It has also been suggested that Aristotle's library was the prototype of the great libraries which were set up in the Hellenistic period at, for example, Alexandria and Pergamum. His actual books were bequeathed to Theophrastus, who left his library, including Aristotle's books, to Neleus, who in turn removed them to his native city of Scepsis in the Troad. After the death of Neleus, his family, who had no interest in philosophy, neglected the books (one report indeed has it that the books were buried in a pit and suffered accordingly!) They eventually came into the possession of Apellicon of Teos who published them in Athens in a corrupt form. The first proper edition of the Aristotelian works was produced by Andronicus of Rhodes in the second half of the first century BC, on the basis, at least in part, of the texts previously possessed by

Apellicon which were brought to Rome by Sulla in 86 BC. It is to this edition that we owe the title *Metaphysics*, which probably means simply the works following those on physics.[10]

What, then, did Aristotle conceive of himself as doing in writing these works and carrying on whatever activities went on in the Lyceum? A substantial part of the Aristotelian works is devoted to what we now think of as science, particularly biology, which seems to have been a major interest of his. Unlike Plato, there is comparatively little concern with mathematics. Another major interest is logic, of which as a formal discipline Aristotle can fairly be said to have been the founder. How that interest arose is a difficult question to answer, but it must have had something to do first with reflection on Plato's concern with methodology particularly in the late dialogues, and second with Aristotle's conception of science itself. It would be a mistake to see Aristotle's conception of scientific methodology as having a close resemblance to the modern one. Experimentation as such was more or less unknown to the Greeks, and there have been many speculations on the reasons why this was so. Directed observation was another matter, but Aristotle did not view that merely as the collection of data. In the first place, the aim of science was to arrive at a systematic knowledge of the reasons for phenomena in terms of their place in a system of species and genera with various essential properties. This meant that the procedure of science was based somehow on demonstration, according to which essential truths could be shown to follow necessarily from principles which were themselves necessary. The middle term in a syllogism so provided would indicate the reason why the conclusion not merely followed necessarily from the premises but was necessary in its own right.

This cannot be conceived as providing what Karl Popper in modern times has called 'the logic of scientific discovery'. It may be an account of science as a finished process – how, that is, its conclusions are to be set out – but it is likely that the whole thing should be seen in the context of the pursuit of knowledge through discussion.[11] In those terms, the aim of demonstration is to convince participants in a reasoned discussion that things should be seen in such and such ways as necessarily so. Aristotle points out that it is the mark of a foolish man to think that everything can be proved or demonstrated; so one has to start from something undemonstrated. This is where dialectic comes in, and Aristotle conceives of this in much the same way as Socrates does his style of argument, which in turn developed into Platonic dialectic. The details of this are a matter of argument among commentators, but it certainly and typically involves starting from general conceptions and beliefs about the matters under consideration. Hence many of the Aristotelian works start with a review of previous views in the field in question – something that turns into history of philosophy and history of science, and may indeed provide something of a justification of those disciplines.

It is not an exaggeration to say that for Aristotle philosophy is dialectic, although he himself would have said, and does say, that wisdom, which is the end of philosophy, consists in a knowledge and understanding of both the premises and the conclusions of demonstration, so that one gains thereby a kind of synoptic insight into nature. But that is not possible for all provinces of knowledge, so that one cannot expect either the same methods or the same kind of knowledge of, say, ethics as one can of physics. But the aim is the same throughout – to provide an understanding of why things are as they are in the area of knowledge in question. In so far as that is a case, as I believe it always was, of convincing those who work with you or even the world at large on these matters, it is probably true that in the end Aristotle's goal is not very different from Plato's idea of creating a blaze in another soul. But the context is different. Plato no doubt worked by means that involve a considerable appeal to inspiration. In Aristotle's case the conviction has at its back a vast panoply of facts and opinions. So Aristotle's philosophy has an encyclopaedic character that Plato's does not have (which is not to say that it is better philosophy – that depends on what is itself a philosophical issue, whether philosophy needs an appeal to data and facts or can rest with being quite *a priori*). It is clearly its encyclopaedic character which underlies the reputation that the Lyceum had in the ancient world, as Cicero testifies, and it is the impression that Aristotle's works still give, even if our view of the facts has changed in many ways. How the average Athenian regarded what went on in the Lyceum is impossible to know, and Aristotle was no Socrates who could be met every day in the market-place or exercise-ground. But the fame of the Lyceum was certainly widespread and Aristotle's intellectual influence was immense. For what it is worth, Diogenes Laertius (V.41) reports a story that when Theophrastus died all the Athenians attended his funeral in honour of him.

THE LATER SCHOOLS

I shall spend less time on the conduct of philosophy in the post-Aristotelian Greek world. There were other philosophical movements which were in existence before and contemporaneously with Aristotle. There was the Megarian school founded by the Eucleides whom Plato visited, and who made considerable contributions to logical issues. Of one of the school, Stilpo, it is reported by Diogenes Laertius (II.119) that when he visited Athens people would leave their work to come and look at him, which says something, if it is true, of the fame of some philosophers at this time. Another, Diodorus Cronus, who left to posterity a so-called 'master argument' concerning the ideas of possibility and necessity, is also reported, very unusually, as having philosophical daughters. There were also schools like the Cyrenaics and Cynics who probably thought of themselves as Socratics but took opposing views on the place of pleasure in life – pro and con respectively. (The eccentric and often scandalous behaviour of Diogenes the Cynic – who, it is said, lived in a barrel and preached the life of a 'dog' as the simplest and most basic form of life without respect to human delicacies – has almost become the stereotype caricature of a certain kind of 'philosopher'.)

Round about 300 BC other schools sprang up, no doubt in partial imitation of the Academy and Lyceum. Zeno of Citium, Zeno the Stoic as he became known, opened a school in the Stoa or Painted Portico, while Epicurus opened a rival school in a garden. In many ways they must have looked back to Aristotle, but they presented different theories (different from each other as well as from Aristotle) about the nature of the world and the place of man in it, involving different views of ethics also. It is sometimes said, for example by W.K.C. Guthrie,[12] that philosophy now had a different motive. Its function, says Guthrie, 'is to bring an assurance of peace, security and self-sufficiency to the individual soul in an apparently hostile or indifferent world'. It was even claimed by Gilbert Murray[13] that the whole set of attitudes which made up the Hellenistic way of thought and of which the new philosophical movements formed a part involved a 'failure of nerve'.

These sorts of claims should be treated with a certain scepticism. From the very beginnings, philosophy had always had as one of its motives the alleviation of a certain concern – a concern about the nature of the world in which we find ourselves and of man's place in it. What marks off philosophy from religion in this respect is that philosophy achieves its result, if it does, through argued understanding. Hence the other side of the coin is that, as Aristotle asserted, philosophy may be said to begin with wonder. The Hellenistic world was one in which social and political change was the order of the day, and this did indeed bring to the surface a concern about human existence. With the Romans, who were by and large an unphilosophical people, philosophy did become assimilated to religion to the extent that at times, as with Stoicism, in particular during the oppressions of the early Roman Empire, it was in danger of becoming a substitute for religion, with a consequent diminution of the intellectual character of the philosophical theses in question. At the same time, that assimilation no doubt contributed to the survival of some philosophical movements, and during the rise of Christianity philosophy – Platonism in particular – was often seen as a rival to that religion, and supported or opposed accordingly. Nevertheless, philosophy never lost its intellectual character entirely nor its attempt to provide that understanding of which I have spoken.

The immediate post-Aristotelian period was one in which there was constant interchange and mutual criticism between differing schools. While the Stoics, first under Zeno and later under Chrysippus, put forward theses on a whole range of matters in a way that almost rivals the encyclopaedic character of Aristotle's philosophy, the Epicureans were more restricted both in the range of their philosophical coverage and in their way of life. Stoicism always maintained a kind of public attitude to affairs – they inherited, for example, the Cynic view of man as a citizen of the world. The Epicureans were much more private in their attitudes. Indeed, there has been speculation about what exactly went on in the Garden where Epicurus set up his school.[14] What is undoubtedly the case is that Epicurus set a premium on friendship and a quiet life in the face of human ills (his thesis that death is not to be feared because it is 'nothing to us' is famous), while the Stoics were more in favour of going out to meet those ills. But both schools tried to set out a view of nature and the world, of man, and of the consequences of all this for ethics. The Stoics also made considerable contributions to logic, following in this respect the Megarians.

In a way, however, what marks off the immediate post-Aristotelian schools is their debate on epistemological issues – the search for, or rejection of, what was termed the criterion of truth.

This may have been dependent on a certain reaction to scepticism. Pyrrho preached scepticism – described as a determination to persist in inquiry and a refusal to be dogmatic on anything, even on what the senses tell us – at about the same time as Epicurus and Zeno. Whether he initiated a formal school is another matter, although one certainly existed later. He may again have thought of himself as a Socratic, and eventually even the Academy became sceptical in philosophical attitudes, under Arcesilaus and Carneades, perhaps again in the belief that they were following the practice of Socrates.

What all this seems to have produced is a constant debate between adherents of the various schools, particularly between the Stoics and the Academy, on whether there existed a criterion of truth (which amounts to a foundation for the attainment of certain knowledge), and if so what it was. One can imagine the disciples of the various participants in the debate eagerly sharing in the argument, like the modern philosophy student enthusiastic about the latest thing in the subject. But of how all this affected the general public one has little idea, although there are reports of a liking for public attention on the part of some philosophers. It is reasonable to suppose, however, that, as was the case with Socrates, but not with Plato or Aristotle, philosophical debate was very much an affair of the market-place, even if the subject-matter of the debate was philosophical in a comparatively narrow and technical sense. One certainly gets the impression of a philosophical ferment during this period, although developments in what we now view as science came from elsewhere, not from the philosophers.

At some time between 90 and 80 BC Antiochus of the Academy broke from the sceptical position maintained by Carneades, claiming to be going back to the original Plato. But he did so in a way which involved interpreting Plato in terms of Stoic and Aristotelian principles. Meanwhile Panaetius, the Stoic, and, following him, Posidonius moved towards a more eclectic Stoicism, with the result that others found little difference between the Academy and the Stoa. Scepticism remained a force as a school of its own, but elsewhere various forms of eclecticism were the order of the day for the next two centuries. This was especially true of the so-called Middle Academy under Albinus and Numenius, who embraced a kind of mysticism based somewhat remotely on Plato with some connections with Pythagoreanism. Numenius indeed is reported to have said that Plato was Moses speaking Greek! Under the Romans, during the early Empire, Stoicism became, as I have already noted, a moral force, a way of life in the face of oppression.

By this time, philosophy was pursued and taught in various places around the Mediterranean. Albinus, for example, gave lectures which Galen heard in Smyrna, while Numenius probably worked at Apamea in Syria. Athens was no longer of necessity the centre for the subject. Alexandria became more and more the place where philosophy flourished, although, in spite of the apparent death of the traditional philosophical schools in Athens in Cicero's time, philosophy continued to be taught in Athens from time to time. Indeed, as already noted, the emperor Marcus Aurelius, who was a contributor to a form of Stoicism in his own right, endowed four chairs of philosophy in Athens (in Platonism, Aristotelianism, Stoicism and Epicureanism) in AD 176, with an annual salary to the incumbent of 10,000 drachmae. It is not clear what a drachma was worth by this time, but by the standard of fifth-century BC Athens this was a formidable salary. Herodes Atticus was given the responsibility for appointing the first holders of the chairs; after that, Lucian (*Eunuchus*, 2) tells us, they were appointed by 'the vote of the best citizens', whatever that means. Lucian goes on, however, to tell a story about the scandals involved in the election of someone to the chair of Peripatetic Philosophy in about AD 179. (The cynic may suggest that it has ever been thus!)

The final philosophical movement in the Greek world took place initially in Alexandria – the Neoplatonic school initiated by Plotinus in the third century AD comprising another form of mystical Platonism. But his main disciple and biographer, Porphyry, taught in Rome. Of the later leading Neoplatonists, Proclus taught in Athens, while Iamblichus taught in Syria. It must be remembered that by this time Christianity was becoming dominant, and Neoplatonism was sometimes seen as a rival to Christianity, and one to be used against Christianity by powers, such as the emperor Julian the Apostate, who wanted to resist the new religion. Porphyry, for example, wrote a polemic against Christianity. On the other hand, Christian writers themselves absorbed elements of Greek philosophy and thought in those terms; St Augustine, for example, was converted to orthodox Christianity from Manichaeanism by reading Christian versions of Neoplatonic works, and much of his philosophy is inspired by Neoplatonism. Plotinus himself owed much to Ammonius Saccas of Alexandria, who wrote nothing himself but who taught not only Plotinus but also the Christian, Origen. Neoplatonism was thus contemporary with some of the Church Fathers. In AD 529 the emperor Justinian, in the interests of Christianity, forbade the teaching of philosophy anywhere in the empire. So philosophy as an institution ceased at Athens, although there is some evidence that it continued in some form in Alexandria. The main Neoplatonic philosophers, such as Damascius, tried, rather unsuccessfully, to carry on their work in Persia. On their return to the Empire they devoted themselves to the writing of philosophical commentaries, particularly on Aristotle. But philosophical argument went on in some form, particularly in a dispute between Simplicius and the Christian Neoplatonist John Philoponus over such matters as the doctrine of creation.

It is difficult to get a firm impression of the practice of philosophy in all this welter of philosophical movements over such a long period. Moreover, its entanglement with the rise of Christianity and its employment as an anti-Christian philosophical 'religion' gives that practice a character which is in some respects local to the period, however much philosophy and Christianity were involved with each other for many hundreds of years to follow. To a large extent, philosophy lost its 'dialectical' character during the closing stages of the Greek period. Plotinus' arguments, for example, are not as such of a very high standard. Even Sextus Empiricus who wrote his compendium of Scepticism, probably in the second century AD, recording a wealth of previous argument against the 'dogmatists', seems somewhat undiscriminating in his sense of what constitutes a valid argument. If it is not true that post-Aristotelian philosophy in general involved a 'failure of nerve', there is a progressive diminution in the quality of argument during the period, despite some exceptions which are inevitably seized upon by scholars.

Nevertheless, from Plato onwards, the practice of philosophy was a function of 'schools', concerned not only to pursue various theories and versions of knowledge but also to teach these to those who could come and be taught. In general, this required in those participating a degree of wealth and a position in society. (It is reported that, under Lyco, who was himself a wealthy man, the Lyceum set fees which made it open only to the very rich.) If a slave could pursue philosophy it would have been only via work done for others (although, perhaps as something of an exception to the rule, Epictetus the Stoic, in the first century AD, was both a professional philosopher and an ex-slave). Philosophy, therefore, had standing in large part because its practitioners had standing. This, at all events, was the general situation, although philosophers often enough received payment for their work, either from students (as with the Sophists) or through grants from some other source (as with the Chairs endowed by Marcus Aurelius – who of course was a philosopher himself). Whichever way it was, to be a philosopher was in general to be a member of a school, so that in that respect at least the situation was not all that different from what held good after the rise of the modern universities, except that the general culture and the presuppositions of scholarship were different. In the Greek world there were schools of philosophy, rhetoric and grammar only. Hence, learning tended to mean philosophy alone, and not just one subject among many others. This is not to say that there were no historians, geographers, or even scientists (we must remember Archimedes, for example), but they remained individuals and did not have a place in the educational establishment or system of learning. Hence, philosophers had a standing all of their own, which perhaps they have never had since – not at any rate as philosophers.

2

THE MIDDLE AGES AND RENAISSANCE

THE EARLY MIDDLE AGES

The period of philosophy which it is conventional to include under the heading of the 'Middle Ages' is a very long one. St Augustine was born in 354 and died in 430; William of Ockham lived from about 1285 until 1349. If these figures can be deemed to mark the boundaries of the period in question, we are concerned with something like 1,000 years. In any case the beginning of the period so delimited overlaps with that already covered for Greek philosophy. There are those who would include Augustine, and perhaps Boethius (c.480–524/5), in the history of Greek philosophy. Augustine, it is true, was converted to orthodox Christianity from Manichaeanism by reading Neoplatonic works put into a Christian form. Boethius translated into Latin Aristotle's logical works and Porphyry's introduction to Aristotle's treatment of the categories, and was thus responsible for the way in which interest in Aristotle's logic survived, when the other Aristotelian works became inaccessible in the west, along with knowledge of Greek. (The Aristotelian works were translated into Arabic, and knowledge of Aristotle, if at times intermixed with Neoplatonism, survived thereby. Translation from the Arabic was the route by which knowledge of Aristotle returned to the Latin world in the thirteenth century.) Moreover, a comment by Boethius on a remark of Porphyry about the status of species and genera generated the much later debate in the eleventh century and after about the status of universals. So these philosophers constitute something of a watershed.

Nevertheless, with Augustine the spirit of philosophy changed and became in a sense subservient to theology and to Christian ideas and concerns. This is evident in Augustine's most popular work, *The Confessions*, which is partly autobiographical, partly philosophical, but supremely religious, written in the form of an address to God. He says that he became interested in philosophy at the age of 18, through reading Cicero's now lost work *Hortensius*. But before he became drawn to the priesthood, in part as the result of a mystical vision which he and his mother, an orthodox Christian who had been pained by his Manichaeanism, had had at Ostia shortly before she died, he had held teaching posts in rhetoric at Carthage, and later at Rome and Milan, where he heard St Ambrose, who was bishop there. He was eventually himself Bishop of Hippo. In spite of the religious background which affects everything that he wrote, there is much in Augustine's works which is recognizably philosophy in such a way that it can be separated from its theological context, and the works are very much part of the history of philosophy. In any case, some of the Neoplatonists reveal in their writings a theological preoccupation, even if one of a different kind from Augustine's. Nevertheless, Augustine was professionally, so to speak, a priest and bishop, and never professionally a philosopher nor a member of a school, as were contemporary and later Neoplatonists. In this he began a tradition which lasted in the Latin west throughout those 1,000 years. (Elsewhere, in Byzantium, Greek philosophy was continued, but in a very second-hand and scholastic way, without any claims to originality, as part of a system of schools; while the revival of Aristotelianism among the Arabs from the tenth century onwards had its own religious context, even if not all its participants were professional theologians.)

In the Latin west it was the eleventh century before that tradition really flowered. Before that, in the ninth century, there was John Scotus Eriugena, who had some knowledge of Greek, acquired perhaps from Irish monks, and so retained some means of access to the previous tradition. It is not clear whether John the Scot, so-called, was a priest himself, but he was asked by the Emperor Charles the Bald to translate into Latin the works of Pseudo-Dionysius which Charles had received as a gift from the Emperor Michael of Byzantium. It was supposed that these were the writings of Dionysius the Areopagite, an Athenian convert of St Paul, although they were probably written at the end of the fourth or the beginning of the fifth century. John also translated the works of the Church father, Gregory of Nyssa, in whom, incidentally, has been seen the beginnings of idealism of a kind similar to that of Berkeley in the eighteenth century.[1] His occupation, after that of royal tutor, may have been that of teaching grammar at Laon, but his main philosophical work, *On the Division of Nature*, which has been regarded as a great metaphysical construction, is both mystical and religious in conception.

I have mentioned that Eriugena probably taught grammar at Laon. He would have done so as a member of a school attached to the cathedral there. Charlemagne, who was crowned as Emperor of the Holy Roman Empire in 800 encouraged the institution of schools as educational establishments, and set up his own palace school. Such establishments were concerned to teach, apart from theology, the seven liberal arts – grammar, rhetoric, dialectic, arithmetic, geometry, astronomy and music. This conception of education goes back, in part, to Plato, although it was influenced also by the more general and traditional Greek view of what was to be taught in the schools. But the teaching of dialectic at this time owed much to the rediscovery of Boethius' account of Aristotle's logic, and those who had a taste for it found that they could apply logical criteria, or supposedly logical criteria, to theology too. The transfer of teaching from the monasteries to schools set up in the shadow of various cathedrals, particularly in northern France, had, therefore, a radical effect of a philosophical kind on theological thinking, and from this emerged new philosophical movements, even if they were still intimately linked with theology. Institutionally, there also emerged from all this the first universities, particularly in Paris, Bologna and Oxford. The University of Paris, for example, was initially formed from the amalgamation of various theological schools (Bologna becoming, by contrast, a centre for law). Such schools were often instituted by scholars, inevitably ecclesiastics of one kind or another, who wished to teach there and collect around themselves interested students. This, for example, was the case with Peter Abelard at Paris in the twelfth century.

ABELARD AND DIALECTIC

The career of Abelard (or Abailard) was a tempestuous one. The story of his love affair with and marriage to Heloise, and his subsequent castration through the agency of her uncle, is well known. It seems not to have affected his reputation as a scholar, although the fact that he had enemies in the church hierarchy, particularly St Bernard of Clairvaux, led to the condemnation of his theology and his eventual excommunication. He was a theological radical, and this no doubt attracted students who wanted to hear him. He was born of a family of minor nobility at Le Pallet, near Nantes in 1079. As a young man he studied under Roscelin of Compiègne, who was famous for his nominalism, maintaining that universals were *flatus vocis* (vocal breathings), whatever he meant by that. He then studied dialectic under various masters, ending up at Paris with William of Champeaux, who was, by contrast with Roscelin, an extreme realist over universals. For a while he set up his own school at Melun, but then returned to Paris, where he ousted William both doctrinally and literally, establishing his own school there. For a time he then studied theology at Laon, returning to Paris after conflict with Anselm at Laon akin to his conflict with William. This was the period of his love affair with Heloise. After his castration, Heloise having become a nun, he stayed at the Abbey of St Denis, intending to become a monk. One of his theological works was burnt at the Council of Soissons. But he soon set up another school at Nogent-sur-Seine for students who sought him out, although he later gave this to Heloise and a group of nuns. After about five years as Abbot of St Gildas in Brittany, he returned to the school in Paris at Ste Geneviève. After the condemnation of his views by the Council of Sens and his excommunication, he retired to Cluny, had some sort of reconciliation with Bernard, and died there in 1142.

I have given special attention to these facts only because they give some picture of how someone with the ability, but also arrogance, of Abelard could practise his discipline by teaching those who flocked to him. Perhaps his most famous theological work was *Sic et Non*, although this was not the work which was condemned at Soissons in 1121, that being *De Unitate et Trinitate Divina*; it was his views on the doctrine of the Trinity which were the subject of criticism at Sens too. The importance of *Sic et Non* was that it involved the application of logical considerations to texts drawn from the scriptures and the church fathers. Abelard set such texts in contraposition to each other, perhaps as an exercise designed to sharpen the wits of theological students, but also to show the need to go behind the mere words to the true meaning. The work was in some ways the inspiration for Peter Lombard's *Sentences*, published in the twelfth century, which provided a systematic presentation of key passages of scripture and the works of the church fathers.

The *Sentences* became an obligatory text for comment as part of university courses in theology throughout the rest of the Middle Ages. Abelard's way of setting out passages and views was a less systematic version of what became with St Thomas Aquinas the standard way of presenting views, no doubt influenced by the practice of disputation, by thesis, antithesis and eventual resolution.

Abelard wrote on dialectic before he wrote on theology, but he continued to publish works on both subjects throughout his life, and it is arguable that logical concerns always loomed large with him, as they did with some of his contemporaries. Abelard's views on universals and on semantics are both subtle and complex, as a result of which his actual position on universals has often been misunderstood. He was sometimes thought to be a nominalist, like Roscelin, on the grounds that he said that universals were *sermones* (forms of speech). Others have said that he was a conceptualist, while his view that concepts were arrived at by abstraction from things suggests an element of realism in his thinking. The truth is probably[2] that he was less interested in the ontological status of universals than in the logical or semantic status of predicates, and in that sense he was something of a forerunner of William of Ockham. For our present purposes none of this matters. It is important, nevertheless, that Abelard was above all a dialectician or logician concerned to apply logical considerations to whatever other domain might be his interest. Since he was of his time, he was a clerk, and later a monk and priest; so theology had to be the main domain of this kind. Exactly the same thing could be said of the other philosophers of the time, although they varied both in their ecclesiastical position and in the degree of their interest in logic. It is not a period, however, in which one can detect a concern with the wider aspects of philosophy. That came only with the rediscovery of Aristotle. The two main factors in the subsequent practice of philosophy in the Middle Ages were that rediscovery and the rise of the universities. Indeed, the two factors soon coincided.

THE MEDIAEVAL UNIVERSITIES AND THE CURRICULUM

The two earliest universities were those at Paris and Bologna. The latter, as I have already noted, became the main centre for the study of law, Paris being the centre for theology. Theology, law and medicine came to be the main concerns of the mediaeval universities, and arts were merely propaedeutic to those subjects. Philosophy only figures to any extent in connection with theology. Hence, it is the latter which is our main concern. The University of Paris arose, as already noted, towards the end of the twelfth century as the result of a coming together of various schools already in existence there, and its pattern was followed elsewhere, including Oxford. A university was in effect a guild of licensed teachers, claiming an international status and open to all students who could meet its requirements for entry. Students could begin study at about the age of 14, provided that they had adequate knowledge of Latin, but the subsequent course was very long by modern standards. The head of a university was the Chancellor, assisted, as at Oxford, by two Proctors responsible for administration; but the teachers who were responsible for the curriculum of the university were the Regents, the *magistri regentes*, those who had qualified and remained to teach. The power given to the university to grant the licence to teach came via a charter and statutes, which laid down the rights and privileges of the constituent members of the university, and were confirmed by either the Pope or the Emperor, or later by other kings. Thus the standing of the university as a *studium generale* was given to that at Paris by a Papal Bull in 1215, which confirmed the standing which it already had by custom. Oxford followed suit in 1254; Cambridge in 1318.

While such rights and privileges could be withdrawn, and occasionally were so for certain periods, the charter and statutes allowed the university to conduct its own affairs without external interference, and, by the licence to teach, gave standing to its degrees. A student proceeding to a qualification in theology would naturally take holy orders. At an early stage religious orders of 'mendicant friars', such as the Dominicans and Franciscans became associated with universities, claiming chairs of theology in Paris, for example. There was initially some resistance to this from the regents, and the orders were limited to one chair each. Students from the orders were known as 'regulars' (i.e. bound by the rules of the order). But 'secular' students were admitted also, and institutions or colleges were set up for the benefit of poor students of this kind. This was the case with the Sorbonne which was founded in about 1257, and some Oxford colleges had a similar origin. Merton College was the first college at Oxford to lay down statutes for its corporate life, and it excluded 'regulars'. In Duns

Scotus' time at Oxford, i.e. at the end of the thirteenth century, there was a long queue of qualified bachelors waiting to give their inaugural lecture in order to become regent masters, and as there was only one Franciscan chair regent masters held the chair for one year only.

A student seeking to qualify in theology was required to qualify in arts first, taking the BA by following courses in the seven liberal arts – first the *trivium* of Latin grammar, logic and rhetoric, and then the *quadrivium* of arithmetic, geometry, music and astronomy. This might take between four and seven years, and the student had to pass the test of disputation, all of course in the academic language of Latin. It was in this part of the course that the study of Aristotle's logic, and later, after the rediscovery of Aristotle, other aspects of his philosophy, came to play its part. The BA entitled the holder to teach arts and to proceed, if it was thought desirable, to the degree of master. But to qualify in theology, after qualifying in arts, the student had to follow lectures on the Bible for four years and then lectures on the *Sentences* of Peter Lombard for another two years. The standard age for qualification as bachelor in theology was 26.

To become a master (which was, in effect, to acquire a doctorate and be equipped for university teaching), it was necessary to spend another period of about eight years, making about thirteen or fourteen years of theology in all, including four years preparing and giving lectures on the Bible and the *Sentences*, and taking part in public disputations. The latter were conducted by a regent master and involved bachelors as 'respondents' and 'opponents', with the regent master giving his final '*determinatio*' or verdict. Disputations could be either ordinary (*ordinaria*, on some specific issue), or on a variety of chosen subjects (*de quodlibet*), and were therefore called *quodlibets* or quodlibetal disputations. The latter were held on formal occasions with some solemnity. Either form of disputation could be published, as could lectures given by the bachelor also, either as an *ordinatio* – a revised and in effect examined version of the original – or as a *reportatio* – a report of the original version. In the case of a *quodlibet*, the publication would naturally be made by the master who provided the *determinatio*. This at all events was the sort of procedure that was generally followed, and it is as a result of it that we have works such as, in the case of Duns Scotus, those entitled *Ordinatio* and *Quaestiones Quodlibetales*.

It should be clear from all this that the aim of the course was to give the student, first, knowledge of texts and what had been said about them, and, second, an ability to argue pro and con about such matters. Hence, the prominence of the lecture in the first instance and the rule-governed disputation in the second. The question which I raised in the previous chapter about what students in the ancient world did with what they were told in lectures arises here too. There are illustrations of students using slates in the Middle Ages, but, as in the ancient world, other forms of note-taking seem ruled out by the scarcity of paper. Since books were in manuscript form too, what access would the normal student have had to them, and how often? It is clear from St Thomas Aquinas' lectures on certain of Aristotle's works, such as the *Physics*, that it was necessary to provide the student with rather precise details of what occurs in the text in question. This gives the works a relentless character which, to me at least, puts them very high on the list of the most boring works ever written! The introduction to an English translation of Aquinas' lectures on Aristotle's *Physics*[3] says 'Aquinas presumes that the reader will be able to consult the text of Aristotle's *Physics*'. Whatever be the case with the published form of these lectures, this cannot be the case with the lectures themselves. Aquinas may have read out the Latin version of each passage being summarized (and the lectures are almost entirely devoted to exposition). But what did the students then do with what they heard? They could make a few notes perhaps, but for the rest it must have been a matter of memory, with perhaps a little opportunity subsequently to consult copies of the texts being discussed. It was not, one might think, an entirely satisfactory situation.

Moreover, the system was not designed to produce philosophical innovation, since, first, philosophical issues were subservient to theology as the queen of the sciences, and, second, the main philosophical occupation turned, apart from logic, on commentary on texts. Even logic was still largely a matter of the refinement of aspects of logical theory derived from Aristotle through Boethius.[4] This is true, for example, of the *Tractatus* or *Summule Logicales* of Peter of Spain (who is probably the later Pope John XXI and lived in the first half of the thirteenth century). Perhaps the one exception to that judgment was the work done on the semantics of terms, which derived from Abelard. This became known as the theory of supposition (a term in a proposition is said to take the place of what it stands or 'supposits' for). That theory perhaps received its most elaborate development in William of Ockham's

Summa Logicae in the fourteenth century, although it can be found earlier in the writings of Peter of Spain and William of Shyreswood (or Sherwood). By the time of Ockham and his contemporary Franciscan, Walter Burleigh, there were also developments in the theory of deductive inferences or *consequentiae*, beyond what Aristotle had provided but owing something to the logic of the Stoics. Hence, in the field of logic there were developments apart from what could be got from mere study of and commentary on texts. But this had been true at least since the time of Abelard.

THE REDISCOVERY OF ARISTOTLE: ST THOMAS AQUINAS

Apart from logic, what I have said about the effects of the system on philosophy certainly holds good. On the other hand, one should not underestimate the effect for the practice of philosophy, within these parameters, of the rediscovery of Aristotle's works other than those on logic. That rediscovery was due to the fact that the knowledge of Aristotle had been preserved by the Arabs and was put to use in the latter half of the twelfth century by Averroes (Ibn Rushd) in Moorish Spain. (It should be remembered that Byzantium was still a great power during this period, and the Emperor Manuel Comnenus made various moves towards the Latin west. It was also the period of the later Crusades. All this meant that there was more knowledge in the west of some form of Greek, if only for diplomatic purposes.) Aristotelian works became available in Latin translations from Arabic translations, and, more or less at the same time, in Latin translations from the Greek. Translation of Aristotelian works became something of an industry in the thirteenth century, and Aquinas, for one, relied extensively on the translations by his friend William of Moerbeke, having little knowledge of Greek himself. It is perhaps worth noting that last fact and the general unwillingness or inability of philosophers to equip themselves with knowledge of Greek before the Renaissance.

The wider knowledge of Aristotle's philosophy was not immediately or universally welcome. When the University of Paris received its charter in 1215, study of Aristotle's works on metaphysics and 'natural philosophy' was prohibited, in part, perhaps, because some non-Aristotelian works, some of them Neoplatonic, were attributed to Aristotle, and also because of 'guilt by association' through the use of Aristotle by non-Christians such as Averroes and certain thinkers judged heretical. The ban was gradually ignored, although it was not until 1366 that study of Aristotle was prescribed for all those studying arts at Paris.[5] But the great reconciliation between Christianity and Aristotle was brought about by, above all others, Aquinas, despite some places where the reconciliation is dubiously successful. (I have in mind the doctrines of creation and the immortality of the soul, neither of which is obviously compatible with Aristotle.) In Aquinas' philosophy we have a compendious presentation of the philosophy of Aristotle seen through Christian eyes, and it provided a framework within which a Christian theology could be expounded. Aquinas wrote many works on particular issues in philosophy, and set himself against the Averroists in these respects, but the two great *Summas*, the *Summa Theologiae* and the *Summa Contra Gentiles*, have, as their aim, the provision of the framework which I have mentioned.

Their method, however, no doubt owes much to Aquinas' experience as a teacher at the University of Paris and his consequent part in disputation. Aquinas, who was the son of the Count of Aquino, was born in about 1225. His family no doubt thought of an ecclesiastical/political career for him, but, on going to the University of Naples in 1239, he became attracted to the life of the Dominican friars and entered the order in 1244, in spite of family opposition. Indeed the Dominican General planned to take him to Bologna and then on to Paris, but Aquinas was kidnapped by his brothers on the way and was imprisoned in the family castle at Aquino for a year. However, he managed to reach Paris in 1245, to study under Albertus Magnus. These events were in one sense the only dramatic events of his career. Aristotelianism was already prevalent in Paris, and there can be no doubt that it was during his period there that he acquired his devotion to that philosopher. Albertus Magnus took him to Cologne from 1248 until 1252, when setting up a Dominican study house there; but he then returned to Paris, where he completed his course in theology, becoming the holder of the Dominican chair there from 1256 until 1259. During the rest of his life until 1272 he taught theology either in Rome or in Paris. He was then sent to Naples to organize a Dominican study house there, and died in 1274 on the way to the Council of Lyons. It was neither a long nor, strictly speaking, a very eventful life.

This is not the place to say anything further about St Thomas' Aristotelianism, how far he was faithful to Aristotle's philosophical thinking, and how successful he was in reconciling Aristotle with

Christianity. It is clear, however, that for Aquinas philosophy was not, and could not be, independent of theology, even if from a theological point of view he may be seen to have established a firm place for reason as against revelation. Moreover, his doctrine of the primacy of the intellect over the will might be taken as a clear indication of the importance of philosophical considerations and philosophical argument. Aquinas wrote many works both of commentary on Aristotle and of argument concerning specific philosophical issues, in spite of the overriding emphasis on theology. We have already seen something of the character of those commentaries when they were the subject-matter of lectures. In all probability, he would have thought that a lecture could have no other character. It was strictly didactic and a place for exposition, not argument.

But the same would not have been true about the practice of disputation at the University of Paris and other universities, and this is reflected in the style of the *Summa Theologiae* (or *Theologica*) above all. For the material presented in that monumental work is set out in the form of questions, in response to which Aquinas plays the role of both respondent and opponent, and finally gives the *determinatio*. Aristotle is frequently invoked as 'the Philosopher' on one side or other of an issue. Hence the treatment of a given question is in the form of a hypothetical *reportatio* of a disputation, in which the position of Aristotle is given great importance. One might say that the form that is observed is a combination of the disputation and the exegesis of texts, these being either religious texts or those of Aristotle. For the argument is not, so to speak, cold. It still involves a considerable appeal to authority of one sort or another, and the religious commitment is obvious also. Hence, one can find in Aquinas illumination about Aristotle, about the scriptures, about theological matters, and sometimes about philosophical issues considered for their own sake. A modern philosopher coming to Aquinas should never forget, however, that the *Summas* are, by intention, works of theology, in accordance with the practice of university study and teaching in the thirteenth century. Although Aristotle came to be regarded in this period as *the* philosopher, no substantial philosophy emerges in the period which is independent of theology. It is thus theological practice which determines the practice of philosophy.

The same is true of the rest of the mediaeval period, and it goes some way to explain what is meant by scholasticism, as mediaeval philosophy came to be called. It is not simply that it was pursued by scholars within universities devoted to the teaching of theology. After all, some universities concentrated on other things, as the University of Bologna did with law, and social philosophy could be pursued in that context. It is rather that the pursuit of knowledge, even scientific knowledge, was in effect limited by having to fit in with some form of inherited wisdom and by being connected with teaching according to prescribed forms. Those forms admit argument, certainly, but argument which conforms to the canons of the *disputatio*. A question is put or contemplated, and what is to be said about it pro and con is set out. Authority in the form of Aristotle's works, and sometimes other things, including the Scriptures, is appealed to where it is judged relevant, and a final determination of the appropriate answer to the question is given. It is perhaps surprising that so much great philosophy came to fruition in this context, given that so much weight is attached to the corpus of previous philosophical thought, and given the fact that, officially at any rate, theology sets the parameters for philosophical inquiry. There is also a sense in which it is easy to see how great a burden of established ways of thinking and accepted beliefs had to be overthrown at the Renaissance, and why Aristotle, somewhat regrettably, was regarded as part of that burden. It was natural that the rediscovery of Plato, or at any rate Platonism, should play some part in that.

DUNS SCOTUS AND OCKHAM

We have not reached the end of the Middle Ages with Aquinas. He was, as we have seen, a Dominican. The two great thirteenth/ fourteenth-century philosophers, Duns Scotus and William of Ockham, were both Franciscans, and, as it happened, both were British by origin. Duns Scotus was almost certainly born in Scotland about 1266, while William of Ockham was born in Surrey about 1285. They both attended the University of Oxford as members of the Franciscan order. They were in many ways very different kinds of thinker, although they both differed from Aquinas on matters of philosophical doctrine. Scotus received the honorary title of 'Doctor subtilis' (Aquinas was called 'Doctor angelicus' and 'Doctor communis'), which may have been one way of noting the difficulty of his thought and style of writing while doing justice to his philosophical and theological standing. (His name, 'Duns', which is probably only a reflection of his place of birth, is also the origin of the word 'dunce', which is a less polite way of recording the same thing.) His career, after he acquired his doctorate, was devoted to lecturing either in Oxford or in Paris, with a possible period in Cambridge. In 1307 he was moved to the Franciscan study-house in Cologne, where he died the following year.

Ockham, by comparison, had a much more turbulent career. He was a much clearer writer than Scotus, but perhaps less of the metaphysician. In many ways his philosophy can be set down as part of the history of logic, although his work on semantics (or 'supposition'), the first part of his *Summa Logicae*, follows the tradition of Abelard. Such matters seem to have been something of a preoccupation of contemporary Franciscans. As a nominalist, though a much more subtle one than earlier nominalists, he was something of a radical thinker, and it would not be altogether misleading to see him as a very early exponent of the empiricism that has been characteristic of British philosophy. However that may be, his career at Oxford was cut short before he obtained the teaching licence by accusations of heresy by the Chancellor of the University directed to his lectures on the *Sentences*, and in 1324 he was summoned to the Pope at Avignon to answer the charges. He remained in Avignon for four years, after which the commission considering the charges declared some, though not all, of the statements in his commentary to be heretical, although no further action against him seems to have been taken.

However, in 1327 he became involved in the campaign mounted by Michael of Cesena, the General of the Franciscan order, against the Pope at Avignon, urging the characteristic Franciscan cause of apostolic poverty. In 1328 Ockham and two others accompanied Cesena, fleeing from Avignon, to put themselves under the protection of the Emperor Louis (or Lewis, or Ludwig) of Bavaria. The Emperor, in alliance with the Ghibellines of Lombardy, was in dispute with the Pope on the question of the powers of the Emperor, including the right of succession. He set up an anti-pope in Rome and was excommunicated by Pope John XXII at Avignon. Ockham and his companions were similarly excommunicated. He spent the next few years producing writings seeking to prove that all temporal properties of the Church really fell under the jurisdiction of the Emperor, and he argued for some form of political representation in the Church itself, opposing Papal absolutism. With him at the Court was Marsilius of Padua, who also wrote against the Pope, although not always in a way of which Ockham approved. However, in 1347, when the Emperor died after having attempted a reconciliation with subsequent popes, Ockham sought his own reconciliation, although it is not clear whether it ever came to fruition. He died, probably of the Black Death, in 1349.

Most of Ockham's strictly philosophical works were written before he went to Munich. Although it is possible to abstract views on political philosophy from the writings written against the Pope, this was not their main point; they were tied to definite practical considerations. Hence, to all intents and purposes Ockham's philosophical writings came from one who was an *inceptor*, one who had not yet fully qualified in such a way as to have the licence to teach. In this respect Ockham was the great exception to the norm according to which mediaeval philosophers at the time also held academic posts, although it does not really affect that norm, since Ockham would certainly have become a teacher like Duns Scotus, had he been able to complete the process of qualification, and had he been a man of a quite different character and temperament.

By contrast, Duns Scotus did qualify and the rest of his career was relatively straightforward. There were some hiccups before he became regent master, though they had nothing to do with him personally; in a way these have already been referred to obliquely.[6] It seems that Scotus had done all that was necessary for becoming a master in theology by 1301, except for giving his inaugural lecture in the chair. As there was only one Franciscan chair in Oxford, and in spite of the fact that qualified bachelors held the chair for one year only, there was a long list of people waiting to give their inaugural lectures. Scotus would have had to wait several years to qualify as master. However, it became the English province's turn to provide a candidate for the Franciscan chair in Paris, one which, incidentally, had more prestige than that at Oxford. Scotus was selected, and went to Paris; he began his commentary on the *Sentences* there in 1302.

However, in 1303 there was a dispute between the French King, Philip, and the Pope, Boniface VIII, over the taxation of Church property, which led to Philip's excommunication and a subsequent attempt by Philip to have Boniface deposed. There was an anti-papal demonstration involving the friars in Paris, following which a royal commission questioned all the Franciscan friars to determine which side they were on. A majority, including Scotus and Master Gonsalvus, who later became head of the Franciscan order, sided with the Pope, and the penalty was exile from France within three days. In response the Pope withdrew the University's right to confer degrees. His subsequent death that same year and the accession of a new Pope led to the lifting of the ban in 1304, and the banished students were helped to return. It is possible, though by no means certain, that it was in this period that Scotus was in Cambridge. Gonsalvus, who became head of the Franciscan order in 1304, named Scotus as the next bachelor to become Regent Master, and it is probable that Scotus finally qualified in 1305. Since he left Paris for the Franciscan study-house in Cologne in 1307 and died towards the end of 1308, it was neither a long career nor indeed a long life. (If he was in fact born about 1266 he must have been about 42 when he died.)

Apart from Ockham's work on logic, the *Summa Logicae*, the philosophy of the two scholars under consideration can best be found in the same sort of works, their commentary on the *Sentences* or *Ordinatio*, and their *Quodlibeta* or *Quaestiones Quodlibetales*. Both kinds of work are ostensibly theological in character, differing though they do in the form in which theological issues are presented – the commentary being, in effect, published lectures, and the other work being a formal report of disputations. To most modern philosophers it must seem extraordinary that philosophy should issue in such forms, and they do not, as philosophy, make easy reading. In that respect, Aquinas' two *Summas*, not to speak of other works written by him on explicitly philosophical issues, can justifiably be regarded, by comparison, as straightforward philosophical treatises.

The theological context does not belie that judgment, even if it does imply the existence of a limit to the scope and style of philosophizing that was possible at this time. To be a philosopher in the Middle Ages from the thirteenth century onwards is to practice theology using a mainly Aristotelian system of thoughts, concepts and arguments. Within this given framework there were sometimes, it need hardly be said, innovations. There are things in Aquinas' works that are not, strictly speaking, Aristotelian. The relative positions taken by him and the Franciscans on the issue of the primacy of the intellect or the will – Aquinas taking the side of the intellect, Scotus and Ockham favouring the will – are not positions on an issue raised by Aristotle. Scotus' doctrine of the formal distinction on the side of the thing (*distinctio formalis a parte rei*), which, at any rate in the applications given to it, involves the idea of a distinction which is a necessary one without being merely conceptual, is, in spite of its obscurity, a genuine innovation. It influenced Descartes, though indirectly, in his idea of the real distinction between mind and body, and the notion of *de re* necessity that it involved has been resuscitated in this century. Aristotle might not have disagreed with the idea, but it is not as it stands an Aristotelian issue. Finally, one can find Ockham saying, as he does over the question of whether philosophy can justify the claim that there is a rational soul distinct from the body, that Aristotle did not speak clearly on the matter but that in any case he, Ockham, does not care what Aristotle thought; the issue is what is true. But then, one might say, Ockham was something of a rebel anyway. Nevertheless, there is a sense in which such remarks herald the break-up of the scholastic way of thought.

THE RENAISSANCE

Scholasticism did not perish utterly in the next three centuries, however, and the thought of Suarez (1548–1617) had some influence on Descartes, to the extent that that philosopher looked back to the past, as was inevitable he should to some extent, and employed scholastic concepts. Nevertheless, the new modes of thought, the new humanism, which the Renaissance brought with it, combined with a rediscovery of Platonism, if not, strictly speaking, Plato, led to a gradual diminution of the Church's authority, and, eventually, to a new flowering of philosophy.[7] That did not happen all at once, however, as is witnessed by the well-known fate of Galileo (1564–1642) at the hands of the Church, and even more crucially perhaps the less-known fate of Giordano Bruno (1548–1600), who was burnt at the stake, having been arrested by the Inquisition for heresy. Bruno was inspired by the doctrine of the earlier Nicholas of Cusa (1401–1464) concerning the coincidence of all opposites, and perhaps by Nicholas's dethronement of the earth as the centre of the universe, not to speak of the more ambivalent attitudes to this matter taken up by Copernicus (1473–1543). Bruno despised Copernicus as a mere mathematician; he himself asserted the unity of the All in the One and denied the geocentricity of the universe. His fate, like the more celebrated but less drastic one of Galileo, is a clear indication of the remaining power of the Church at this period.

Most of the philosophers of the Renaissance were, however,

ecclesiastics, which to some extent explains the Church's attitude to them. Nicholas of Cusa was a priest who eventually became a Cardinal and Bishop; Marsilio Ficino (1433–1499), who is thought of as one of the main sources of the resuscitation of Platonism, became a priest at the age of 40, when he had already published commentaries on some of Plato's dialogues but still had substantive works to come; Bruno became a Dominican, although he left the order in 1576 when accused of holding heretical opinions. Apart from the revival of Platonism (not always clearly distinguished from Neoplatonism), what distinguished all these thinkers (and indeed others of the period) was their flirtation with mysticism. Both Ficino and Bruno were influenced by Hermetic ideas (views attributed in the early centuries AD to Hermes Trismegistus, the 'thrice-great' Hermes). None of these ideas fitted well with orthodox Catholicism, but this was, of course, the age of the Reformation, and the ideas put forward are symptoms of a ferment of new ways of thinking which in one way or another constituted a rebellion against the Catholic Church's dominance. The curious thing about the philosophers whom I have mentioned is that they still operated from within that Church.

During the years leading up to Descartes and Cartesianism there were revivals of other, and older, philosophical ways of thinking, apart from Platonism. There was a resuscitation of atomism in the thought of Pierre Gassendi and Thomas Hobbes.[8] There was also a revival of Scepticism arising from a new translation into Latin of Sextus Empiricus, and a use of Sextus' arguments by Montaigne (1533–1592). Francis Bacon attempted to codify the principles of the new science in a way which, perhaps somewhat unfairly, manifested an opposition to Aristotle. By the time of Descartes things were ripe for a complete overthrow of the ways of philosophizing which had been established in scholasticism. Here I stress the phrase 'ways of philosophizing', for, despite the legacy of scholasticism which scholars have found in Descartes, the leading philosophers of the seventeenth and eighteenth centuries were new men with a new approach to the subject. Hence, when we ask, with reference to this time, 'What was it to be a philosopher?' we receive a different answer from that which has held good hitherto. For this we must turn to the next chapter.

3

THE SIXTEENTH AND SEVENTEENTH CENTURIES

THE LATE RENAISSANCE: BACON AND HOBBES

One thing that is striking about the practice of philosophy during the periods so far surveyed is that it has nearly always been carried on within a definite institutional set-up. From Plato onwards in the ancient Greek world the practice of philosophy presupposed the existence of schools engaged both in the development of philosophical theory and in teaching. Even when an individual was not an actual member of such an institution, as was the case, for example, with Cicero, philosophy was pursued against the background of such schools and would not have existed without them. In the Middle Ages there is, first, the all-pervasive influence of the Church; every philosopher was not only a Christian but a cleric of some kind. (It was different among the Arabs, where the main philosophers were not clerics despite their allegiance to Islam. Both Avicenna and Averroes, for example, practised medicine for some time.) Second, there was the institutional framework provided by the schools of theology. Initially, it is true, these were established by individuals, but they operated generally in the shadow of the great cathedrals; and from them developed the mediaeval university system within which theology and therefore philosophy were taught and pursued. There were rebels like Abelard and Ockham, who to some extent carried on their activities in a unorthodox way; nevertheless their heterodoxy presupposed the system. The Renaissance changed all that but only gradually. I have already noted some Renaissance philosophers who occupied offices within the Church, and the Church, particularly perhaps the Jesuits, had a great intellectual influence until the seventeenth century and beyond. But the greatest philosophers of the seventeenth and eighteenth centuries were very much individuals, with a variety of forms of employment and patronage.

This was of course a post-Reformation world, and that fact made a great difference where, as in Britain, the Catholic Church had a greatly diminished influence. This was evident in England even during the period which might be held to be still the Renaissance. Here the most notable philosophers had nothing to do with the Church and had to depend on other means of support in order to pursue their interests. Equally, while they often attended a university at some point, they were not part of the university system. Francis Bacon (1561–1626), for example, who was in many ways the proponent of the new science initiated by, amongst others, Galileo, was also much involved in the affairs of the courts of Elizabeth I and James I. He was constantly concerned to get royal favour, in part in order to obtain support for his plans for the furtherance of science. He eventually became Lord Chancellor and Viscount St Albans. As a philosopher he was mainly concerned with, first, the prejudices or 'idols' which stood in the way of the proper acquisition of knowledge, and, second, the methods which should be followed for discovering the forms of nature. So his interests were in a sense epistemological, although there is an implicit metaphysics lying behind that epistemology, involving a conception of the world which was consistent with Galileo's discoveries. In Bacon's view, this was opposed to the Aristotelianism which had previously held sway, although much of the language in which his views were expressed was at bottom Aristotelian. At the same time, his concerns were very different from those of the scholastics, as was his social and intellectual position. As is clear from what I have already said, apart from his own standing he depended on royal patronage for the pursuit of his aims.

The somewhat later British philosopher, Thomas Hobbes (1588–1679), in fact overlapped with Descartes, to whose *Meditations* he contributed objections on the invitation of the Abbé Mersenne, who functioned somewhat as a philosophical impresario in France. As a proponent of atomism he had much in common with Pierre Gassendi in France (1592–1655), who began life as a priest, then taught at the University of Aix-en-Provence, where he was a straightforward scholastic, but later, as professor of mathematics in Paris, adopted Epicureanism. Hobbes's metaphysics and philosophy of mind are also basically Epicurean, involving a form of atomism, but his political philosophy is not. His observations on the role of the state in his *De Cive* (1642) and particularly in his *Leviathan* (1651) were stimulated by the Civil War. His defence of absolute sovereignty, backed by his version of the doctrine of the social contract, was suspected by both sides in the dispute between King and Parliament, but both *De Cive* and *Leviathan* were in fact published while Hobbes was in France, the latter during the Commonwealth. He had fled to France in 1640 because he thought his life was in danger as a consequence of what he had written on political philosophy up to that time. Whether he was reasonable in having such fears is a matter for argument, as was his precise motivation in publishing *Leviathan*.

Hobbes spent most of his life, after leaving Oxford, as a tutor, mostly with the Earls of Devonshire, and subsequently in 1646, after he had fled to France, with the future Charles II. His service with the Devonshires enabled him to travel to the Continent with the Earl in 1634 until 1636. (He had been abroad before in 1610 with the young Devonshire and again in 1629 with the son of Sir Gervase Clinton during a period in which the Countess of Devonshire temporarily dispensed with his services as an economy.) During the 1634–6 period he became a member of Mersenne's circle and also visited Galileo. Subsequent service with the Devonshires also brought him into contact with contemporary politicians in England, and this, combined with the fear of the possible consequences of his own writings on social and political philosophy, brought about his flight to France in 1640. After he returned to England in 1651, having come to feel isolated in France, he remained a private citizen. After the Restoration, despite fears about Charles II's possible attitude to him because of his return to England in 1651, he was granted a pension by the King. He was engaged in scholarly controversy during his later life, but not public controversy. It is clear that the practice of philosophy, in Hobbes's case, amounted to publishing works which were made possible by patronage and employment as a tutor to persons of influence. There is no real institutional background to this; although Hobbes was at the University of Oxford as an undergraduate, his pursuit of philosophy had nothing to do with the university.

It would be wrong, however, to underestimate the part played at this time by intellectual discussion among philosophers, and by, in particular, the focus provided by Mersenne, with the approval of Richelieu. The Abbé was a friend of René Descartes, who consulted him regularly, particularly about his relations with authorities, and was responsible for collecting pre-publication objections to the *Meditations* to which Descartes wrote replies. Mersenne befriended Hobbes when he went to France, and Hobbes apparently met Descartes once in 1648. While the meeting was amicable, subsequent correspondence was not; for one thing, Descartes accused Hobbes of plagiarism in his views about optics, while Hobbes disapproved of Descartes' temporizing with the Church. Both perhaps were over-conscious of the originality of their approaches to philosophy. It has to be noted, however, that both were remarkable for one thing – the fact that, while they still published some works in Latin, they also published in the vernacular. This was itself a sign that philosophy had emerged from scholasticism.

DESCARTES AND CARTESIANISM

In some ways, in Descartes' case, the emergence from scholasticism is not altogether unambiguous. Descartes relies extensively, for example, on the language of scholasticism. But in his approach to philosophy and in his establishment of 'Cartesianism' as a mathematical and scientific system he was astonishingly new. While his scientific system was caught up and overtaken by Newton, Descartes was in it building, but in a novel way, on what Galileo had started. In that respect Cartesianism became the dominant intellectual movement of the seventeenth century, although Cartesian physics came to be accepted in university circles in France only when it had been superseded by Newton. Likewise, as the result of Descartes' approach to philosophical issues, philosophy has never been the same again. Opinions may differ about whether that has been a good thing, but as a fact it is undeniable. All this is in spite of Descartes' somewhat nervous attitude to the Church, to the Jesuits and to what he thought of as the dominant intellectual authorities generally.

Descartes was educated at a Jesuit college at La Flèche, and perhaps at the University of Poitiers, near which he was born in 1596. His attitude to the Jesuits, which was a mixture of nervousness and warm respect, is perhaps not surprising. He subsequently joined the army for, as he put it, educational reasons, served in the Netherlands and Germany, and was present at the battle of Prague. (His father, who was a gentleman of a good family, had been in military service.) During his army career he had dreams which suggested to him that he might found a complete science of nature based on mathematics. After the battle of Prague he left the army, travelled for a time, and then lived in Paris. In 1628 he went to the Netherlands, where he stayed at various places for twenty years, until in 1649 he was persuaded by Queen Christina of Sweden to live in Stockholm and teach her philosophy. Unfortunately the cold weather and having to give lessons to the Queen at 5 a.m. was too much for him and he died there in 1650. Nearly all his main works were written during his time in the Netherlands, including a work entitled *Le Monde*, which was meant to present his system of nature in accordance with his dreams, but which he suppressed when he heard of the condemnation of Galileo by the Church. When he did publish his system in his *Principles of Philosophy* in 1644, it was in Latin and in a much more didactic form. It has been described as a Jesuit school text, but it was dedicated to the Princess Elizabeth of Palatine, to whom he was introduced in 1642 while she was living at the Hague, and with whom he had some correspondence on philosophical matters, including the relation of the soul to the body. Meanwhile, he had in 1637 published his *Discourse on Method* and then works on optics, physics and geometry, all in French with, apparently, the aim of gaining popular support for his views.

In 1641 he published his *Meditations on First Philosophy* in Latin, though it was translated into French with his approval. It has come to be regarded as his central work, but he met with hostility from the theological and other forms of establishment, so that his hope for both recognition and approval from them was never fulfilled. Indeed, in 1663 his works were placed on the Index. His attitudes to official hostility and his almost obsessional craving for recognition have led to subsequent charges of hypocrisy and cowardice, but it cannot be denied that he had something to fear. He did not yet live in a period of enlightenment, and the official 'Enlightenment' when it came in the next century still had to meet resistance from the Jesuits, the Church in general, and the French establishment. Things were somewhat different in Protestant countries, which explains to some extent Descartes' stay in the Netherlands, although the official story was that it was the place where he could best work undisturbed. The Netherlands universities in fact accepted Cartesianism, at any rate his cosmology, when it was still forbidden in France.

The Abbé Marin Mersenne died in 1648, but until that time he was a good friend of Descartes, enabling him, through his rather selfless organization of intellectual discussion, to come into contact with most of the leading philosophical and scientific figures of the day. These included not only Hobbes but Gassendi and the young Jesuit priest, Antoine Arnauld, who later became known for his argument with Leibniz and who was the leading figure in the movement set up at the abbey of the Port-Royal, which was responsible for the so-called *Port-Royal Logic*. Although Arnauld was a Jesuit, the main theological impetus of the movement was an Augustinian one, following the doctrine of the sovereignty of divine grace and the subordination of reason to faith, which was put forward by Cornelius Jansen, Bishop of Ypres (1585–1638). Blaise Pascal (1623–1662), the distinguished mathematician and also author of the posthumously published *Pensées* which put forward the view that in relation to God the heart has its reasons, was also a member of this Jansenist movement. It became the official reaction to Cartesianism, but it could not have existed without Descartes, and in many ways it reflected the ways of thinking which Descartes introduced. Cartesianism indeed became very popular, fashionable and influential, despite the official, disapproving, attitudes of the Church and the establishment, which led to Descartes' works being placed on the Index in 1663 and to Louis XIV forbidding the teaching of Cartesian physics in 1671.

Descartes' own attitude to authority of all kinds was, as already indicated, exceedingly anxious (the reasons for which can only be a matter for speculation). He dedicated his *Meditations* to the Faculty of Theology at the Sorbonne in the hope of allaying suspicions already induced by his earlier *Discourse on Method*, but without real success. Some, including, as we have already noted, Hobbes, were inclined to despise him for temporizing with the theological authorities, but to do so was not only part of his own nature but was also due to the social and historical context in which he found himself. What is remarkable about the two works just mentioned, from both a stylistic and a philosophical point of view, is the strikingly autobiographical way in which they were written. In the *Discourse* he sets out his own thinking about the method to be pursued in seeking knowledge as if it is an autobiographical account of his own ruminations, rather than, so to speak, a research programme. Equally in the *Meditations* the 'search for certainty' there set out starts from a use of the so-called 'method of doubt' which is presented in the form of a description of the train of thought involved in very first-person terms. Philosophy had never been pursued and offered for consideration in this way before.

Apart from the philosophical style of Descartes' writing in these works, in the '*Cogito ergo sum*' which, notoriously, Descartes saw as the conclusion of the 'method of doubt' and the main foundation for certainty in our knowledge of the world, he put great weight on the privileged access we have to the contents of our minds, as opposed to the properties of the so-called external world, apart from what geometry tells us about them. Descartes is sometimes said to have initiated the 'age of epistemology', during which the theory of knowledge and the search for certainty were given priority within philosophy. Since he had great concern with certain metaphysical issues – the nature of the mind, of bodies, and the relation between these – this description of the situation is something of a caricature (especially when one considers too the concerns of other continental philosophers who followed him). But the epistemological and autobiographical approach to these issues cannot be denied; nor can Descartes' concern with knowledge of what is, so to speak, private to us. How he came to have this latter concern is one of the great puzzles in the history of philosophy. It has been suggested, for example, by Jonathan Rée[1] that 'the rise of capitalism was accompanied by an increasing preoccupation with individual subjectivity', and that this had a connection with the Protestant ethic. While such suggestions are not utterly absurd, they cannot be regarded as providing the real explanation of the phenomenon; nor can anything resulting from an appeal to the facts of Descartes' upbringing, although these may well do something to explain his attitudes to authority.[2]

It is clear that because of what he came to think of as his mission to present to mankind the new science of nature and to reveal, against received doctrine, the firm foundations of this new knowledge, he felt it incumbent on himself to set out the processes of thought which he had personally gone through or would go through to that end. In spite of the over-cautious attitudes to authority, it was he, Descartes, who was to present that vision. And if he could do it, so could others. One can see in this some of the reason for the popularity that Descartes' ideas acquired. He was in a sense a popularist, tilting, if not against windmills, at least against something that was becoming a façade, with the gradual decay of the Church's authority, the rising importance of experimental science, and the changing political structure of society. Descartes did not see himself in a way parallel to Socrates' description of himself as the 'gadfly of Athens', but the role of the philosopher as a critic of received opinions and ideas was beginning to be reinstated. In spite of some rebels, the attitude of philosophers had been different in the Middle Ages. That, in a way, went along with the position of the philosopher as an individual, unbacked by any institutional set-up. Both Descartes and Hobbes were nervous of authorities, although for different reasons; they were both very concerned to establish their own originality, although it is Descartes for whom this is the greater preoccupation. But worry about the acceptability of their ideas became, almost naturally, the disease of seventeenth-century philosophers, a disease to which different people reacted in different ways. We shall see more of this later.

Cartesianism was, however, extremely influential, not merely as a movement in its own right which acquired popularity, but in its effect on the thinking of others. As far as concerns the theological establishment, I have already mentioned Arnauld, who was not a Cartesian but could not have held the philosophical views which he did if Descartes had not existed. Perhaps a more direct influence on philosophico-theological thinking is to be found in the works of Nicholas Malebranche (1638–1715) who was a priest at the Oratory, and who, despite holding Augustinian views on theology, was much opposed to the Jansenist movement in general and Arnauld in particular. Malebranche was much impressed by Descartes' *L'Homme*, published posthumously in 1662 in Latin and in 1664 in French. His own *Recherche de la vérité*, published in 1674, with its Cartesian-inspired title, was in effect an attempt to reconcile Descartes with Augustinianism. He tried to bring this about by, among other things, adopting the 'occasionalist' doctrine of the relation of mind to body put forward by some followers of Descartes, particularly Arnold Geulincx (1624–1669), according to which God puts into our minds ideas of physical events on the occasion of those events occurring. Malebranche's Augustinian gloss on this is that we therefore see all things in God.

Other more indirect influences exerted by Descartes, not to mention his effect on Spinoza, Leibniz and the British philosophers to which we shall come, tended to go in the direction of a reinforcement of the scepticism at least implicit in the 'method of doubt'. The impetus to this was given weight by Pierre Bayle's *Dictionary* (1695–7), an idiosyncratic work in the form of a biographical dictionary which gave Bayle the opportunity of expressing many critical and sceptical opinions. There is, finally, the French Enlightenment of the eighteenth century, personified by the so-called *philosophes*, the centre-piece of which is the *Encyclopaedia* edited by Diderot and D'Alembert. Although this is scarcely a major philosophical work it embodied the sceptical, critical and anti-religious spirit of the age, and was bitterly opposed by the establishment, particularly the Jesuits.

SPINOZA

The major philosophical movements which took place in the rest of the seventeenth century came through persons who, although undoubtedly influenced by Descartes, were philosophically independent in all sorts of ways. Once again they tend to stand as individuals, outside the establishment and having comparatively little to do with the universities or any other determinate institution. First, there is Spinoza (1632–1677). Benedict de (or Baruch) Spinoza was born in Amsterdam of Jewish parents who had come as refugees from the Inquisition in Portugal. In spite of an orthodox Jewish upbringing he developed views sceptical of that religion, although we know little of how that came about or indeed of his education in general. Because of his views he was eventually excommunicated from the synagogue. He spent the rest of his life working as a lens-grinder, refusing the offer of a chair at Heidelberg in 1673 because he thought that a philosopher should avoid official commitments. For a while he took part in discussions of the 'new philosophy' of Descartes with a group of enlightened Christians, but eventually he left Amsterdam to live in various Dutch villages in seclusion. He died in 1677 of consumption, a contributory cause of which must have been dust from the lens-grinding.

He had correspondence during his life with Henry Oldenburg of the Royal Society in London and with scientists such as Christian Huygens, but although he was visited by Leibniz he was largely unknown. His main work was published only after his death and was first greeted with incomprehension. This work, *Ethics*, is a systematic working out in geometrical style of a set of ideas about reality as a single substance, which is God or nature; it deals also with the nature of the mind, the emotions and human freedom, which is to be seen in a form of blessedness which lies in the intellectual love of God. It is a magnificent though perhaps rather austere work, and it is unrelenting in its attempt to derive the theses which he wishes to maintain from certain initial premises according to the method of geometry, which Descartes had advocated as the supreme science.

Many have seen Spinoza as the archetype of the philosopher, committed solely to the working out of his philosophical ideas without respect for any other considerations, and without much concern for their acceptability to others. He hardly fits, however, any prototype of the philosopher which we have so far met. On the whole, the philosophers reviewed so far, who have had anything like the same singleness of mind, have at least been concerned to teach their philosophy to others. This is not the case with Spinoza, except that he did, of course, write books in which his views are set out. But the works which he published in his lifetime were either published anonymously or, as was the case with his exposition of Descartes' philosophy in geometrical form, disavowed as his own views.

Spinoza established no philosophical movement and had no direct influence on others, however much Leibniz, for one, saw his own views as opposed to those of Spinoza, although in a similar intellectual context derived from Descartes. The search for the truth, the correction of the understanding, and the attainment of a state of virtue which is that blessedness which is the intellectual love of God are indeed Spinoza's aims. There is, of course, a religious dimension to all this, a message for mankind, but Spinoza's main concern is to get that message straight. In that kind of single-mindedness, Spinoza is almost unique in the history of philosophy. Wittgenstein, as we shall see, had some of it. Unlike Wittgenstein, however, Spinoza did not reject others; he merely concentrated on getting at the truth, whatever others had to say.

LEIBNIZ

Leibniz (1646–1716), like Spinoza, published very little in his lifetime. Indeed he published only one book, the *Theodicy*, concerned with natural theology and arising out of discussions with Sophia Charlotte, the daughter of the Electress Sophia of Hanover, who was to become Queen of Prussia. This work is hardly representative of his philosophy. He wrote several other books which remained unpublished until after his death. The *Monadology*, which was supposed to be the exposition of his mature philosophy, was written with the encouragement of Sophia Charlotte. The *Discourse on Metaphysics*, which many have seen as his central work, was sent to Arnauld, from which resulted a considerable correspondence. His *New Essays Concerning Human Understanding*, a commentary on and reply to John Locke's *Essay Concerning Human Understanding* was left unpublished on Locke's death in 1704. There was also left unpublished a mass of papers on a great variety of subjects. Leibniz engaged in correspondence with a whole host of scholars and scientists, including correspondence with Samuel Clarke in which Leibniz in effect criticized Newton's theory of space and time and Clarke acted as Newton's mouthpiece. The complete collection of Leibnizian writings is vast, and it is undoubtedly surprising that so little was published in his lifetime. Indeed, Bertrand Russell, in his book on Leibniz,[3] maintained that, while nearly everything he wrote was designed to persuade some individual, the bad parts of his philosophy, including what he did publish, were designed to please princes and, particularly, princesses. Whether or not the last point is true, it is certainly the case that Leibniz spent a good deal of his life trying to obtain royal favour and also convince other leading scholars of the truth of his views.

In this, and in other ways too, he could hardly be more different from Spinoza, with whom he spent a month at one time, whose views he thought quite wrong, and on whose *Ethics* he wrote extensive notes when it was published after Spinoza's death. Leibniz was a very public figure, an indefatigable traveller and correspondent, and a man with a vast range of interests, well beyond the bounds of philosophy as conventionally conceived. But, like Descartes, he was very anxious that his views should be accepted, and he was very concerned to have the patronage of important people, including royalty. Like Descartes too, he practised philosophy as an individual, without any institutional backing except what patronage and relations with the intellectual élite could bring. This can be said in spite of the fact that he attempted to get royal backing for the setting up of academies like the Royal Society of London, with which he had dealings when he travelled to London in 1673 on behalf of the Elector of Mainz, and in spite of the fact that he was successful in this at Berlin where he was made President for life.

Leibniz's father was Professor of Moral Philosophy at the University of Leipzig, and died when Leibniz was 6. His mother, who also died before he left university, saw to his early education, and his precocious grasp of Latin enabled him to have free range of his father's library, where he read widely, mainly in the classics. He learned and was excited by logic, as it was then taught at school, and at 15 went to the University of Leipzig to continue those studies, although philosophy as taught at such universities was still scholastic. At the same time he continued his private reading. He at first intended to be a lawyer and wrote a thesis on law which the University of Leipzig refused to accept on the grounds of his youth (he was 20). It was, however, accepted by the University of Altdorf, although Leibniz declined a post there. In 1668 he became in effect a diplomat in the service of the Elector of Mainz. In this capacity he was invited in 1672 to Paris to explain a project to the court of Louis XIV, and he remained there for four years (apart from the brief visit to England in 1673) studying mathematics and meeting French scholars and philosophers. It was at the end of this period in 1676 that he made his discovery of the differential calculus, which Newton had discovered independently but did not publish until 1693, after Leibniz had done so in 1684. This was also the period of his visit to Spinoza.

For the rest of his life he was in the service of the Dukes of Brunswick at Hanover where he was officially appointed librarian. He was engaged to write the history of the house of Brunswick, and he travelled extensively to gather material for this and other purposes, such as the compilation of a code of international law. His relations with the princesses of the house have already been referred to, but when they died he fell into disfavour with the court at Hanover, in part because of his absences in order to seek the support of other royal families for the setting up of academies. When the Elector of Hanover became King of England as George I in 1714, Leibniz was instructed to remain in Hanover, where he died two years later after illness and neglect. It is perhaps surprising that Leibniz wrote as much on philosophy as he did during this period, even if he did not publish it, for nearly all his main works come from this time. Nevertheless, Russell blamed Leibniz for wasting his time on the history of the house of Brunswick and so not producing his *magnum opus*. Whether that criticism is deserved is a matter of opinion.

The bare facts of his life reveal, however, what being a philosopher meant in his case, although Leibniz was clearly much else besides. The range of his interests and writings is astonishing – from logic to jurisprudence, with many other things in between. Among philosophers, however, he is mainly known for his espousal of a metaphysical system, based on the idea of an infinite, but organized, plurality of spiritual entities which he called monads, each one having the status, as he said, of the ego (*le moi*) in ourselves, in being simple while reflecting an infinite plurality. In this he was quite opposed to Spinoza's single unified reality. He was also opposed to Spinoza's rejection of the idea of the freedom of the will in any ordinary sense, although whether Leibniz was successful in avoiding a similar position to that of Spinoza has exercised scholars and commentators.

Apart from his very wide-ranging philosophical interests, he was a contributor to the physical theory of the period, and, as we have seen, he discovered, independently of Newton, the differential calculus. He made great contributions to the development of formal logic on mathematical principles, and he had the hope that it might be possible to produce a logical calculus such that, in the face of problems, it would be possible to say quite simply 'Let us calculate'. Not all these aspirations have been fulfilled or have proved long-lived, but Leibniz's optimism in these respects, as well as in his general metaphysical belief that God has produced the best of all possible worlds (an idea caricatured by Voltaire in his *Candide*), is notable.

All these ideas and projects were pursued by him as an individual, to the extent that this was made possible by his employment and patronage. He was in constant contact with the other intellectual and scientific figures of the age, but, as with the other philosophers whom we have noted, his activities had little or nothing to do with the universities, despite his wish to institute academies like the Royal Society. Nor was Leibniz at all concerned with teaching, except in the marginal way provided by his contact with intellectually interested royalty. He was concerned to argue with other philosophers such as Arnauld, by way of correspondence, but in the main simply with the aim of persuading them of the acceptability of his own views. While, like Descartes, he was concerned to maintain his relation with figures of influence, such as royalty, he did not have Descartes' fear of ecclesiastical authority and theological establishment. But then, it might be pointed out, Leibniz came from, and in the main lived in, Protestant Germany, not Catholic France; that fact cannot be unimportant. At the same time he did not have Spinoza's single-minded dedication to the truth as he saw it, without regard for anything else. He was nothing if not a man of the world, even if it was a world of intellectual ferment.

LOCKE

For the last main figure in seventeenth-century philosophy we must return to England, a country which was also Protestant, but which was politically troubled (it is the period of the 'glorious revolution' which led to the succession to the English throne of William of Orange). John Locke (1632–1704) is generally opposed, in histories of philosophy, to Descartes, Spinoza and Leibniz, as an empiricist against those of a rationalist persuasion. It is true that in his main work, his *Essay Concerning Human Understanding*, Locke was very critical of the doctrine of innate ideas, which one can find to some extent or other in the works of these rationalist philosophers, though whether he had them in mind in writing as he did is a matter of dispute. He did try to argue that all our ideas are derived ultimately from experience (as indeed Aquinas had done), but in his account of knowledge itself in the fourth book of the *Essay*, rationalist influences are evident, and to that extent Locke was of his time. He was also of his time in rejecting what went on in the name of philosophy in the universities.

Locke, who was the son of a West Country lawyer, went to Westminster School and from there in 1652 to Oxford, where he encountered philosophy, although only in the scholastic form which seems to have been persistent at universities of the period, with a slight qualification as regards Cambridge.[4] He seems to have absorbed some of its concepts, although he thought little of it, being much more excited by a private reading of Descartes. It was in fact the style of Descartes' philosophizing which impressed him rather than the opinions expressed, but, as already indicated, Cartesian influences were evident in the fourth book of the *Essay* when it came to be written and published in 1690. At all events, when Locke had completed his BA and MA in 1659 he was elected to a Senior Studentship at Christ Church for life. He later became Lecturer in Greek and then Reader in Rhetoric and Censor in Moral Philosophy until 1664. He must therefore have done some teaching, although enthusiasm for actually taking degrees was not notable among undergraduates of the period. However, he did not continue his career in that direction, since, according to the practice of the time, this would have entailed him taking holy orders, for which he had no taste. Instead he set about taking a degree in medicine, which, after some difficulty, he obtained, being awarded a Doctorate in Medicine in 1674. However, although he practised medicine occasionally, he did not take it up as a career. Instead, he temporarily took up the post of secretary to a diplomatic mission.

When this came to an end in 1666, Locke returned to medical studies in Oxford, until he met Lord Ashley, who was later to become the first Earl of Shaftesbury and was one of the most influential politicians during Charles II's reign. In 1667 Locke entered the service of Ashley as medical adviser and secretary, and when Ashley became Earl of Shaftesbury and Lord Chancellor of England he was given an official position. Shaftesbury was in and out of office until 1683, and Locke's own position varied accordingly. He returned to Christ Church for a while, but in 1675 he went, for the sake of his health, to France, to take the cure at Montpellier. But he remained in France for four years, met Cartesians, and became a friend of a pupil of Gassendi, all of which must have been influential on his philosophical views. On his return he spent some time in Oxford, but was still associated with Shaftesbury in one way or another. Shaftesbury fled to Holland in 1682 in fear of what were in effect renewed charges of treason, and died there the following year.

Locke himself felt unsafe and he also fled to Holland in the autumn of 1683. He remained there, for a time in hiding because of fears of extradition, until 1689, after the 'glorious revolution'. During that period he wrote his *Essay*, a Latin version of his *Letter on Toleration*, and his *Two Treatises on Civil Government*. On return to England he lived for two years in Westminster, refusing diplomatic office which was offered by King William, with whose supporters he had been associated in Holland, accepting instead the sinecure of Commissioner of Appeals. The *Essay* and the *Two Treatises* were published in 1690. In 1691 he became the permanent guest of Sir Francis Masham at Oates in Essex, having long been admired by Lady Masham. He remained there as a member of the family, involved in philosophical and other controversies until 1704, when he died. He was a Commissioner for Trade for four years from 1696, until ill-health forced his retirement, and he in consequence spent part of his time during this period in London. In 1702 the University of Oxford formally condemned his *Essay*, which Locke claimed be 'a recommendation of the book'.

In the light of the above, it cannot be said that Locke had nothing to do with a university, although it is fairly clear that the progress of his philosophy owed little or nothing to the University of Oxford.

On the other hand, Locke was not, like Leibniz, a constant correspondent with, and associate of, a wide range of men of intellectual and scientific understanding in Europe, despite those whom he met during his stay in France. Perhaps typically English, Locke had an association with others which was much more domestic. The most famous correspondence which Locke engaged in and which was published in his lifetime was with the Bishop of Worcester, who thought that his remarks about the soul were consistent with materialism. Moreover, it is of some significance that in the 'Epistle to the reader' which prefaces the *Essay*, Locke says that the book originated in a discussion 'on a subject very remote from this' between 'five or six friends meeting at my chamber'. This discussion led to questions about the limits of the understanding. So, he says, 'Some hasty and undigested thoughts, on a subject I had never before considered, which I set down against our next meeting, gave the first entrance into this Discourse; which having thus begun by chance, was continued by entreaty.' He goes on to emphasize the disjointed way in which the book was eventually written. It went through four editions during his lifetime, of which a recent editor[5] reckons that something like 3,200 copies in all were printed. Locke was preparing a fifth edition, which appeared in 1706, when he died, with a printing of perhaps 900 copies. A sixth edition appeared in 1710, and there were regular reprintings of it thereafter. This suggests that whatever the University of Oxford and other authorities thought of it, the book was a considerable publishing success and had a certain popular appeal, which is, in a way, what Locke hoped it would have, as the general tenor of the 'Epistle to the reader' makes plain. (It was also translated into French (1700) and Latin (1701).)

In a sense Locke was following the example of Descartes in trying to write plainly and simply with a minimum of technical terms and a minimum of reliance upon scholastic notions. Like Descartes too, he does not always succeed in this aim. He still relies, for example, on notions such as that of 'substance', construed, at least in part, in a scholastic way. Locke is also notoriously vague on certain points, and it is arguable that total consistency was not his strong point. However that may be, he certainly followed Descartes to the extent that he embraced the Cartesian 'way of ideas', basing his conception of human knowledge on the ideas that are to be found in the human mind, even if he disagreed with Descartes when he argued that all those ideas originate in perception. But whatever influences on his thought came from the Continent in this way, his own views were immensely influential on the subsequent development of thought in France, particularly in respect of the *philosophes* of the French Enlightenment, such as Condillac and those associated with the *Encyclopaedia* produced by Diderot and D'Alembert, to which reference has already been made.

This particular influence came mainly through the views expressed in the *Essay*. Those views are almost entirely epistemological in character, presenting a theory of the nature of knowledge and its presuppositions. Like Descartes, Locke inevitably has recourse to metaphysical considerations at times, but these play a lesser role in his thought than did similar ones in the thought of Descartes, let alone in that of the other rationalist philosophers whom I have discussed. Locke's 'Englishness' and his lesser involvement with the tradition of scholasticism, which was so entrenched in the thought of the Catholic Church establishment, meant that his metaphysical thinking is considerably more casual than that of Descartes. Moreover, Locke was very influenced by the kind of scientific thinking which was dominant in England, particularly the thought of Robert Boyle, and the idea of the movement of the minute parts of bodies (the 'corpuscular hypothesis'). In consequence, Locke's view of the physical world is in many ways different from that of Descartes. Moreover, he was not a mathematician, and the *Essay* shows little sign of any contact with the sort of mathematized physical theory which is associated with the name of Newton. (Newton's *Principia* was published in 1687, three years before the publication of Locke's *Essay*.) On the other hand, some of the things which Locke says about reason in the fourth book of the *Essay* are very critical of the tradition of logic that was dominant in his time, although, in contrast with Leibniz, there is no attempt to put anything in its place. Rather, what he has to say is a criticism of the kind of insistence on syllogistic argument and its reliance on supposedly accepted general truths or maxims, which was typical of the disputations employed in Oxford at that time.

What Locke initiated primarily was a concern with the limits of the human understanding, a concern which was taken further by Hume and Kant. But his approach to this via his adaptation of the Cartesian 'way of ideas' was both level-headed and at times rather casual. The same is true to a large extent of his political thinking. The first *Treatise of Civil Government* is an attack on the theory of the divine right of absolute monarchy put forward by Sir Robert Filmer in his *Patriarchia*, and is now of merely parochial interest. The second *Treatise* was meant to defend the principles lying behind the 'glorious revolution' and was influential, via Montesquieu, in the setting up of the American Constitution. It has more permanent philosophical interest, for, among other things, its defence of natural rights, particularly the right to property. It has the same qualities of sanity, combined with a certain casualness. Locke had none of the great originality of Descartes, none of the single-mindedness and systematic character of Spinoza, and none of the vast philosophical range of Leibniz. However, Leibniz took him seriously and thought of him as having an importance sufficient to justify his writing a section-by-section commentary on and criticism of the *Essay*. Moreover, in his concern with the limits of the human understanding Locke set up a tradition of his own which has been persistent and rewarding.

THE INTELLECTUAL MILIEU AND THE LIMITATIONS OF THE UNIVERSITIES

It is difficult in the case of thinkers like those discussed in this chapter to trace exactly what they owe to whom in the intellectual milieu of their times. All those with whom we have been concerned owed much, although in varying ways and amounts, to their commerce with the philosophers and scientists of their age, or at least to their published works. With the exception of Spinoza, they were enabled to pursue their interests as a result of forms of patronage, or at least of modes of employment which amounted to something like patronage. They were not as such men of wealth, although they associated with leading figures of their day. But they were enabled by their circumstances to have an intellectual independence. It would be, of course, a little misleading to say that that is how philosophy was in the seventeenth century; for in paying attention to these men we pay attention only to those who have come to be thought of as the leading philosophers of the century. There were hosts of lesser figures, most of whom were associated with universities in ways in which the leading philosophers were not. Although Locke was a student of Christ Church for life and worked there for some part of his life, his employment as a teacher at Oxford was relatively short-lived. None of the other major philosophers had as much connection with universities as that. But those lesser figures, as we now regard them, who did work in the universities of Europe were in general still buried in scholastic approaches to philosophy, both in their ideas and in the forms in which they thought those ideas should be pursued and taught.

We have already noted Locke's poor opinion of philosophy as it was taught in Oxford in his day. Such philosophy was, he believed, just an excuse for indulgence in obscure notions for their own sake. Moreover, the practice of disputation, which was still the main examination method for philosophy students, put a premium on a method of argument which relied on unexamined premises. All this, he thought, was vastly inferior to the newly developing sciences, both in respect of content and method. In consequence, there was some tendency for Locke, in a way that was taken further in the next century by Hume, to think of the right philosophical method as itself 'experimental', just as Descartes and Spinoza had thought of the right philosophical method as akin to that of geometry, while Leibniz had the ambition to solve problems by an appeal to a calculus. There was indeed something approaching an obsession with new methods in the seventeenth century, none of which has in the long run turned out to be acceptable as *the* philosophical method. But the intellectual milieu, of which both the new philosophy and the new science were part, was beneficial to both in enabling the legacy of the past to be discarded to a great extent, even if never completely or absolutely. It is indeed arguable that it was the ability of those philosophers, whom I have discussed, to talk to and argue with the leading scientists of their day, or at any rate their representatives, which marks them off from their predecessors. It is also true that it has rarely been the same since then.

At the same time, whatever may be said about this sort of thing and about how it affected the methods of these philosophers in a way that distinguished them from what went on in the universities of the period, their philosophy would not have been what it was if Descartes had not initiated the revolution which was inherent in his way of presenting philosophical problems. I mean by this both his relatively non-technical style of philosophizing and the autobiographical approach which is explicit in his *Discourse on Method* and *Meditations*. None of the other philosophers with whom we have been concerned had quite the same approach, but they were undoubtedly affected by it. Moreover, in spite of the ambiguities of

Descartes' attitudes towards the authorities of his day, his approach to philosophy was fundamentally anti-establishment, involving an appeal to whoever was prepared to listen and discuss the issues. As we have seen, he was considerably helped in this by the selfless activity of Marin Mersenne; but discussion with leading intellectuals, no matter what their persuasion, became a regular feature of philosophical practice, whatever the Church and other elements of the establishment might think. Thus, in a way, the non-involvement of these men in the characteristic activities of the universities was beneficial in furthering the revolution; they were not inhibited by such institutional ties, even if they were still under whatever restrictions governments and politics imposed on their private lives and writing activities.

But, from the point of view of what had been the case in previous centuries and what was to be the case again, the curious thing was the lack of connection at this time between the most fruitful pursuit of philosophy and the teaching of it. Whereas we have today come to think of that connection as almost essential, it was all but totally lacking at this time. Such teaching of philosophy as went on in universities and similar institutions had nothing to do with what we now think of as the real progress of philosophy. Hence, those who had experience of such teaching in the name of philosophy cannot have been in contact to any great extent with the movements in philosophy which have come to be seen as really valuable. Moreover, in the case of Spinoza and Leibniz at least, they published so little in their lifetime that there was little opportunity for the student to get to know what they thought. Knowledge of that, to the extent that it existed, must have been a matter of hearsay. It was of course different with Hobbes, Descartes and Locke. We have already noted the relatively large numbers of printed copies of Locke's *Essay* which were published, and the works of Descartes seem to have been very accessible. But Locke's *Essay* was formally condemned at Oxford, so that it cannot have been on any reading-list at the university; similarly, Descartes' works cannot have been accessible at Catholic universities and colleges once they were placed on the Index. In general, therefore, one can be confident about the lack of connection between the pursuit of real philosophy and the teaching of philosophy during this period.

Historically, this might be set down as an anomaly, although the same thing is true of at least the first part of the following century. That it is so can be thought of as something of a comment on the state of the universities at this time, and a partial rectification of the situation came only with changes in some universities in the eighteenth century, particularly in Germany, where new standards of scholarship were introduced. In Scotland too, though for different reasons (in part connected with the fact that an earlier tradition of compulsory philosophy – logic, methaphysics and moral philosophy – for all students was retained), philosophy flowered in a university context in the eighteenth century. But of England, that is to say of Oxford and Cambridge, where the seventeenth and eighteenth centuries were a period of apathy and neglect,[6] it was not until well into the nineteenth century that anything similar can be said. For different reasons again (this time connected with the dominance of Catholic thought and Catholic philosophy there), the same is true of France and other Catholic parts of Europe.

This must be part of the story of the next chapters. It is curious, however, that we have come to think of the seventeenth and early eighteenth centuries, when the progress of philosophy had little to do either with the universities or with any institution for the teaching of the subject, as one of the greatest periods of philosophy – indeed a classical age. Apart from the intrinsic merits of seventeenth- and eighteenth-century philosophy, philosophers then spoke for the learned in general and were associated with the great minds of the day, by direct contact or correspondence. They were, as such, respected by the powers that be, by royalty and the aristocracy. This was the reason for the patronage that made their pursuits possible. But there was, partly in consequence, comparatively little popular diffusion of the subject by modern standards, in spite of what I have said about, for example, the fashionableness of Cartesianism and Locke's publishing success. Nor was it possible, as was the case in both the ancient and mediaeval worlds, for the young to come and sit at the feet of the master. For the leading philosophers were not concerned, in general, to perpetuate the subject or their views on it by such methods. All this adds to the paradox; for, considered as an institution, that was what seventeenth-century philosophy was. I shall return to this issue in my Conclusion.

4

THE EIGHTEENTH CENTURY

THE ENLIGHTENMENT

At the beginning of the eighteenth century things were much as they had been in the previous century, except perhaps in Germany. In that country, with exceptions in the nineteenth century to which we shall come in due course, the practice of philosophy became almost indissolubly associated with the universities, at any rate from the time of Christian Wolff (1679–1754), who put forward a somewhat corrupt form of Leibnizianism. Moreover, Wolff originally published his philosophical works exclusively in German, only turning to Latin when he sought a wider audience. Partly because of this, his philosophical system became the established philosophy in Germany until the time of Kant, whose teacher, Martin Knutzen, was a Wolffian. Wolff corresponded with Leibniz from 1704 until the latter's death. He accepted with modifications a good deal of the apparatus of Leibniz's system. He had, however, a closer connection with scholasticism than Leibniz did, and also maintained, in Cartesian fashion, a firm distinction between soul and body, in a way which implied a considerable restriction on and modification of Leibniz's monadology.

The details of this do not matter much for our present purposes. Wolff was in effect the leading figure of the German Enlightenment, but, unlike the leading figures of the French Enlightenment, his activities were very much part of the university system. He was in fact appointed Professor of Mathematics in 1707 at the University of Halle, which was thought of as the leading German university at the time. He was also elected to the Berlin Academy on Leibniz's recommendation. But in 1723, at the instigation of the Lutheran Pietists, he was exiled by William I of Prussia. He then moved to the Calvinist University of Marburg, only to return to Halle, on the accession of Frederick the Great in 1740, as Professor of Law and Vice-Chancellor, becoming Chancellor in 1743. Hence, despite the hiccup in the middle, he had a very distinguished academic career, was influential even outside Germany, and received high honours, including being made a baron of the Holy Roman Empire for his services.

In his person as an established university figure, therefore, philosophy received considerable public recognition, whatever may be thought of his particular contribution to it. We shall return to some of the details of the sequels to this later, but it might be worth noting now that Freiherr von Zedlitz, Minister of State to Frederick the Great from 1771 to 1788, to whom Kant dedicated his *Critique of Pure Reason*, and who offered him a chair and title at Halle, wrote to Kant extolling the value of philosophy over professional and what he called 'bread and butter' studies. The application of these professional studies would occupy men a few hours a day 'but in these and all the remainder of the day they are men, and have need of other sciences'. It is difficult to think of a present-day Secretary of State for Education writing similarly, at least in this country.[1] But the public prominence given to philosophy in eighteenth-century Germany, which this story reflects, owes much to Wolff.

Things were not thus in France and other Catholic countries. In France the universities were still thoroughly scholastic and impervious to the intellectual changes going on elsewhere, including the various Academies which Leibniz had done so much to further. In consequence, the universities there were as moribund, although perhaps for somewhat different reasons, as they were at the time in England (despite the position that the great Isaac Newton had at Cambridge). Teaching took place in Latin in French universities until the latter half of the eighteenth century. Philosophy was, along with the humanities, merely propaedeutic to theology, law and medicine, according to the mediaeval pattern. Its content remained relatively unchanged during the period, in spite of the increasing dominance of Cartesianism in the eighteenth century, at a time when things were moving on elsewhere. Although the attitudes of the French universities to physical theory and cosmology were more open than those to the more traditional aspects of philosophy, it remained true that Cartesianism took hold there when it had to all intents and purposes been superseded by Newtonianism. All this meant that, unlike in Germany, the French universities played no part in the Enlightenment. The philosophical contributions to that came from elsewhere.[2]

The actual participants in the French Enlightenment, which centred on Diderot and D'Alembert's *Encyclopédie* (referred to on pp. 60, 68) were individuals, intellectuals without institutional backing, and united more or less only by their opposition to the establishment, both religious and political. The most well known perhaps is François Voltaire (1694–1778), who was a contributor to the *Encyclopédie*. His work did much to bring about the eventual breaking of the Church's influence over the intellectual scene, something which reached its culmination in the French Revolution. These men were not great philosophers, although Jean-Jacques Rousseau (1712–1778), Swiss by origin and in many ways an impossible man, is a central figure in the tradition of political philosophy. They were considerably influenced by Locke, both in respect of his political philosophy and in respect of his epistemology. The epistemological influence is particularly evident in the case of the attempt of Etienne Bonnot de Condillac (1715–1780) to analyse all the mind's operations in terms of sensations and their derivatives. The *philosophes* were all, in spirit, humanist, empiricist, anti-religious, anti-establishment and to some extent materialist. The most evident indication of the last is provided by the title of one of the main works of Julien Offroy de la Mettrie (1709–1751) *L'homme machine*; but Denis Diderot (1713–1784) and Claude-Adrien Helvétius (1715–1771) were equally materialist in tendency, and their views were judged scandalous, to the extent that Helvétius was forced to retire from the royal service. The *Encyclopédie* itself came under opposition from the Jesuits and was suppressed for a while.

Nevertheless, it was all meant to embody the spirit of the 'age of reason', in spite of the opposition to it. Despite that spirit, it was, in philosophical content, somewhat second-hand, and except for the influence which Rousseau's doctrine of the 'general will' had on later political thinking, especially that of Hegel, it had no real philosophical legacy, whatever influences it had of other kinds. Some of Condillac's views were in a sense developed later by Maine de Biran (1766–1824), who emphasized what he called *l'effort voulu*, in effect the part played by the will and resistance to it in providing an impression of 'exteriority' beyond our sensations, so that we can have knowledge of the so-called external world. Biran has been called the 'French Kant', but he remains relatively unknown. He combined philosophy with a life of political activity at the time of Bonaparte and afterwards. He received the recognition of the *Institut de France* and the Academies of Berlin and Copenhagen. He remains the last philosopher of note in France for some time, and his pursuit of the subject took place once again outside the universities.

The state of the English universities in this period has already been noted. Things did not improve during the eighteenth century, despite a gradual abandonment of the mediaeval system of awarding degrees and the institution of the tradition of *Literae Humaniores* at Oxford at the end of the seventeenth century. Written examinations came in at Cambridge in 1772, and at Oxford when a new statute was passed in 1800. The state of the universities did not prevent the existence of real scholarship in certain areas, as is witnessed by Newton and Richard Bentley, the classicist, at Trinity College, Cambridge. But neither university produced any philosophy or philosopher worthy of mention after Locke. The two great names in British philosophy during the early to middle eighteenth century are of course those of Berkeley and Hume. The former was born in Ireland, the latter in Scotland. In the later eighteenth century it was Scotland that was the centre of philosophy in Britain, and, as was the case in Germany, this was very much a product of the university system. It is thus not an exaggeration to speak of a Scottish Enlightenment and to see some relationship between philosophy in Scotland and philosophy in Germany, although the connection was never a very direct one. We must first, however, consider Berkeley and Hume.

BERKELEY

Berkeley (1685–1753) was born near Kilkenny in Ireland, took a degree at Trinity College, Dublin, and became a Fellow of the college in 1707, although he also entered the priesthood, being ordained in 1710. The course at Trinity College was a general one, and Berkeley became acquainted with the views of Locke, Boyle and Newton – the 'new philosophy', as it was termed. Indeed, in 1705 Berkeley formed a society to study it. The influence of Locke upon Berkeley was considerable, although Berkeley thought that he did not go far enough in his empiricism. His attitude to Newton was respectful, though critical. It was during his period as Fellow of Trinity that his main works, *An Essay towards a New Theory of Vision*, *A Treatise Concerning the Principles of Human Knowledge* and

Three Dialogues between Hylas and Philonous were published. Hence, there is a sense in which Berkeley's philosophy was a product of the university system. But this is so only in a tangential way since Berkeley was not a teacher at the university; Trinity merely provided, through the Fellowship, the means for him to present his own ideas arrived at through his study of other philosophers and scientists.

The *New Theory of Vision* is a work on visual perception and, in particular, the problem of distance perception, in the tradition of Descartes' *Dioptrics*, and Malebranche's writings on optics. (Berkeley does not mention the latter, although he knew of Malebranche's other ideas.) The other two works take the theory of perception further in terms which justify the assertion that Berkeley was an idealist, perhaps the first one. Probably the best account of that is Berkeley's own at the end of the *Three Dialogues*. There he speaks of 'the truth which was before shared between the vulgar and the philosophers: the former being of the opinion, that *those things they immediately perceive are the real things*; and the latter, that *the things immediately perceived are ideas, which exist only in the mind*', and he adds 'Which two notions put together, do, in effect, constitute the substance of what I advance.' In Berkeley's metaphysics there exist only spirits and ideas. He thought that the notion of substance which Locke clung to was not only misconceived but also a possible source of both scepticism and atheism. For that reason he criticized Locke's theory of knowledge, particularly his doctrine of abstract ideas, for admitting such notions. At the same time, the insistence on extreme empiricist principles which all this entailed led him to reject Newton's views of absolute space, time and motion, and, worse still perhaps, some parts of mathematics, particularly the use of the notion of infinity in geometry. Such views set him against the supporters of Newton, but he continued to maintain them, although with modifications, in later publications.

In 1713 Berkeley went on leave to London, to publish the *Three Dialogues* and to seek friends in the literary and intellectual world of that city. He was a friend of Swift, despite the latter's suggestion that a consequence of his idealism was that one ought to be able to walk through closed doors. Dr Johnson's suggestion that one might refute Berkeley by kicking a stone is well known. Berkeley was also befriended by Addison, Steele and Pope. After a period on the continent as chaplain to the Earl of Peterborough, he was due to return to Trinity, but did not do so. Instead, he had a further period abroad, returning to Trinity in 1721, where, perhaps surprisingly after what were, on Berkeley's own admission, murmurs about his absence, he became Senior Fellow.

He was now seeking ecclesiastical preferment, and was made Dean of Derry in 1724. However, he never took up residence there, because he became involved in a project to set up a college in Bermuda, largely for missionary purposes. Impatient with government delays in supporting the project, he went in 1728, having now married, to America, where he settled on Rhode Island and established contact with a Dr Johnson of Yale College. He returned to England in 1731, without success in his project because of lack of government support. There were some grumbles over his spending his time in this way rather than serving the cause of Protestantism in Derry, but in spite of them he remained in London. He was appointed Bishop of Cloyne in 1734, and returned to Ireland to carry out his duties there, subsequently publishing only one more substantial work – a strange book, *Siris: a Chain of Philosophical Questions and Inquiries concerning the Virtues of Tar-Water, and divers other Subjects connected together and arising one from another.* Apart from claims, put to use among the local population of Ireland, for the medicinal virtues of tar-water, the 'divers other Subjects' include the nature of the universe, God and the doctrine of the Trinity!

Berkeley's career was clearly unusual for a philosopher, and it is perhaps important that his most well-known works date from his twenties, before he had embarked on anything ecclesiastical. Like Locke, Berkeley pursued his philosophical ideas from a university context, without that philosophy being put to practice within that institution. Trinity College made it possible for him to be the eminent, though often misunderstood, philosopher that he was. But his way of practising philosophy was, as with Locke, to publish books in order to present his philosophical ideas and arguments to the intellectual public. Thus his first visit to London, which enabled him to meet the leading intellectual figures of the day there, was the important event in his philosophical, as opposed to ecclesiastical, career. Locke had died before Berkeley published anything, so that Berkeley never met the man who was the most eminent philosopher in England before him; and there was no other philosopher of note remaining there. Hence, Berkeley's philosophical career was to some extent a solitary one, even if one gets no sense of a concern that this was so. Involvement with the leading literary and intellectual persons in England was enough, and the way in which Berkeley was, even as a young man, received by such persons is notable.

Nevertheless, the actual practice of philosophy in his case, and in general at the time, was a matter for the individual, and the individual's publications were directed at those of the public who would read them, not at other philosophers, though correspondence with other learned men might ensue.[3] There were in that sense no philosophers who could be called professional outside the universities, and no worthwhile philosophy went on inside them. Locke had been no different from Berkeley in that respect, and it was in fact the order of the times; but it is a point to be remarked on when one considers the importance attached by philosophers, both before this and afterwards, to argument and discussion with other philosophers.

HUME

David Hume (1711–1776), was like Berkeley in not being English, though this time we have to look to Scotland. He was born in Edinburgh of a family of poor landed gentry who thought of themselves as a branch of the family of the Earl of Home (or Hume, as was David Hume's preferred spelling). As he himself said, he 'passed through the ordinary course of education with success' and went to the University of Edinburgh in 1723, from which he probably did not graduate, perhaps preferring not to, as was the custom then both there and in Oxford. Edinburgh University did not then have, in any case, the same distinction in Scotland as Glasgow or Aberdeen, and it was in those universities that philosophy flowered in the eighteenth century, beginning with Francis Hutcheson who held the chair of moral philosophy at Glasgow from 1730 until his death in 1746.

It is perhaps worth noting the age at which Hume went to university (12 or 13, compared with the age of 20 at which Locke went to Christ Church, and that of 15 at which Berkeley went to Trinity College, Dublin). Scottish universities were still very mediaeval in conception, and the course that Hume took would normally have included humanities (Latin, if not exempted, and Greek), logic, moral philosophy and natural philosophy. The compulsory philosophy – a tradition which persisted until quite recently – was a somewhat mixed blessing for philosophy itself. While it brought about a university-based pursuit of philosophy in Scotland in the eighteenth century on a scale and with a breadth that the new tradition of *Literae Humaniores* at Oxford did not produce in the same way, the teaching curriculum remained mediaeval. At King's College, Aberdeen, for example, the regent-system, according to which a professor had to teach a batch of undergraduates in all subjects from the beginning until their graduation, was still in place when Reid took up a chair there in 1751. On the other hand, Hutcheson insisted on lecturing in English rather than Latin (and, indeed, without notes) when he took up his chair at Glasgow, and this did give an impetus to philosophy.

However this may be, Hume claimed that he got little from his time at Edinburgh University, and that his real education came from subsequent reading, which he persisted with in spite of his family's wish that he should take up law. It was probably during this period that he began writing his *Treatise of Human Nature*, although at the end of his life, when he wished to disparage and even disown that work, he claimed, improbably, that he began it 'before he left College'. But all this led to some kind of breakdown or 'vapours', which involved, as he put it, 'coldness and desertion of the spirit'. As a result in 1734 he abandoned philosophy for a while, and started working for a trader in Bristol. But this lasted only for a few months, and he decided to continue his studies in France, living frugally on a small income. Strangely enough, in the light of his subsequently published opinions on religion, he spent some time at the Jesuit college at La Flèche, which Descartes too had attended. He returned to London in 1737, where he arranged for the publication of the *Treatise*, now completed. The first two books of that work appeared in 1739, the third in 1740. Notoriously, Hume later claimed that the work 'fell dead-born from the press'. This seems to have been an exaggeration, although reviews were not good, and one long review in particular was both condescending and critical of his style of philosophizing. Perhaps as a result, Hume never wrote in the same free style again.[4]

In 1741 Hume produced anonymously an intentionally popular volume of essays, *Essays, Moral and Political*, followed by a second volume in 1742. (These essays were acknowledged by him in 1748.) In 1744 he applied for the chair of Philosophy ('ethics and pneumatic philosophy') soon to be vacant at Edinburgh, but he failed to get it, probably because of opposition to him in Edinburgh as a result of his religious views. In spite of this failure to obtain a university appointment, Hume remained friendly with Hutcheson at Glasgow until the latter's death in 1746, and he had a close friendship with Adam Smith who was in 1751 appointed to the chair of logic at Glasgow. Indeed, when Smith moved to the chair of moral philosophy there in 1752, Hume applied for the logic chair, but was again unsuccessful. He had meanwhile had an appointment as tutor to the Marquis of Annerdale at St Albans, which improved his finances, but not much else, as the Marquis was insane; he had also accompanied General St Clair on some rather dubious expeditions to Britanny and Turin, out of which emerged, if nothing else, a rather unflattering description of his appearance by Lord Charlemont who met him in Turin.[5]

During this time too came the publication of the two *Enquiries* and other works. Hume by then felt better off and this gave him the means for such literary work. He now insisted that the *Enquiries*, rather than the *Treatise*, should be deemed as containing his real philosophy, although posterity has not entirely agreed with him. In 1751 he took up residence in Edinburgh with his sister and her husband, both he and his sister, he said, 'loving order and frugality'. After his failure to get the chair at Glasgow he was elected in 1752 to be Librarian of the Advocates' Library in Edinburgh, where he remained until 1757, with a small salary but access to the resources of the library. He now turned to history, rather than philosophy, publishing his *History of Great Britain* (from James I to the Revolution) and then, in reverse chronological order, his *History of England*, first the Tudors and then the period from Julius Caesar until Henry VII. Hume acquired a great reputation and made a good deal of money from these works. He was indeed for some time thought of as a historian rather than a philosopher.[6]

The rest of his life until his retirement in 1769 was spent in diplomatic roles, especially as *chargé d'affaires* in Paris, where he had gone with Lord Hertford, the Ambassador there. He was a considerable social and literary success in Paris ('No lady's toilette was complete without Hume's attendance' reported Charlemont), in spite of his bad French, his unprepossessing appearance and general lack of grace. On returning to London he was Under-Secretary of State until 1768, and his pension was thereby increased. He died after a longish illness in 1776, expecting that his mind would suffer at death the same fate as his body. It is recorded that after his funeral a mob swarmed around his grave, presumably expecting some sign from heaven over the burial place of the infidel, and watch was kept over the grave for about eight nights; such was Hume's popular reputation in Scotland, whatever his social success in Paris and the verdict of posterity on him as a philosopher. His *Dialogues Concerning Natural Religion* were published only after his death, but Hume's reputation as an atheist made him hated in religious circles, in spite of Adam Smith's attempt to show, in giving an account of his death, that Hume, like Epicurus, had died a dignified and unfearing death in accordance with his philosophy.

I have gone into considerable detail concerning Hume's life and circumstances partly because of the mixed reputation that he had (Paris versus Edinburgh, one might say) and partly because, as far as concerns Scottish academic life, Hume stood on a threshold which he was unable to cross, perhaps because of the reputation that he had in Scotland. His appearance and manner no doubt told against him in certain circles, but he seems to have been able to overcome such obstacles. What he could not transcend was the effect of his expressed beliefs, at any rate in Scotland, although it was a different matter in the fashionable circles of Paris. Hume continued the empiricist tradition that had been laid down by Locke and Berkeley, but he took that tradition almost to its limits, nearly, if not entirely, to the point at which he could be seen as the supreme sceptic. Commentators have differed on whether such scepticism was his dominant motivation or whether his aim was to maintain a consistent naturalism. Certainly Hume's moral philosophy was naturalist in that it saw the foundation of morals as lying in the contribution that actions make to the satisfaction of natural desires. Moreover, there is an appeal to human nature at the centre of many of Hume's solutions, if that is what they were, to such problems as the source of our belief in causal necessity and belief in a so-called external world. Indeed, one view of Hume's philosophy is that it was an attempt to follow the example of the great Newton in attempting to establish a science of human nature, as well as other aspects of nature.

But many of the 'solutions' to problems of which I have spoken must have seemed negative. Consider, for example, the well-known claim in *Treatise* I.iv.2 about belief in the existence of bodies independent of our minds: 'We may well ask, *What causes us to believe in the existence of body?* but 'tis vain to ask, *Whether there be body or not.*' Some may well think that this is just to evade the question, even if the view expressed follows more or less directly from the first principles of his philosophy – that all we are confronted with is impressions and ideas, and that every simple idea is a copy of a corresponding impression. Indeed, the somewhat later Scottish philosopher, Thomas Reid, thought that Hume's conclusions were absurd, that his arguments were valid, and that the fault must therefore lie in his premises, which involved those doctrines about impressions and ideas. On that view, which has much to be said for it, Hume had taken Berkeleian empiricism, with its theory of perception according to which all that we directly perceive are ideas, but without Berkeley's God, and he had pushed the consequences of that theory to its limits in a kind of absurdity. Nevertheless, the arguments themselves and the insights involved are at such a high level that Hume's great reputation in the history of philosophy is abundantly justified. That said, it has to be added that that reputation was not constant after his death. Notoriously, Kant said that a reading of Hume woke him from his dogmatic slumbers, although it is not entirely clear how much of Hume Kant had read. But in Britain Hume had to be rediscovered in the nineteenth century, since which time there has been no looking back.

SCOTTISH UNIVERSITIES AND THE SCOTTISH ENLIGHTENMENT

Hume was 'Mr Hume, the atheist' to his contemporaries, and such success as he had was a *succès de scandale*. But the scandal was enough to keep him from the fulfilment of his ambition to hold a Chair in a Scottish university. It was an ambition which was attained by Francis Hutcheson (1694–1746), who concerned himself with the parallels which he took to exist between the moral and aesthetic senses, and by Hume's great friend Adam Smith (1723–1790). Adam Smith is now most well known as a political economist for his work *The Wealth of Nations*, in which it is argued that self-interest best preserves the social and economic well-being of society; but he also wrote about the moral sentiments, following Hume to some extent, putting weight on the idea of sympathy and the role of an imaginary impartial spectator in assessing our actions. Although Hume did not achieve his ambition to occupy a Chair, it was in effect an ambition which, so far, no leading eighteenth-century philosopher in Britain, outside Scotland, had had. Apart from the earlier Locke, there was activity at this time in England in the field of moral philosophy, of which perhaps the two main examples are provided by Joseph Butler (1692–1752)[7] and Richard Price (1723–1791); but of these the former was an Anglican bishop and the latter a Unitarian minister. Other, more obscure, English figures, often clerics, had philosophical pretensions too, but there are no corresponding university figures to speak of.

Historically, therefore, it is of some importance that it was in Scotland that Hume's ambition was pertinent. Moreover, it is significant that the ambition was to hold a Scottish chair. In the two English universities of the time, the work of teaching undergraduates was carried out by college tutors. As Gibbon made clear, professors often did nothing. This was not the case in Scotland. The late persistence of the 'regenting' system gave the prime responsibility for teaching to the holder of a chair, and when that gave way to a more specialized form of teaching it was the giving of lectures by a professor which had pride of place. Hutcheson's abandonment of Latin for that purpose, as well as his style of lecturing, made the professorial lecture course more accessible and so boosted philosophy.

It no doubt affected it in another way too. It has sometimes been said that the character of British philosophy today, by comparison with that of much continental philosophy, owes much to the fact that philosophy teaching is primarily carried out by way of the tutorial, with the opportunity that that gives of criticism of the student's work and discussion of it. That entails a kind of 'Socratic' approach to philosophical issues, without the formality involved in a mediaeval disputation. But it was not the primary practice in Scotland in the eighteenth century any more that it was in Germany. Hence the exposition of a philosophical point of view, and the impetus that that gave to system-building, was what inevitably had pride of place there. The great Scottish philosophers of the eighteenth century, such as Smith, Thomas Reid (1710–1796) and their successors, tended to produce treatises. Their students no doubt acquired familiarity with that way of thinking, not the Socratic one, let alone the ideal of a life lived together so as to produce the transmission of a flame from one mind to another, which Plato extolled, whether or not he practised it.

But Hume was not party to what did go on in the Scottish universities; in particular, he was never involved in teaching. Like the other seventeenth- and eighteenth-century philosophers whom we have discussed, he wrote for a public who were assumed to be educated enough to follow, if not understand, let alone accept, what he wrote. In Paris, this made him the intellectual of the hour; in Scotland – at any rate with the public at large, and also with the ecclesiastical establishment – it produced only scandal. As is well known, Hume was sometimes prey to doubts about his views, and appealed to nature as the remedy, saying that a dinner, a game of backgammon and conversation with friends can make philosophical speculations appear 'cold, and strain'd, and ridiculous'. Whatever one might think of such a remedy, and a really consistent philosopher ought perhaps to think that it is not good enough, Hume could not have had recourse to it if he were not a socially inclined sort of person. That was no doubt what saved him, given the position that he found himself in as a result of his persistence in being Socratic, at least to the extent of insisting on 'following the argument where it leads'.

The Scottish Enlightenment has some strange features, or at any rate seems to do so at first sight. As late as 1697 a student was executed in Edinburgh for blasphemy – the blasphemy in question apparently amounting to little more than a certain scepticism about religious matters.[8] But at about the same time the presbyters introduced into the Scottish universities reforms based on the Dutch example after the 'Glorious Revolution'. These reforms included an opening up of the universities to a wider circle of students, with bursaries for the less well-off, and the institution of the study of modern, not simply ancient, philosophy. In spite of resistance to some of these reforms by Andrew Fletcher in Edinburgh, they became the rule. A university curriculum in arts involving a substantial amount of philosophy persisted in Scottish universities until very recently. The Scots felt themselves to be in a difficult position after the 'Union' with England, because of the comparatively greater economic success of England and the tendency for political power to gravitate towards London. There came about a belief that Scotland would at all events be intellectually predominant, and the existence of an 'educated public' reinforced that belief. There had to be a balance between the values represented by the Presbyterian Church and those represented by a secular culture, and this is what the system aimed at.[9]

The place of the universities in all this, and the place of philosophy in the curriculum of the universities, gave philosophy an almost pre-eminent role to play in the intellectual life of Scotland, in spite of what many would regard as the dominance of Presbyterian theology. Humean scepticism, the results of which, as we have seen, even dogged his funeral, was followed by the institution of a Scottish philosophical 'school of common sense' by Thomas Reid, who thought that Hume's arguments were valid but his conclusions absurd, so that the error had to lie in the premises of his arguments (see p. 83). Reid saw as those premises the whole of Hume's epistemology with its reliance on a doctrine of impressions given to the senses and their corresponding ideas. Much of Reid's philosophy thus involves a critique of Hume's epistemology, a better account of sensation and perception (one almost unique in the history of philosophy), and an insistence on what common sense is supposed to tell us about our natural and 'original' faculties, both in the field of knowledge (the realm of our intellectual powers) and of conduct (the realm of our active powers). In the latter case, Reid, like some others at about the same time, for example Richard Price, put a great weight on what in morals he supposed to be a matter of intuition, and this included both rules of conduct and belief in freedom of the will.

Reid was educated at Marischal College, Aberdeen and became Librarian there for a time, resigning from the post in 1736 to visit England and subsequently to enter the ministry. He was appointed Professor of Philosophy at Aberdeen in 1751, although he had by this time published only one philosophical paper. He published his *Inquiry into the Human Mind on the Principles of Common Sense* in 1764, and in the same year moved to Glasgow (which was the most notable Scottish university at the time) to succeed Adam Smith in the Chair of Moral Philosophy there. Reid gave up his chair in 1780 in order to devote himself to writing, and thereafter published his two sets of *Essays* on the intellectual and active powers respectively. But it was as a proponent of the philosophy of common sense that he was most influential, both in Scotland and in certain colleges in America, where 'Scottish philosophy' became, towards the end of the nineteenth century, a kind of textbook philosophy. Reid had an ardent disciple in Dugald Stewart (1753–1828), and a very critical follower in Thomas Brown (1778–1820). The school culminated in the nineteenth century in the work of Sir William Hamilton (1788–1856), who not only edited, with copious notes, Reid's own writings, but also tried to link Reid with German philosophy, particularly Kant. He came under attack from John Stuart Mill, who was an Anglicized Scot, and Scottish philosophy as such never really recovered.

What is clear from all this is that, whatever role was played by

Scottish philosophy of the Enlightenment in the social, intellectual and political life of Scotland, it was in its essentials an academic movement. Its home lay in the universities, particularly Glasgow and Aberdeen. (Edinburgh University was less prominent then, and St Andrews University, although as ancient as Glasgow and Aberdeen, was moribund in the eighteenth century, in spite of the fact that the regenting-system was abolished there in 1747.) But because philosophy was so widely accessible to educated people, due to its central place in university education, the philosophers could think of themselves as addressing an educated public. It was still a public restricted to Scotland's main cities, but it was a wider one than Locke, say, could have depended on in England, where no similar situation existed in the universities. It is perhaps less clear that the 'educated public' understood exactly what was going on in the name of philosophy in the universities. Thomas Carlyle, writing anonymously in his *Signs of the Times* in the *Edinburgh Review* in 1829, complained that metaphysics and the moral sciences were in a state of decay almost everywhere, and that what he called the 'Philosophy of Mind' had ceased to exist in Scotland with the death of Dugald Stewart, who had died the previous year.[10] This was in spite of the existence of Hamilton, not to speak of James Mill, the father of John Stuart Mill (though Carlyle might not have been willing to count him because Mill was too obviously an empiricist).

THE GERMAN UNIVERSITIES: KANT

I said earlier in this chapter that it is possible to see some relationship between philosophy in Scotland and philosophy in Germany. The Scottish tradition, and the temperament of individual Scots, induced the belief that they were, by nature, metaphysically inclined; in due course Scottish philosophers were drawn to German metaphysical thinking, in spite of Carlyle's complaint of the decay of that subject. In that respect, German metaphysics meant Kant, and Kant was both the product and a part of a parallel university system. There are of course differences between the system in Germany (and indeed on the continent in general) and that which has grown up in Britain. It has to be remembered that at the time there were only two universities in England compared with four in Scotland, while the system in Germany was widespread. Nevertheless the situation in Scotland, with the end of the regenting-system, was like that in Germany in some respects. The dominant role was given to the university professors, whose lectures students might attend (sitting at their feet, so to speak) in order to prepare themselves for final assessment by means which are the relics of the mediaeval disputation (particularly in the oral defence of a thesis, which is still an essential part of the continental system).

In the eighteenth century, the bachelor's degree in Germany tended to be merely a matter of attending university for a couple of years, and masters' degrees had lost their reputation; so the doctorate tended to be the norm, as in effect it had been in the Middle Ages, if not under that title. In Scotland there were university colleges, in which students resided, but they did not have the independence from the university that Oxford and Cambridge colleges had. In Germany there has been, by contrast, the phenomenon of the migrant student, who may sit at the feet of whichever professor is judged to be the one from whom learning is to be derived. There has also existed a freedom to present one's thesis where one chooses. Scotland was in this respect something of a compromise between the German and English extremes. But for present purposes the point which requires emphasis is the power and influence of the professor. (The elaborate steps that have often had to be taken in Germany to acquire that position, via that of the *Privatdozent*, are legendary.)

As far as concerns the eighteenth century, philosophy in Germany after Wolff means, to all intents and purposes, Immanuel Kant (1724–1804), and Kant is almost the archetype of the philosopher as university professor. He lived in Königsberg all his life, went to the university there, and after a period of poverty as *Privatdozent*, was professor there until three years before his death. His life was the epitome of regularity, including daily walks at the same hour, and although he is said to have liked some form of social life, including the company of good-looking, educated ladies, the rest of his life was very much taken up with his duties as university professor. The universities in Germany were rather in the doldrums during the eighteenth century, and student numbers suffered. There were attempts at reform towards the end of the century and further attempts, particularly through Wilhelm von Humboldt, in the early part of the next century, although there were serious proposals in the 1790s for the actual closure of universities, and some did indeed close.[11]

The philosophical faculty, of which philosophy formed just one part (the rest including other arts and sciences), had for some time been thought inferior to the other faculties, theology, law and medicine. In 1798 Kant argued for the equality of the philosophical faculty with the other faculties, especially theology. Later Fichte campaigned for philosophy as the queen of the sciences, in conscious opposition to utilitarian conceptions of education, and urged that ability, not birth, should be the criterion for university attendance, with all the demands for financial support of students that that entailed. (Fichte was the first Rector of Humboldt's new university at Berlin, but he resigned after one semester, as the result of a dispute with university teachers who were less stern than he was with regard to the conduct of students.) The early part of the nineteenth century was the high-point of university-based philosophy in Germany.

Kant claimed that a reading of Hume (or some part of Hume's writing) woke him from his dogmatic slumbers. Kant's teacher was, as noted at the beginning of this chapter, Martin Knutzen, who was a Wolffian, but the general atmosphere of Königsberg was Pietist. Kant was influenced by C.A. Crusius, who maintained, amongst other things, the limits of the human understanding. Crusius inspired Kant's fundamental question 'How is synthetic *a priori* knowledge possible?' It is thus not altogether clear how large Hume's influence was in fact, except that Hume's general empiricist, and one might say sceptical, approach to philosophy stood in clear opposition to the received tendencies of post-Wolffian metaphysics in Germany. Kant's main contemporary was perhaps Moses Mendelssohn, the Jewish philosopher (1729–1786), with whom Kant corresponded, and who initially replied to Kant's *Critique of Pure Reason* (1781, 2nd edn 1787) by saying that he could not follow the argument and that his nervous disposition excluded 'all exertion'. This perhaps pardonable reaction did not prevent him from characterizing Kant as the 'all-slayer'.

The first *Critique* represented, however, a considerable shift from Kant's pre-critical writings, and Kant himself described his new approach – a form of idealism, anti-metaphysical in many ways, but a kind of metaphysics itself all the same – as a Copernican revolution in conceiving objects as conforming to our 'faculty of intuition' rather than vice versa. In conformity with his so-called 'transcendental idealism', Kant argued that space and time were *a priori* forms of intuition, conditioning experience or appearances, for which a reality consisting of 'things-in-themselves' was somehow responsible, though in a way which was quite unknowable. Thought, manifested in judgment, had to conform to certain *a priori* principles if it was to be objective, and attempts, such as those made by traditional metaphysicians, to go beyond what the understanding, combined with sensibility, can provide could produce only illusion. This emphasis on the limits of human understanding, and what this could show about reality, was and is of the utmost importance, whether or not valid, both for philosophical thought generally and for the development of philosophy in its historical context. All this emerged from one who was the epitome of the university professor as popularly conceived.

It would not be right here to enter upon any further exposition of Kant's system, which compasses, not only epistemology and metaphysics, but ethics and aesthetics too.[12] These last two subjects were dealt with particularly in the other two *Critiques*, those of *Practical Reason* and *Judgement* respectively (the last of which not only put aesthetics firmly on the philosophical map but also offered a critique of the notion of teleology). Kant characterized previous metaphysics as concerned with God, freedom and immortality. Whether or not that is an accurate characterization, Kant certainly had a position to maintain on these matters and on many others. His ethics, with its emphasis on duty, is part of the system, although it is often seen as very Protestant in character.

Kant's writings are generally regarded as severe and perhaps even unapproachable, although his lectures at the university were said to be very different – witty, and with amusing digressions, nothing of which is detectable in the three *Critiques*. In spite of his influential writings on aesthetics, he appears to have had little, if any, aesthetic sensibility. He had a great interest, however, in politics, with opinions which were often radical, although he took no practical political action on anything. His philosophical standing has proved to be immense, however, and his influence, nearly all derived from his published works – his treatises, so to speak – has been equally great. It is easy to be sympathetic with Moses Mendelssohn in his difficulty with Kant's argument, and it has to be admitted that the works are far from easy to read, but Kant stands supreme as an academic philosopher – and indeed as a philosopher in general. Many a philosophical tyro has tried to grapple with Kant, almost before any other philosopher; his philosophy is nothing if not a challenge, and so it is often treated. Kant's philosophy is a fitting conclusion to the eighteenth century, a kind of template for what was to come, even when that fell short of his high standard. Whatever was the case elsewhere (and only Scotland affords any kind of parallel), the professionalism of philosophy as a university discipline was now established in Germany.[13]

5
THE NINETEENTH CENTURY

THE GENERAL SITUATION IN ENGLAND

In at any rate the first half of the nineteenth century the situation which I have described as applying in the eighteenth century still held good. Changes in university systems gradually took place more or less everywhere, however. In England, until University College London was instituted in 1827, in deliberate opposition to the policy of religious tests which restricted holders of fellowships and the like at Oxford and Cambridge to members of the Church of England, the universities of Oxford and Cambridge remained the only universities in England; and not much in the way of philosophy went on there. Religious tests continued in Oxford and Cambridge until the Test Act of 1871, but in 1850 the first of a series of Royal Commissions was appointed which led to reforms in those universities, including the abolition of the condition that fellows of colleges must not be married, and a gradual increase in the powers of the university in relation to the colleges.

The undergraduate study of philosophy in Oxford was still restricted to degrees in *Literae Humaniores* ('Greats'), and this meant that there was still some bias towards ancient, as opposed to contemporary philosophy, unlike in Scotland. In Cambridge, where philosophy figured in the Moral Sciences Tripos, the situation was somewhat different, but the numbers of those involved in philosophy there were much smaller than those in Oxford; and this situation has remained in being up to the present day, in spite of all sorts of other changes. It is still not possible to take an undergraduate degree in Oxford in philosophy alone; but the number of students there who gain at least some taste of philosophy far exceeds that in any other university in England – and in Scotland too, since the decision was made in most universities there to give up compulsory philosophy.

There were no philosophers of note at either Oxford or Cambridge, however, until the last quarter of the century, and by this time most of them had embraced some form of idealism of a Hegelian kind, although Hegelianism as such had diminished in influence in Germany. This was the case with T.H. Green (1836–1882), probably the first philosopher worthy of comment to appear in nineteenth-century Oxford, to be followed, if with differences of doctrine, by Bernard Bosanquet (1848–1923) and, particularly, F.H. Bradley (1846–1924). At Cambridge were James Ward (1843–1925) and J.M.E. McTaggart (1866–1925), both of them idealists though with differences between them, together with a critic of idealism, though largely restricted to ethics, in Henry Sidgwick (1838–1900). Bertrand Russell (1872–1970), also at Cambridge, was initially an idealist too, and was converted from that philosophical point of view in part through the influence of G. E. Moore (1873–1958), who was, as much as anyone, responsible for the move to philosophical realism, which, in one form or another, had become dominant on the continent of Europe. With the partial exception of Russell, who really belongs to the next century, all these philosophers were university philosophers of a very academic kind.

J.S. MILL AND NINETEENTH-CENTURY ENGLISH PHILOSOPHY

The same could not be said of John Stuart Mill (1806–1873), the leading British philosopher of the earlier part of the nineteenth century. I say 'British', not 'English', because Mill was Scottish by origin. His father was James Mill (1773–1836), also a philosopher, who, along with the later Alexander Bain (1818–1903), professor of logic at Aberdeen (although mainly concerned with psychology), was responsible for the revival of traditional British empiricism in psychological dress. However, although James Mill was Scottish he lived most of his life in London (an example of the gravitation towards London that tended to take place with Scottish intellectuals, including also Carlyle). There he met and was greatly influenced by Jeremy Bentham (1748–1832), the founder of modern utilitarianism and a radical thinker, who devoted his life to legal reform based on the philosophical principles of utilitarianism. Bentham and the

Mills were all very much involved in the Reform Movement, and John Stuart Mill even went to Paris in 1830 to observe the July Revolution there. The rigorous education that James Mill prescribed for his son is legendary; I shall not go into the details of it here. James Mill was, for most of his life in London, an examiner in the office of the East India Company, and his son followed him in the employment of the company, beginning as a clerk in 1823, until the company came to an end in 1858. After a period in which John Stuart Mill described himself as a recluse, he was elected to Parliament as a working-man's candidate in 1865, only to lose the seat in 1868. He spent most of the rest of his life in Avignon, where he had a cottage, and continued some writing, although his main publications appeared in the years between 1843 and 1865.

J.S. Mill was much involved in the radical politics of his day. For a time he hoped to build up a new radical party; he supported socialism as it appeared in France and elsewhere and explicitly set himself up as a proponent of working-class rights. But he was not a total success as a practical politician. Perhaps he was too true to his principles; he was certainly too much the philosopher, and too much concerned with the truth. Some of his works, certainly those on *Representative Government* (1861) and *The Subjection of Women* (1869), and, in a way, his *Essay on Liberty* (1859), have very practical purposes and implications. But others of his works are definitely theoretical, particularly his *System of Logic* (1843), his *Examination of Sir William Hamilton's Philosophy* (1865), and what is perhaps his most well-known work, *Utilitarianism* (1863). The first and third of the last three works, along with *On Liberty*, remain the most read. Indeed, *On Liberty* presents a classic thesis about the scope of individual freedom, which is much referred to when such considerations arise today, as they have done over, for example, pornography, homosexuality and the like. Mill's general attitude was that individuals should be free to do whatever does not impinge upon the rights of others; they should have complete liberty to do whatever is not other-regarding. There are obvious questions that can be raised about exactly when our actions have no effect on others – indeed whether they ever have no such effect.

Utilitarianism takes further the approach to ethics initiated by Bentham (although the ideal of promoting 'the greatest happiness for the greatest numbers' had been put forward earlier in those terms by Francis Hutcheson). Bentham based his ethics and social philosophy on an analysis of the human mind, according to which pleasure and pain are the 'sovereign masters' of mankind. But a large part of Bentham's motivation derived from a concern for legal and social reform, in opposition to the legal principles enshrined in the works such as Blackstone's *Commentaries*. Bentham quite rightly saw those principles as cruel in practice, especially when applied, as they were, in the prevailing system of punishment. In his view, punishment should be carried out in accordance with what he saw as the principles of psychology, expressed in terms of the pursuit of pleasure and the avoidance of pain, the overall aim being the greatest happiness of the greatest number. J.S. Mill was to introduce refinements on that point of view, in the interests of consistency and realism. But utilitarianism, which basically involves the idea that human actions should be judged in terms of their utility, given the general aim of furthering human well-being and happiness, has remained a force ever since, even though it is often opposed to a 'Kantian' emphasis on duty and the good will.

The radical and reforming movement which Bentham, with the co-operation of James Mill, and later John Stuart Mill, initiated was an extremely active one. Bentham set up, at his own expense, a new journal, *The Westminster Review*, as the mouthpiece of the movement, in opposition to the Whig *Edinburgh Review* and the Tory *Quarterly*. After a change of ownership in 1828, when for a time both Mills ceased to write for it, it came back later into the ownership and under the editorship of J.S. Mill, as *The London and Westminster Review*. The Benthamite movement was also responsible, on the suggestion made in a letter to *The Times* in 1825 by Thomas Campbell, for the institution of University College London. This was opened to students in 1828, and because of its secular character, its willingness to admit students of any or no denomination, became known as 'the Godless institution of Gower Street'. (Bentham's clothed skeleton and mummified head have been preserved in University College, although Bentham was not personally the founder of the College – the founding being the work of what Bentham termed 'an association of liberals'.)

In the following year, as a counterblast, there was founded King's College in the Strand, an institution intended to be based on 'the doctrines of the United Church of England and Ireland', the teachers of which were, with some exceptions, to be members of that Church, as with Oxford and Cambridge. King's College received a charter, but University College did not, although it claimed to be the University of London. After various arguments – and against the opposition of Oxford and Cambridge to the conferment of degrees by London – a new University of London was given a charter in 1836 as an examining body. The two colleges were not made constituent members of the university until 1898. By this time other new universities, in Durham and Manchester in particular, had been founded, soon to be followed by other metropolitan universities. So ended the restriction of English universities to the two ancient foundations of Oxford and Cambridge, where religious tests for the holding of posts were abolished in 1871. It was from about this time that the professionalism of philosophy in England began. It is probably no coincidence.

To return, however, to J.S. Mill, it has to be noted that the period of his lifetime was one of striking developments in science, particularly in the person of Charles Darwin. Mill's *Logic* evinced a strong interest in scientific method (mainly as regards the physical sciences, although its final part was concerned with the social, or what Mill called the 'moral', sciences). Indeed, one might argue that Mill's account of the 'four methods of experimental inquiry' is the part of the *Logic* which has attracted the greatest attention since its composition. Mill came in for criticism in this respect from a philosopher who was part of the university system, William Whewell (1794–1866), who was Professor of Mineralogy and Moral Philosophy (a professor, as was said, of the science of things in general) at Cambridge. Whewell was in many ways a traditionalist, both in his epistemology and his political attitudes, but his account of scientific method, which relied on the idea of what has become known as the 'hypothetico-deductive method', is more in tune with contemporary thinking on these matters than is Mill's account. Mill used Whewell's *History of the Inductive Sciences* (1837) for many of his examples, but Whewell's later writings were tellingly critical of Mill's thinking in this sphere. But the philosopher who in many ways supported Mill on various issues, but who was also the expounder of the principles of evolution which Darwin introduced, was Herbert Spencer (1820–1903). He started out as a railway engineer, but gave that up for a literary career and was for a time sub-editor of *The Economist*. Spencer was much more sweeping in his ideas than Mill was, and acquired almost a world-wide reputation as the prophet of evolutionism, as applied to a great variety of issues. But he was like Mill and unlike Whewell in not being an academic.

The other philosopher to set beside and against Mill is, of course, Sir William Hamilton, to whom Mill more or less gave the philosophical death-blow (Hamilton in fact was already dead) in his *Examination of Sir William Hamilton's Philosophy*. Hamilton had been Professor of Logic and Metaphysics at Edinburgh and a continuer of the Scottish philosophical tradition initiated by Reid. He was a man of great learning and had a great reputation in his lifetime. He made contributions to logic as well as forging the links between Scottish and German philosophy referred to in Chapter 4. Whatever one thinks of Mill's *Examination* as a positive philosophical work (and only one chapter, that which embodies Mill's 'phenomenalistic' account of our knowledge of the external world, is still much read), it was devastating in pointing out Hamilton's inconsistencies and the lack of the systematic qualities to which he had laid claim. The 'Scottish' school of philosophy which Reid began, and which has sometimes been known as the school of commonsense, never recovered, although, as already noted, it had some influences in the USA. Subsequent Scottish philosophers, such as James Ferrier (1808–1864), though still very much a part of the university system there, tended to be philosophers of a different kind. (Ferrier, indeed, who attended university at Oxford, and who eventually became Professor of Moral Philosophy at St Andrews, became interested in metaphysics, under the influence of Hamilton. He was an admirer of Berkeley but advocated a rigorous philosophical argument leading to the identification of what is absolute. He might be regarded as of a part with the trend towards Absolute Idealism – the British version of Hegelianism – which became dominant in Oxford in the last part of the nineteenth century.) Although the English universities followed Scotland in the professionalism of philosophy, Scottish philosophy, as such, lost its distinctive character from this point.

It should be clear from what I have said that in England, at any rate in the first two-thirds of the nineteenth century, philosophy was carried on by a number of individuals, who maintained themselves in a variety of ways, but who were independent of any single institution to which philosophy might belong. Some of them, such as Carlyle and the Mills, were examples of the gravitation from Scotland to London, which many eighteenth-century Scots feared. They were also part of a literary and political scene which had its outlet in the various *Reviews* of which mention has already been made. There is arguably a certain amateurish quality to some of their writing, considered as philosophy; it has none of the character of the work of the seventeenth- and eighteenth-century giants. It cannot be denied, however, that J.S. Mill was a major philosophical figure, although a very English figure philosophically speaking, in spite of his Scottish origins. He belongs in many ways to the tradition of the British Empiricists, as Russell was to do later, and his work does not have the systematic character of the German philosophy of the time. Some may think that a defect, but it is perhaps all to the good. It is also arguable, however, that if Mill had been a 'university philosopher' his philosophy, or at any rate its style, would have been very different. That, however, is an empty supposition, in that the professionalism of philosophy in England had not yet begun. When it did begin, in the latter part of the century in Oxford and Cambridge, the philosophy which was pursued was in many ways a copy of what philosophy had been in Germany earlier – even if with an English flavour.

JOURNALS AND PHILOSOPHICAL SOCIETIES

Before turning to the state of affairs in Germany, it is worth noting the rise of certain institutions, outside the universities, which were to become organs of the professionalism that was coming. I have in mind the beginnings of philosophical journals and of certain philosophical societies. Although a few learned journals had existed before this time, the oldest being the *Journal des savants* (1665–), it was not until the nineteenth century that they appeared in any great numbers. Journals concerned with philosophy sprang up in a number of countries during the latter half of the nineteenth century. Not all of these journals have had more than a relatively ephemeral existence, and others which have had a reasonably prolonged life have ceased publication for certain periods for reasons which have nothing to do with their philosophical standing. Some have ceased publication or have had gaps in their publication because of wars and other public events and calamities. In Britain the longest running journal, the earliest to commence there, and the one on which I shall concentrate, is *Mind*, which was started in 1876, the same year as the beginning of the *Revue Philosophique* in France. It was the brainchild of Alexander Bain, who was Professor of Logic at Aberdeen from 1860 to 1880. Although he was nominally a professor of logic, Bain's main interests and publications were in the field of psychology and philosophy of mind, and for that reason it is perhaps no surprise that the journal, when it appeared, was subtitled 'a quarterly review of psychology and philosophy' (in that order). So it remained until 1974, when I myself was editor, although it is arguable that in the light of the journal's typical contents the subtitle should have been changed years before, so as to make reference to philosophy only.

Bain consulted various people – Croom Robertson, who was Grote Professor of the Philosophy of Mind and Logic at University College London and whom Bain appointed as the first editor, Herbert Spencer, and Venn and Sidgwick at Cambridge. He gained their support but found a publisher, appointed the editor and started the journal himself and at his own expense; indeed he supported the journal financially for the first fifteen years of its history, when Croom Robertson resigned the editorship. Then Henry Sidgwick took on the financial sponsorship, but in 1900 set up the Mind Association in order to secure backing for the journal from subscriptions. So it has continued. The philosophers at Oxford were at first deeply suspicious of the new journal, as they were of the Aristotelian Society (to be discussed later), as London organizations; and there was a certain jubilance in Oxford over the founding of the Mind Association with an Oxford secretary, given that the second editor, G.F. Stout, a Cambridge man by origin, had in 1899 been appointed Wilde Reader in Mental Philosophy at Oxford. There were complaints from Cambridge that *Mind* was to be an Oxford 'house journal'. Eventually, however, *Mind*'s status was recognized by all.[1] (Another cause of annoyance was Stout's decision to start *Mind* all over again when he took up the editorship in 1892, with a 'New Series'. The decision, which affected the numbering of issues, has been a great source of confusion ever since.)

The original form of *Mind* was more or less what it continued to be – it contained articles, critical notices of important books and shorter notices of others. There were then also abstracts of important articles in foreign journals. Article writing was not, however, second nature for academic philosophers of that time, who tended to prefer the more traditional practice of book writing. Consequently it was only gradually that journals such as *Mind* came to be seen as a major tool of philosophical publication and, more particularly perhaps, of philosophical progress. Indeed, in the 1940s there was a tendency for G.E. Moore, under whose long editorship *Mind* was, arguably, the leading English-language journal, to publish long series of articles, most notably those by John Wisdom on 'Other minds'. Such publications might at other times have taken a book form, but this was, of course, during the Second World War. In any case, *Mind*, soon after its commencement, had a rival in the *Proceedings of the Aristotelian Society*, a fact which takes me to my second point concerning the initiation of new philosophical institutions.

The existence of philosophical societies of one kind or another was nothing new. They existed wherever people thought it worthwhile to meet to discuss philosophical issues which interested them. For example, Bruce Kuklick, in his *The Rise of American Philosophy*,[2] emphasizes the role of the Metaphysical Club in Boston, Massachusetts, followed by others when it came to an end in 1879, in bringing about the dominance of Harvard over the American philosophical scene at the end of the nineteenth century and the beginning of the twentieth. Such societies were often motivated by religious or theological interests. In the USA it was from this background that there was founded in 1867 in St Louis the *Journal of Speculative Philosophy*, the first technical philosophical journal in the USA and probably the first philosophical journal in the English language, which lasted until 1893. (Of the leading American journals of philosophy which still exist the *Philosophical Review* was set up at Cornell in 1892, and the *Journal of Philosophy* at Columbia in 1904.) The Aristotelian Society was set up in London in 1880 by Shadworth Hodgson with the deliberate aim of involving philosophically interested amateurs. In spite of its title it was never particularly concerned with Aristotle; it had more concern with the British empirical tradition in opposition to the Oxford Idealism of the time, and was much distrusted by Oxford. It published records of its proceedings between 1888 and 1896; then, for four years, papers given were published in *Mind*, until in 1900 a 'New Series of Proceedings' commenced publication. Publication of the proceedings of symposia, in conjunction with the Mind Association and, initially, the British Psychological Society, began in the form of Supplementary Volumes in 1918 and has continued ever since. The society's concern with amateurs gradually decreased, this role being taken over to a large extent by the Royal Institute of Philosophy, which published *Philosophy* (initially called the *Journal of Philosophical Studies*) from 1926.

I spoke earlier of these institutions as ones which were to become organs of the professionalism in philosophy that was developing. It is thus of some interest that, although the journals which I have mentioned, and others like them, were set up explicitly as technical publications, societies like the Aristotelian Society originally had other motivations. They were concerned to respond to interests in philosophy that existed in the general educated public. Membership of the Aristotelian Society was not originally large – about sixty or seventy members in 1900. That is very small in comparison with membership today, when the *Proceedings* tends to be a record of technical papers given to meetings attended by a rather small selection of members and guests, but read (it is hoped) by a very much larger membership, as well as those who use academic libraries. On the other hand, the motivation of the founders of the Aristotelian Society was not in a real sense educational; it was not concerned explicitly to spread interest in, and knowledge of, philosophy to those who were unacquainted with it (the Royal Institute of Philosophy was to have something of that educational mission); but the Aristotelian Society was meant for those already interested and at least partially initiated into philosophy. It was inevitably a minority interest, given the restricted scope for becoming acquainted with philosophy except through access to published books. The same no doubt applied to similar societies elsewhere, but the Aristotelian Society, through the publication of its *Proceedings*, gained a reputation which was unique.

THE NEW UNIVERSITY OF BERLIN: FICHTE

I have concentrated in the above on the situation in Britain (where other journals subsequently came into existence), but the situation was not untypical of developments in many European countries, as well as in the USA. With all this in mind, let us now return to affairs in Germany, where, as I have emphasized, professionalism in philosophy was much more advanced than in Britain. Even in Germany, however, as we shall see, there were certain notable exceptions to the general rule.

The final years of Kant's life were the years of the French Revolution followed by the Napoleonic era. In France the effect of the revolutionary movements was the closure of the universities. Napoleon instituted a single Imperial University, which was in effect a ministry of education, responsible for the supervision of the *baccalauréat* and the provision of public lectures. The role of providing higher education, including research, on a competitive basis, though still mainly with practical and utilitarian aims, was given to the new *grandes écoles*. There were similar pressures in Germany, especially as a result of the political upheavals produced by Napoleon, whose eventual fall led to a period of increased political repression there. The result of all these pressures was university reform, although only the better universities survived (others being closed), and it incorporated the ideal of research. *Wissenschaft* became the order of the day, and, with it, the idea of teaching by means of the seminar. Institutes and seminars grew up everywhere in Germany during the nineteenth century, and this put increasing weight on the doctorate as the essential component of a university education.

A new University of Berlin was set up by Wilhelm von Humboldt in 1810 for the Prussian government. It was initially meant to be generalist in conception and to provide in those terms a model for other universities, but it too came under the universal banner of *Wissenschaft*. Apart from von Humboldt, the two main sources of the idea of the new university were Schleiermacher the theologian and Fichte the philosopher. The former was the head of the commission responsible for setting it up, while Fichte was the first rector, although he resigned, as noted earlier, after a few months, because his ideas of conduct at the university were too severe for colleagues to accept. Nevertheless, the new university was non-utilitarian in conception, even if its aims were to produce the contemporary version of philosopher kings – that is to say philosophically educated members of the state administration. It is clear that philosophers played an important role in the development of university education in Germany at this time. But as far as concerns the new University of Berlin, philosophy came to have an even greater part to play, in the person of Georg Wilhelm Friedrich Hegel (1770–1831).

As I have already indicated, Johann Gottlieb Fichte (1762–1814), who perhaps embodied the first reaction in German philosophy against Kant, in the direction of a more comprehensive Idealism (to be described as 'absolute idealism'), played a large part in the setting up of the University of Berlin. Fichte thought that the philosophical faculty (arts and sciences) in general, and philosophy in particular, should play the dominant role in university education (as against the older faculties of law, medicine and theology); but that education should be aimed at bringing about a general knowledge and thereby the intellectual development of the student. This vision was even supposed to inform the lectures given by the professors, so that they might present their ideas for critical reception on the part of their listeners, by contrast with the previous practice of lecturing from textbooks. The development of knowledge would then take place between all concerned. But all this was to be accompanied by a discipline which became unacceptable to those involved, and it was this which led to Fichte's resignation from the rectorship of the university.

Fichte was not a man to pour oil on troubled waters and the event in question was not untypical of him. He was, from 1797 to 1800, during four years of its short existence, co-editor of the *Philosophisches Journal einer Gesellschaft Deutscher Gelehrten*; but his publication in it, in 1798, of an article concerning belief in a divine order led to accusations of atheism and the suppression of the journal everywhere except in Prussia. He was also forced to resign from his chair at the University of Jena. He subsequently gained a chair at Erlangen, but his coming into favour in Berlin was at least in part due to his *Addresses to the German Nation*, given in Berlin, attacking Napoleon. The ideas of Hegel, the dominant figure of the early University of Berlin, fitted in with Fichte's conception of the university to some extent, in that he saw philosophy as providing a universal system of knowledge. The extent to which this had any lasting effect on the University of Berlin is another matter. The trend towards specialism was perhaps an inevitable consequence of the emphasis on *Wissenschaft*.

HEGEL AND THE HEGELIANS

Hegel was a student at the University of Tübingen, where he became a friend of Schelling and the poet Hölderlin. Friedrich Wilhelm Joseph von Schelling (1775–1854) was originally a theologian (as Fichte had been also), but moved into philosophy, becoming a student of Fichte's at Jena. He was for a while professor at Munich, before moving to a post in Berlin. There, like Fichte, Schelling preached the doctrine of the key role to be played by the philosophical faculty, but during the period when Hegel was dominant in philosophy at Berlin (1818–31) he remained philosophically silent, in spite of his belief in the superiority of his own 'absolute idealism', which he asserted openly after Hegel's death. Hegel and he co-edited the *Kritisches Journal der Philosophie* from Tübingen in 1802/3, after which it ceased publication. In it Hegel published several articles. By then Hegel had obtained a position at the University of Jena, and there he wrote his *Phenomenology of Spirit*, finishing it on the eve of the battle of Jena in 1806, in which the Prussians were defeated by Napoleon. This led to the closure of the university for a time and he had to seek other employment. For a while he was Rector of a 'gymnasium' in Nuremberg. He had already begun writing his *Science of Logic*, and with the invitation to take up the post at Nuremberg came the suggestion that he should write a new textbook in logic for school use, a project which was not exactly what he had in mind. However, he continued with the *Science of Logic*, which was duly published in three parts between 1812 and 1816.

In the autumn of 1816 he became Professor of Philosophy at Heidelberg and in the following year there appeared his *Encyclopaedia of the Philosophical Sciences*, of which there were new and much enlarged editions in 1827 and 1830. The *Philosophy of Right* was published in 1821, after he had moved to the University of Berlin in 1818, where he remained until his death from cholera in 1831. His appointment there was, to some extent, an imposition on an unwilling faculty by the Ministry of Education. The conception of the *Encyclopaedia*, with its division into logic, the philosophy of nature, and the philosophy of mind or spirit, the latter including some social or political philosophy and overlapping with the *Philosophy of Right*, fitted in many ways the generalist conception of the University of Berlin. For in it, Hegel tries to present a conspectus, from a philosophical point of view, of all phenomena. It is also, in many ways, imperialist in relation to the rest of the philosophical faculty in that it provides a view of most other subjects covered by that faculty, again from a philosophical point of view. When one puts this together with the lectures which Hegel gave at Berlin on the same subjects as well as on the philosophy of art, history, religion and the history of philosophy, the truly encyclopaedic character of Hegel's view of things becomes very obvious, whatever one thinks of the results. Philosophy was indeed claiming to be the queen of the sciences, and to be the dominant subject in the philosophical faculty and through that in the university.

Notes on Hegel's lectures were kept both by himself and by students who, so to speak, sat at his feet. After his death these notes were put together and added to editions of the *Encyclopaedia*, and other relevant works, as *Zusätze* – additional remarks on the matters under discussion. Ludwig Boumann, who was responsible for some of this in the collected edition of Hegel's works published after Hegel's death, said (in the case of the part of the *Encyclopaedia* concerned with the philosophy of mind or spirit published in 1845) that 'Hegel lectured with great freedom, and what he said had all the enchanting freshness of a new thought-world created at the moment, but such more or less total improvisation unfortunately led to unwitting repetitions, vaguenesses, divagations, and sudden jumps'.[3] Such lectures, it is clear, were quite in the spirit of Fichte's conception of what the role of lectures should be at Berlin. It is also evident that Hegel had a remarkable following. It was not, however, universal. The story is well known that Schopenhauer, when appointed as *Privatdozent* at Berlin (as he was for about two years from 1820, on the basis of his published works and a viva voce examination in the course of which he later claimed to have caught Hegel out), scheduled his lectures at the same time as Hegel's – and nobody came. This was at a period in which there was some rebellion on the part of *Dozenten* against the tyranny of professors – a rebellion which was eventually to good effect in that increased facilities were made available by the state to all university teachers. (Berlin was the first university to guarantee all teachers down to the rank of *Privatdozent* a heated lecture room!) However, Schopenhauer's behaviour had other motives too, and he exhibited throughout his life a passionate and bad-tempered hatred of Hegel.

This is not the place to go into the details of Hegel's philosophy; it is something of an impossible task in any case, such is its comprehensiveness, difficulty and obscurity. Fichte had already claimed to go further than Kant, in retaining the idealism but in crossing the bridge which Kant had asserted impossible to cross, between the individual's representations and the reality that supposedly lay beyond them in things-in-themselves. For Fichte that reality was constituted by an active self which posits something absolute outside itself as a condition of self-knowledge, but an absolute which exists only for it and is thus in a sense created by the self. Schelling held, with modifications, much the same view. There is perhaps a certain arrogance in this assertion of the all-powerful ego, which may well have fitted in with Fichte's personality. A similar imperialism, although a multi-faceted one, is evident in Hegel's philosophy.

The *Phenomenology of Spirit*, which Hegel described as a voyage of discovery, starts from what is, in many ways, the same starting-point as Kant's – the fact that something is presented to us in sense-consciousness and is brought under concepts in judgment. But for Hegel this leads far beyond the point which Kant allowed one to go, to an identification of the self with reality itself, and consciousness of other things with consciousness of self. The unpacking of what is said to be involved in self-consciousness leads in the end to a conspectus of the whole of reality and its phenomena, with the one absolute being a form of complete concept (*Begriff*). Within it is to be found the whole of history, and various forms of culture, art, religion and philosophy. But since all this is the product of an exercise in philosophy, philosophy becomes on this conception, not just the queen of the sciences but all that such sciences can in the end amount to.

The *Encyclopaedia* is an attempt to spell all this out in a much drier way than the *Phenomenology*. It perhaps also makes more evident what Hegel saw in what was for him the supreme philosophical procedure, that enshrined in dialectic. For Kant, dialectic was that part of philosophy concerned with those places where reason attempts to go beyond what is possible for the human understanding. Kant's first *Critique* was concerned to show its limitations in this respect, by reference to the idea that reason, in seeking the unconditional, gives rise to various forms of paradox or contradiction. For Hegel, reason is capable of transcending such antinomies by, to use the technical term, an *Aufhebung*, by which the two opposing standpoints of thesis and antithesis are somehow annulled yet preserved in a synthesis. To proceed from thesis to antithesis and, from this, to the synthesis of the opposing standpoints is the method of dialectic. But it has no firm rules, and success in it is to be judged only by reference to the efficacy or force of the individual arguments. Many commentators have been appalled by the ambition of the project and by the relentless way in which it is pursued; others have been full of admiration for it. It is arguable that Hegel's way of thinking fitted the circumstances of contemporary Prussia. Certainly his political philosophy, set out in his *Philosophy of Right*, with its great emphasis on the role of the state in comparison with the individual, and on *Sittlichkeit*, the overriding role of social ethics, fitted in with the governmental attitudes of the rulers of Prussia, in reaction to the French Revolution and Napoleon, on their road to dominance in Germany.

Hegel's philosophical system was to have immense influence. Most subsequent philosophers in Germany were affected by Hegel's ideas in one way or another, and that influence permeated the thought of philosophers in other European countries too, including, eventually, France. I have already referred to the rise of an English Hegelianism or Absolute Idealism in T.H. Green, Bernard Bosanquet and F.H. Bradley in Oxford and J.M.E. McTaggart in Cambridge. Not all these forms of Hegelianism were orthodox; the philosophers concerned were too much affected by the tradition of British Empiricism, most recently in the person of J.S. Mill, even when they were severely critical of that movement. Bradley, for example, disliked Hegel's formal dialectic, referring to 'a ballet of bloodless categories' (categories being the general ideas or concepts in terms of which the Hegelian system was set out), although much of his argument was Hegelian in spirit. Similar things could be said about Josiah Royce (1855–1916) at Harvard in the USA, although he was thought deviationist by the British Absolute Idealists. In Britain the dominance of Hegelian ways of thinking in academic philosophy persisted into the next century, until the realist movement initiated by G.E. Moore in Cambridge took over.

In Germany, however, the Hegelian influences were of a rather different kind, and opposition to them began rather earlier than it did elsewhere, and in a different way too. Hegelian philosophy was in many ways a substitute for religion; it could certainly be regarded as religious in tendency, in spite of its rationalistic and overwhelmingly intellectual character. Theology for a while was given Hegelian dress, even if, as we shall see, there were objections to this in certain quarters. The most obvious example of this tendency can be seen in the work of Ludwig Feuerbach (1804–1872), who argued that religion is concerned with the relation of man to his own nature or species, so that the proper study of theology ought to be anthropology. Feuerbach began his career as a theologian at Heidelberg, but he turned his attention to philosophy, going to Berlin where he worked for the doctorate under Hegel. He was appointed *Privatdozent* at Erlangen, but then retired into private life, and published the works by which he is known, particularly *The Essence of Christianity* (1841), outside an institutional context.

Feuerbach was at one time, however, a member of the group of so-called 'Young Hegelians', which included also Max Stirner (1806–1856) and Karl Marx (1818–1883), most of whom were radical in their thinking and also materialist in one way or another. The little which I have said about Feuerbach's views indicates the materialist leanings of his theological standpoint, and he claimed, as did Marx in a slightly different way, to turn speculative philosophy upside down. The politically radical views of the Young Hegelians were also quite different from those of Hegel, even when they were influenced by him. Hence it might rightly be said that Hegelian ways of thinking quickly led into what was heterodoxy by strict Hegelian standards. The same is true of Hegel's influence on the university scene. 'Perhaps never', it has been said, 'has such great intellectual influence been dissipated so rapidly as after his death.'[4]

THE CRITICS OF HEGEL: SCHOPENHAUER AND MARX

The remark just quoted is true of Hegel's philosophical influence, as opposed to other kinds of influence including academic ethos, only if we judge the situation by strict Hegelian standards. For critical opposition can be a form of influence – and there was plenty of that. The first criticism of that kind has already been noted, that of Arthur Schopenhauer (1788–1860), who, as a major philosopher, provides an exception to the pattern which has held good hitherto, whereby the practice of philosophy in Germany is a function of an academic context. Schopenhauer was a *Privatdozent* at Berlin for a very short while, but his abandonment of that career, as already noted, was for very different reasons from those of, say, Feuerbach. One might think that his scheduling his lectures at Berlin at the same time as Hegel's was an act of folly for a young man at the outset of his academic career. But Schopenhauer's attitudes to other contemporary philosophers were already well formed by then.

Schopenhauer's father had a business in Danzig, which was moved to Hamburg when Danzig was annexed by Prussia in 1793. His mother was a novelist who moved in literary circles, which included Goethe, with whom Schopenhauer later had some correspondence, particularly over Goethe's anti-Newtonian theory of colour, on which Schopenhauer wrote an early essay. His father, who died in 1805 and left him relatively well provided for out of his business, wanted his son to continue in commerce and gave him a somewhat unorthodox education accordingly (quite different from the concentrated education that James Mill gave John Stuart Mill). Nevertheless Schopenhauer seems to have had some affection for his father, but little for his mother, from whom he eventually became estranged.

This does not have any special relevance for Schopenhauer's

philosophy, nor does his melancholy and perhaps unbalanced temperament, except that we need perhaps to know something of his reasons for the opposition to Hegel. Schopenhauer initially went to the University of Göttingen to study medicine, but moved into philosophy under the influence of G.E. Schulze of that university, who acquainted him with the philosophies of Plato and Kant. (Schulze, incidentally, thought of himself as a sceptic, following the tradition of the Greek sceptics, but he is mentioned by Hegel in his lectures on the history of philosophy as an example, almost the only example, of modern, as opposed to ancient, scepticism, which Hegel considered to be bogus.) Schopenhauer constantly expresses an admiration for Plato in his works, and he invokes the Platonic Ideas or Forms in his treatment of art. But his admiration for Kant is of a quite different order, even if it was a critical admiration. He added, as an appendix to the first volume of his main work, *The World as Will and Representation*, a critical examination of Kant's philosophy, but prefacing it with some words of Voltaire: 'It is the privilege of true genius, and especially of the genius who opens up a new path, to make great mistakes with impunity.' Schopenhauer thought that more recent philosophers, from Fichte to Hegel, had betrayed that genius.

Schopenhauer went to Berlin to attend Fichte's lectures in 1811, because Fichte, who had once been a follower of Kant, had the highest reputation at the time among German philosophers. But he was already prejudiced against him and he annotated his notes on Fichte's lectures with uncomplimentary remarks and worse. Hegel received similar treatment; Schopenhauer can hardly refer to these men in his works without abuse. It is clear, however, that these attitudes were formed long before Schopenhauer experienced the unenthusiastic reception of his own published works – a lack of enthusiasm which was redeemed only at the very end of his life when Hegelianism was on the wane in Germany. (Wagner sent him a copy of the libretto of the *Ring* in 1854, expressing admiration, but without any accompanying letter. Schopenhauer did not acknowledge the tribute, but the admiration was, in any case, decidedly one-sided. Nevertheless, the enthusiasm shown by Wagner is perhaps typical of reactions to Schopenhauer; he has had more influence on artists of one kind or another than he has had on philosophers, with one or two exceptions.)

Schopenhauer presented his doctoral thesis *On the Fourfold Root of the Principle of Sufficient Reason* at Jena, and published it at his own expense in 1813. It did not attract much notice. He then worked in Dresden on his main work which was published in 1819. This was the basis of his application to Berlin for an academic post. His subsequent career, after his failure there, was for the most part, a solitary one, marked by occasional further publications and revised versions of the main work, which received substantial attention only at the very end of his life. He had by then been awarded a prize by the Norwegian Scientific Society in 1839 for an essay *On the Freedom of the Will*, but his submission of *On the Basis of Morality* to the Royal Danish Academy for a similar prize in 1840 met with rejection, in spite of the fact that he was the only candidate. (The comments of the judges were somewhat unclear and ambiguous, but part of the reason for the rejection no doubt lay in his abusive attitude to Hegel. It is perhaps of some interest that the Danish philosopher Søren Kierkegaard praised him for the same attitudes both to Hegel and to academic philosophy generally, indeed for being in those respects as 'rude as only a German can be'.) It was, however, the publication of a collection of articles, under the title *Parerga and Paralipomena*, in 1851, that marked the turning of his philosophical fortunes. He had great difficulty in getting the book published, despite the efforts of his main disciple and subsequent editor, Julius Frauenstädt. But those essays have come to be regarded in many quarters, unfortunately, as the main route into Schopenhauer's philosophy, and have emphasized his somewhat quirky views on a number of subjects, including women, sex and death.

Almost immediately on publication of the essays, however, his name came to public note. Curiously enough, his cause was helped by the publication in Germany of a translation of an article, originally published in *The Westminster Review* for 1853, which saw Schopenhauer as an ally against metaphysical transcendentalism, for which current German philosophy was supposed to be responsible. But Schopenhauer was no empiricist of the kind that Mill was; it was only his opposition to Hegel that put him on the side of those who saw Hegel as bolstering up theologically inspired metaphysics (and on this it is worth noting that Kierkegaard saw Hegel as undermining true religion in distorting the relationship that he, Kierkegaard, took to exist between the individual and God). Schopenhauer thought of himself as carrying on the true tradition of Kant, in spite of the fact that he thought he could do something which Kant thought impossible, in identifying the nature of things-in-themselves, the reality which underlies what alone is available to sense-perception.

Strangely enough Fichte had thought that he could do something similar and had also emphasized something that was crucial to Schopenhauer's identification of the single thing-in-itself – activity or agency. But although it seems likely that in this respect Schopenhauer had derived more from Fichte than he was prepared to admit, Fichte did not maintain, as Schopenhauer did, that the 'Aesthetic' of Kant's *Critique of Pure Reason* (the theory of sensibility and its spatial and temporal forms) was 'a work of such supreme merit that it alone would have been enough to make Kant's name immortal'. Nor did Fichte identify the thing-in-itself with will, which Schopenhauer came to see as a sort of cosmic force, the key to the identification of which is to be found in the unconditional knowledge of our own will, by contrast with the conditional knowledge of all else. But the most important thing in all this is that Schopenhauer argued in a Kantian style, even when he went, illegitimately as Kant would have thought, beyond the limits which Kant argued existed for the human understanding. It is perhaps no surprise that interest in Schopenhauer returned when Hegelian ideas went out of favour, as they did by the middle of the nineteenth century. But that interest was exhibited mainly in a relatively small circle of philosophical adherents and a wider circle of non-philosophers who thought, as did, for example, Wagner and Freud, that some of Schopenhauer's ideas were similar to theirs – often at the cost of the distortion of Schopenhauer's ideas when removed from their context of argument. (I say this in spite of the influence that some of Schopenhauer's thoughts had on the later philosopher, Ludwig Wittgenstein, at any rate when the latter was a young man.)

It follows, then, that Schopenhauer has to be seen as something of a lone wolf baying aginst the dominant academic philosophy of his time. On his own admission he was trying to maintain and continue a previous academic philosophical tradition, that of Kant. But he did it in a very different way (and, incidentally, with a different and beautiful literary style of writing, none of which can be attributed to either Kant or Hegel). Despite the eventual existence of university courses on his philosophy, and in spite of what I have just said about Wittgenstein, his thought has lived on, mainly in the writings of artists and literary figures, and perhaps also, given Schopenhauer's great interest in Hinduism and Buddhism, in orientalists. He presents the perhaps unusual example of a philosopher who has been thought fascinating even though he perpetuated no living philosophical tradition.

That cannot be said of the second kind of critical influence that was generated by Hegel – that of Marx. I have already mentioned Marx's membership of the group of 'Young Hegelians', which also included Max Stirner, Feuerbach and Friedrich Engels (1820–1895), and which was led by a lecturer at the University of Berlin, Bruno Bauer. Marx was born in Trier, was a law student at Bonn, but moved to Berlin where he turned to philosophy. The Young Hegelians were politically radical. They were also philosophically radical in the sense that were opposed to the dominant Hegelian emphasis on *Geist* or spirit (something that produced at least the illusion that Hegel was an ally of the theologians) in the direction of materialism. Hence they tried to interpret Hegel materialistically. One might think, with some justice, that this could lead only to confusion and incoherence; for there is nothing in Hegel's thinking that suggests the possibility of a valid materialism. Hence, we are confronted here with the apparently paradoxical fact that Hegel's ideas were at this time so dominant and persuasive that they could lead people to think in Hegelian terms while involved in systems of belief that were fundamentally non-Hegelian. Marx and the other Young Hegelians were thus not thorough critics of Hegel, as Schopenhauer was. They were opposed to him and what he stood for, but they were still Hegelian, at least in the kind of terms which they invoked and within which they worked. The early works of Marx, such as *The German Ideology* and the *1844 Manuscripts*, are certainly Hegelian in tone. But, unlike Hegel's philosophy, they are materialistic; in that sense alone perhaps, Engels was right in saying that Marx meant 'to stand Hegel on his head'.

Marx's doctoral thesis was on Epicureanism, but he sent it, not to Berlin, but to Jena, which had something of a reputation for producing doctors of philosophy! He then joined Bauer in Bonn, still with the hope of getting a university post, although this required the publication of an additional dissertation. But he eventually broke with Bauer and the Young Hegelians, and he also quarrelled with his mother in Trier and became estranged from his family, losing their financial support. Much of Marx's life, at least for the period following this, was devoted to political preoccupations. He initially moved from Berlin to Cologne, where he edited the paper, the *Rheinische Zeitung* in 1842. But that paper was suppressed by the authorities in 1843. Marx then married and soon moved to Paris, where he and his wife remained until 1845, Marx being much involved with socialist ideas and beginning there his friendship with Friedrich Engels. He was eventually expelled from Paris, and moved to Brussels, where he became leader of the Communist League. He was forced to leave Brussels again in 1848, but he was allowed to return to Paris after the 1848 revolution there. After a brief return to Cologne, Marx and his family moved in August 1849 to London, where he spent the rest of his life, working, as is well known, in the British Museum Reading Room. Whether his activities and writings during this period can be considered truly philosophical (rather than, say, political and concerned with economic theory) is a matter for argument.

Marx's *Theses on Feuerbach* ends with the famous sentence, 'Philosophers have only *interpreted* the world in different ways; the point is to change it.' To the extent that that remark can be taken seriously, it suggests a radically different conception of the practice of philosophy from any which we have so far considered. It is a product of Marx's socialist and revolutionary activities. But although the remark has been taken up by scores of later 'Marxists', it is not clear that it can be taken totally seriously. Marx criticized Feuerbach for not seeing that man's 'species-life', his essence in effect, is the 'totality of social relations' and cannot be abstracted from the 'historical process'. He criticized Stirner for adopting a kind of egoism, in opposition to the conception of a human essence, when Stirner insisted on the ego's self-determination. He thought that Stirner's ideas, even though opposed to those of Hegel, were a product of a bourgeois society, and once again ignored real historical relations. The emphasis on human practice was in one sense salutary in that it was designed to bring thinking down to earth after all the vast abstractionism of Hegel's philosophy. But it was not so easy for one in Marx's position to free himself from the style of philosophizing which Hegel introduced, and in the earlier works Marx employs Hegelian ideas and indeed methods of presenting and organizing them. There is some argument as to how much this survives in Marx's later works, such as *Capital*, which are in some ways much more dominated by economics, and about how exactly the economic base which Marx posited is related to what he called 'superstructure' (which includes all that seems merely cultural). Nevertheless, in arguing about this, Marx is clearly theorizing, not simply urging ways in which the world might be changed.

Philosophy is not so easily kicked out. As Horace said about nature, if you remove it with a pitchfork, it will come back all the same.

ROMANTICISM: KIERKEGAARD AND NIETZSCHE

It might be said that Marx and Schopenhauer are hardly typical as regards the practice of philosophy in Germany in the mid- to late nineteenth century. Did not philosophy continue to be practised in the universities, with all that that entails about its professionalism and academic character? Unfortunately the bigger philosophical names of the period are untypical if that is the norm. In any case we are approaching the time, in the late nineteenth century, which saw the birth of a number of disciplines, which were initially connected with philosophy, but which were later to have an independence – psychology, sociology, logic and the foundations of mathematics, to give just some examples. Most of these movements stemmed from people who were part of the university system, but they brought with them their own forms of technicality and their own influences and protagonists. There was, as a result, a kind of fragmentation of philosophy for a while, so that its history becomes rather complicated.

I shall not try to chart the whole of this history, since, in any case, as the next century progressed there was a tendency for the process to be reversed. The other disciplines which I have mentioned acquired their own autonomy, and, although there may still be room for argument on the scope of philosophy *vis-à-vis* those other disciplines and indeed on their interrelationships, there has been, on the whole, a delimitation of the field of philosophy. This delimitation has arisen from the growth in the professionalism of the subject and from the attempts on the part of its practitioners to establish its frontiers. It is arguable that what look like the great exceptions to that general rule and to the direction in which things were going were a product of the romanticism which had such a great influence on nineteenth-century thought in general, particularly, but not exclusively, in German-speaking countries. It is perhaps no exaggeration to say that certain popular conceptions of philosophy today derive from an identification of philosophy with forms of it which belonged to the romantic movement. At all events, it is the residual influence of romanticism which has in part led to the resuscitation in recent times of interest in those figures who are, by certain criteria, philosophical rebels. I have in mind particularly Kierkegaard and Nietzsche, although the former is not, of course, German.

Of these two it is probable that it is Kierkegaard who provides the odder case as far as concerns the practice of philosophy, although Nietzsche became insane towards the end of his life and lived in the care of his sister who became a kind of high-priestess of a Nietzsche cult, while he poured out books which were in one way or another a mixture of philosophy, poetry and rhetoric. Søren Kierkegaard (1813–1855), who is generally regarded as the founder of Existentialism, was born in Copenhagen in Denmark. His father came from peasant stock in Jutland, but acquired a fortune from a wool business in Copenhagen, where he became a prominent figure among the élite, intellectual and otherwise. The father was an intensely religious man, of Protestant faith, and these attitudes were transmitted to his son, in spite of a lapse, probably sexual, on the father's part. This was connected with his marriage, after the death of his former wife, to Kierkegaard's mother, who had been a servant, and who had a child shortly after the marriage. There is a suggestion in Kierkegaard's *Journals* that his father revealed the misdemeanour while tipsy, and for a while the son lapsed, with the shock of the revelation, into a period of dissipation and neglect of his theological studies at the University of Copenhagen. Søren pulled himself together after his father's death in 1838, and resumed his studies, only to be involved in another crisis which has given him a certain notoriety.

He became engaged to a girl of the Copenhagen bourgeoisie, Regine Olsen, who was 16 years old. But he immediately began to have doubts, ostensibly as to whether someone of his melancholy disposition was suitable for Regine (though whether that was the real reason might well be wondered). For him to break off the engagement was a serious matter for a girl in her position. For a while he played the philanderer, in order make people believe that he had provided cause for Regine to break off the engagement. But this deceived nobody and he finally broke off the engagement himself in November 1841 and fled to Berlin. There he began to write, and, on returning to Copenhagen, produced, from 1843 onwards, a series of somewhat strange books, mostly under pseudonyms. His religiosity remained, as did the effect of his experience with Regine (though it can be argued how far the results of that episode extended). He spent a great deal of time towards the end of his life in controversy with the official Danish state church, which he characteristically regarded as perverting the original message of Christianity.

In his first book, *Either/Or*, he set out a contrast between the 'aesthetic' and 'ethical' ways of life, while revealing in the end that both of these are to be opposed to a third, the religious, the cardinal principle of which is that 'as against God we are always in the wrong'. It is a curiously constructed book, amounting to a series of essays on the aesthetic and ethical ways of life, including in the first case a novelette, 'The Diary of a Seducer', and followed by a sermon by an unnamed priest who sets out the principle of the religious way of life. The aesthetic life is the life of the senses in all forms, including the pursuit of pleasure and eroticism (there is much about Mozart's *Don Giovanni*); the ethical life is a life concerned with duty in a very Protestant sense, and it is argued that the fulfilment of duty can also enhance the aesthetic, even in marriage. But, as we have already noted, it is the relationship with God that really matters.

Most of his other books have the same emphasis, if not exactly the same theme. *Fear and Trembling* takes the biblical story of God's command to Abraham to sacrifice his son, as a starting point to discuss the idea of a particular duty to God which might override all ethical obligations however universal in scope; in that sense it sets itself in opposition to the Kantian idea of the good will which manifests itself in a conformity to a completely general and universal maxim. *Philosophical Fragments* discusses how God and the eternal can have a place in time and history, while *Concluding Unscientific Postscript*, his last work, written under the pseudonym Johannes Climacus, but in such a way as to reveal the true identity of the author (it surveys Kierkegaard's earlier works), argues, against Hegel, that truth is subjectivity and that the existence of the individual cannot be adequately dealt with in terms of a system such as that of Hegel. Johannes Climacus refers back to the words of the priest which conclude *Either/Or*: 'Only the truth that edifies is the truth for you.' It is all a matter of the relationship between the individual and God. The intense religiosity of all this, and of other works, must be evident, and Kierkegaard has sometimes been regarded as having more concern with theology than with philosophy. It is the emphasis on individual existence that justifies the claim that he was the founder of Existentialism. But he did not see himself as the originator of a movement and little attention was paid to him during his lifetime even in Denmark. His views were given recognition only many years after his death.

In some ways Kierkegaard saw himself as a kind of Socrates, and he certainly had a great admiration for that philosopher. He was not himself the gadfly of Copenhagen, as Socrates was of Athens, but he was, especially in his later life, a persistent critic of the established religion, and his emphasis on personal integrity and self-knowledge was certainly Socratic. But the religious context was different from that of Socrates, and there were no contemporary figures in the same position as the Sophists were in the time of Socrates. Even the opposition to Kant and Hegel that was expressed in his works was less than explicit. The same lack of explicitness about other philosophers held good to some extent of Wittgenstein in the next century, but Kierkegaard derived much less than Wittgenstein from the tradition of philosophy, much less even than Marx, who was like him only in that they both operated outside an academic context.

One cannot really use the examples of these two philosophers to argue that the seventeenth- and early eighteenth-century pattern of the practice of philosophy by individual scholars persisted into the nineteenth century. Kierkegaard and Marx were simply exceptions to the general rule. They provide good examples, nevertheless, of the fact that it was possible for such exceptions to arise because of special but differing local conditions. That possibility has become less and less real with the increasing professionalism of philosophy. It is difficult to think of a Kierkegaard appearing today. On the other hand, there have certainly been Marx-copies since Marx's time, although none of them has great importance in the history of philosophy as such, whatever importance they may have had in other ways.

Is the situation different in the case of Nietzsche? Friedrich Nietzsche (1844–1900) is often seen as a rebel against the prevailing tradition of philosophy, and has been treated as someone with a message for mankind which some, both philosophers and others, have found both attractive and suggestive. In his case, the one philosopher who had any influence on him was Schopenhauer, although Nietzsche's will to power was very different from Schopenhauer's will to live. Nietzsche's initial interest and expertise was mainly in classics rather than philosophy, although this included a concern with Greek thought, an aspect of which he set out in his first book, *The Birth of Tragedy out of the Spirit of Music*. This outlines, among other things, the clash between the Apollonian and Dionysiac approaches to art, culture and life, especially in ancient Greece. The Apollonian urge is concerned with dreams and visions, the Dionysiac with drunkenness, intoxication and, in a way, with life. Nietzsche was later to express dissatisfaction with this work, but in it there are already suggestions which are taken up in later writings, particularly the emphasis on life. It also expresses Nietzsche's opposition (in a way which sets him in complete contrast with Kierkegaard) to Socrates, whom he saw as putting an undue emphasis on reason, and in consequence, influencing Euripides, the tragedian, in the wrong way.

There is an evident romanticism in all this and it is taken further in later works. These set out the doctrines of the will to power, and of the superman who will affirm life joyously, but in complete mastership of himself, by contrast with the 'slave morality' of ordinary men; these later works also put forward a doctrine which does not obviously fit with the rest, that of the eternal recurrence of events. Despite what he had inherited from Schopenhauer, he would not accept the type of metaphysics which Schopenhauer derived from Kant, let alone that of Hegel. For Nietzsche, truth itself is subjectivity, though not in the way that Kierkegaard suggested; for him truth is power, though in a way which puts a premium not on the individual but on society. This is not the place to go into the details of this, although it has had considerable influence on some recent continental philosophers. What is clear is that Nietzsche presents a vision of what human beings can be, along with a diagnosis (part of what he called a genealogy of morals) of why they were not generally so. Like Kierkegaard, he poured out books, often, like *Thus Spake Zarathustra*, distinctly poetical in form.

He was for some time an academic at Basle in Switzerland, where he repudiated his German origins and took Swiss nationality. But his post was one in classics and Greek philosophy; he was never part of the philosophical profession proper in the universities. It was while he was teaching in Basle that he became friendly with Wagner, who was then living at Tribschen, near Lucerne. For Nietzsche, Wagner was the epitome of the artist. Moreover, Wagner was, like Nietzsche, an admirer of Schopenhauer, although he certainly misinterpreted what Schopenhauer meant by the will to live (which had nothing to do with the power or otherwise of love), and, as we have seen, the admiration was never reciprocated. Nietzsche at first thought that Wagner had in mind something nearer to his own views, but he became disillusioned with him, and there was a progressive estrangement and a final break. (It has been claimed that Wagner's *Parsifal* was Nietzschean in inspiration, but, if so, Wagner was mistaken yet again over what he saw as the source of his ideas; Nietzsche himself thought *Parsifal* the antithesis of what he intended, in that the ideal presented in it was one involving both chastity and Christianity, both of which he saw as a denial of life.)

Nietzsche gave up his professorship in Basle in 1878 because of ill health. He lived thereafter a more or less solitary life, painfully producing further works. In 1889 he became insane and lived the rest of his life in the care of his sister, as already noted. The madness infects some of the later works. But there can be no doubt that Nietzsche has become a cult figure, although one who has had different effects on different people. One can mention Bernard Shaw as an example of one kind of influence, and the radical students and thinkers who see him as anti-establishment, especially in the connection that he made between truth and power, as another. For subsequent German philosophy he has become part of the history of existentialism. What is very evident is that he was a romantic who does not fit into any definite mould or compartment. Equally he left no precise disciple, even if he has influenced many. As far as concerns the practice of philosophy in his time, he does not conform to any pattern. Unlike Marx and Kierkegaard, he was an academic for part of his life; but he was not, strictly speaking, a teacher of philosophy, and much of his philosophical work stands outside any academic context. In the German-speaking world he was perhaps the last figure of this kind.

LATE NINETEENTH-CENTURY GERMAN PHILOSOPHY

In German academia, after the decay of Hegelianism, there tended to be a return to Kant and epistemology, although there were, even within that movement, some recalcitrant metaphysicians, particularly J.F. Herbart (1776–1841) and his successor R.H. Lotze (1817–1881) at Göttingen. The most influential German-speaking philosopher at the end of the nineteenth century was Franz Brentano (1838–1917), who through his disciples, particularly Alexius Meinong (1853–1920) and Edmund Husserl (1859–1938), originated the phenomenological tradition in philosophy, which has dominated twentieth-century European continental philosophy. Others who have been influential in a quite different way include Gottlob Frege (1848–1925) and Ernst Mach (1838–1916); but these were more specialist in their philosophical influence. Frege has been immensely influential among English-speaking philosophers interested in logic and philosophy of language, from Bertrand Russell (with whom he corresponded) onwards; but he was for most of his lifetime professor of mathematics at Jena. Mach was also extremely influential among philosophers of science. He studied at Vienna, held a chair in mathematics at Graz, and then one in physics at Prague. In 1895 he was appointed to a chair in philosophy in Vienna, with the title 'Professor of the History and Theory of the Inductive Sciences'; but in 1897 he had a stroke which left him paralysed on the right side of his body, and he resigned his post in 1901, devoting the rest of his life to writing. (When Ludwig Boltzmann (1844–1906), who was much opposed to Mach's positivism over science, succeeded him, Boltzmann retitled the chair 'Professor of Theoretical Physics and Natural Philosophy', so enabling him to avoid making reference to his predecessor, as would otherwise have been customary!)

Brentano was originally an Aristotelian scholar. He wrote his doctoral dissertation on 'The Several Senses of Being in Aristotle'. He taught for a while at the University of Würzburg and was then appointed to a chair at Vienna. Freud attended his lectures there for three years. He had become a Roman Catholic priest in 1864, but he left the Church in 1873 after controversy concerning papal infallibility. In 1874 he published his most famous book *Psychology from an Empirical Standpoint*, the title of which signalled two things: (a) an opposition to the prevalent metaphysical tendencies of contemporary German-speaking philosophy, including the neo-Kantianism already noted; and (b) an interest in philosophical psychology (in an age which was seeing the rise of experimental psychology through the influence of, in particular, G.T. Fechner (1801–1887), H. von Helmholtz (1821–1894) and, above all, W. Wundt (1832–1920)).

That interest was one which had already manifested itself in Herbart and Lotze, and was there at the same time in the English Idealists, as well as William James in America. But Brentano expressed the interest in the form of a general psychological theory which purported to set out the essence of mentality. For this purpose, he had recourse to a notion which reflected his scholastic origins – that of intentionality, the tending of the mind towards certain objects. Brentano thought that the mind was to be defined in terms of three kinds of mental acts (those of representation, judgment, and what he called 'the phenomena of love and hate'), each of which is directed to a kind of 'intentional object' which has *in*-existence, i.e. exists only in relation to the act in question. It was different aspects of this view which led, on the one hand to Meinong's theory of objects, and on the other to Husserl's phenomenology. The latter view has been held, though perhaps arguably, to have returned in the end to a form of idealism. But Brentano's philosophy certainly involves a kind of empiricism, in its reliance on data provided by experience, though not an empiricism of the kind embraced by the British Empiricists.

So ended nineteenth-century German-speaking philosophy. Before leaving it, however, it may be important to note one further thing. In Britain there has never, at least until very recently, been any tradition according to which philosophy of some kind is taught in schools. This is not the case on the continent of Europe. In most Catholic countries this is because of the persistence of the old tradition of liberal arts and because of the place that philosophy has in the scholastic tradition; it follows equally that the teaching of philosophy in such cases is not likely to be progressive (although the same might be said of philosophy teaching in the universities there too). Some philosophy was, however, taught in German gymnasia in the nineteenth century. (It will be remembered that Hegel was asked to write a textbook in logic for use in gymnasia.) Some of the major figures in German-speaking philosophy whom we have noted turned to philosophy at university after starting on some other subject (something that still happens in contemporary universities). However, where philosophy is taught in some form at school age, this obviously affects the place that philosophy has in the general culture. It is also bound to have some effect on the practice of philosophy.

THE SITUATION IN FRANCE

It is arguable that the practice of teaching philosophy in schools in France has had a more profound effect, and not always a good one, on the subject there. As we have seen, the French Revolution led to the closure of the universities in France (they were vulnerable because of their connections with the Church), the setting up of the *grandes écoles*, and eventually the institution of the Imperial University by Napoleon. Also under Napoleon (who had a slight experience of philosophy) there was set up the *baccalauréat*, to be administered by the Imperial University. This had philosophy as a compulsory element, though very much linked to the history of the subject. The practice of including philosophy in the *baccalauréat* as a compulsory part has persisted in France until the present time, with results concerning which there might be much argument. For one thing, there is inevitably a concentration in the teaching of it on what is necessary for the passing of examinations. (There have no doubt been some exceptions to this practice, one of the most notable being the course which Simone Weil gave at the lycée for girls at Roanne in the year 1933–4, and which has been preserved in notes by a pupil, Anne Reynaud-Guérithault.[5])

The nineteenth century was definitely not a high-point of French philosophy. After Maine de Biran, to whom reference was made in Chapter 4 (see p. 75), there was no outstanding general philosopher until Henri Bergson (1859–1941) at the very end of the century. He became professor of philosophy at the Collège de France, which survived the Revolution as an institution for advanced students, in 1900. Bergson's philosophy put emphasis on life, and the idea of a vital spirit, as against intellectualism. There was a link and a similarity between his views and those of William James in America, especially in relation to James's later philosophy, when James understood Bergson as urging him to 'dive back into the flux'. Even earlier there had been a similarity between the idea, expressed in Bergson's first work *Les Données immédiates de la conscience*, of the temporal continuity of consciousness and James's idea of the 'stream of thought'. Much of this, in both philosophers, can be construed as something of a reaction to Hegelianism.

Earlier there was Auguste Comte (1798–1857), the founder of positivism, with whom J.S. Mill was associated. Comte was influential in the growth of sociology, but he never managed to obtain an academic post. There were also a number of lesser figures, such as Victor Cousin (1792–1867), who was eclectic in his philosophy but who wielded considerable power over the philosophical scene, including teaching appointments, as director of the École Normale and minister of public instruction. He thus tried to ensure the dominance of philosophical eclecticism in the teaching of philosophy in France, probably to the detriment of French philosophy during that period. Neo-Kantianism also played a role in French philosophical thinking, as it did in Germany and elsewhere. Mention should, however, also be made of Pierre Duhem (1861–1916), physicist, and philosopher and historian of science, who has had influence more recently because of his emphasis on instrumentalism in scientific theorizing, something that fits in to some extent with the pragmatism which has had a large place in philosophy in the USA.

Apart from what I have said about Cousin's influence, part of the reason for the low state of philosophy in France in the nineteenth century might be sought in the correspondingly low state of the universities as they revived after the Revolution and the Napoleonic reforms. But there existed also other institutions, such as the *grandes écoles*, the École Normale and the École Polytechnique, with which most of those who had some philosophical repute were connected in some way or other. Nevertheless, there was nothing in France corresponding to the seminar system in Germany, and it may well be that the general atmosphere was not favourable to progress in philosophical research. The emphasis on teaching, both in the schools and in the universities, and the demands of the examination system seem to have produced something approaching a form of scholasticism in philosophy, even if that scholasticism was not of the same kind as held good in more committed Catholic countries, where Thomism was still dominant.

But the situation was, in some ways, not much different elsewhere in Europe, outside German-speaking countries. Hegelianism had a belated influence in Italy and Holland, as it did in effect in England. But all this is in the context of the university institutions which existed in those countries. It was becoming the general rule that the practice of philosophy should be embedded in whatever university institutions existed, and, despite the 'rogue elephants' whom I discussed earlier, it was becoming less and less plausible that philosophy should have a large place outside those university institutions. Philosophical amateurism, if that is the right way to describe non-professionalism, was becoming a thing of the past, although, as we shall see, there are still some exceptions to that rule, for special reasons, even in the twentieth century.

THE RISE OF PHILOSOPHY IN THE USA

The transition from amateurism to professionalism was particularly obvious in the USA, where the shift took place in a comparatively short time. As Bruce Kuklick has pointed out,[6] philosophy in the USA was, in the nineteenth century, most often the province of amateurs, but by 1900 it was the activity of the professor. Moreover, the centre of the transition was Harvard. There had been earlier philosophical figures, including Jonathan Edwards (1703–1758), but most of them, like Edwards, were theologians, and their interest in philosophy stemmed from religious considerations. Intellectual life in Boston, where Harvard is situated, was, in the early nineteenth century, dominated by Unitarian ideas, and it was from this source that there emerged so-called American transcendentalism, in the person of Ralph Waldo Emerson (1803–1882). He was influenced to some extent by Hegelianism, which had a place in St Louis with W.T. Harris who, as noted earlier in this chapter, founded the *Journal of Speculative Philosophy*. Emerson had some possible influence on Nietzsche and Bergson, but he was not a philosopher in the orthodox sense – more of the sage. He believed in a kind of unity of souls with God – what he called the over-soul – but the general character of his 'philosophy' was both derivative and home-spun. He nevertheless had considerable influence on both American literature and American thought generally. Towards the end of his life a summer school was set up at Concord, Massachusetts, where he lived, and this was followed by similar ventures. In Boston, a Metaphysical Club was set up, on the suggestion of William James, but Harvard's philosophical activity gradually became dissociated from the amateurs who mostly made up the membership of that club.

The President of Harvard towards the end of the nineteenth century, Charles Eliot, was a great admirer of German *Wissenschaft* and scholarship, but he was strongly opposed to any system of government-supported universities. Paradoxically perhaps, he was also opposed to the emphasis being put on research in the university, wanting Harvard to be more like an extremely efficient liberal arts college. All that changed later, and the situation was different in any case in other American universities, even if they had a lesser role to play in the growth of academic philosophy. (By American standards, Harvard, Yale and Princeton were ancient universities, going back to the seventeenth and eighteenth centuries, but other universities were coming into existence in the second half of the nineteenth century, and these were less based on the older college system. Johns Hopkins, in particular, put emphasis on postgraduate teaching.) William James (1842–1910), one of the great figures of

Harvard at the turn of the century and member of a talented family which also included his brother, the novelist Henry James, agreed with the disapproval of postgraduate teaching, referring to the 'Ph.D. octopus'. But all that gradually changed, despite James's fears of the university taking the factory as its model 'like other American institutions'!

James had a medical training and was initially appointed to a teaching post in physiology at Harvard. But he had travelled in Europe and admired the way in which psychology was developing in Germany. He had no formal training in either psychology or philosophy and claimed that the first lecture in psychology that he heard was his own. But he introduced a course on the relations between physiology and psychology at Harvard, which led to his giving demonstrations in experimental psychology. Indeed James was responsible for the setting up of a psychological laboratory at Harvard, although he eventually became somewhat disillusioned with experimentation in psychology. But before that, in 1878, his psychology course was transferred to the philosophy department (such still being the prevalent view of psychology), and he was appointed as professor of philosophy in 1885. The main, and great, product of this move was his *Principles of Psychology* (1890), in which he set out a view of the mind in terms of the various mental functions characteristic of human beings. He also put forward in that work a famous account of the stream of consciousness, which had similarities to the views almost simultaneously being put forward by Bergson, with whom he came to have a fairly close relationship.

The *Principles* remains a very philosophical work in many ways. James became more and more the philosopher. His last work (posthumously published), *Essays in Radical Empiricism*, is the most Bergsonian, emphasizing an ontology of pure experience provided that it takes due account of life. In between, apart from his *The Varieties of Religious Experience*, came *Pragmatism*, which applied, or, as is often suggested, misapplied some ideas of C.S. Peirce (1839–1914) which connected meaningfulness with rational usefulness, so as to suggest that truth itself is a matter of usefulness. Thereby, pragmatism, the main, and perhaps typical, American philosophical theory, or approach to philosophy, was born, to be carried on later and applied by John Dewey (1859–1952), so that in that respect, if in no other, James's philosophy has been enormously influential.

C.S. Peirce, who is arguably the greater philosopher, but who was relatively unknown during his lifetime, and whose thought survives simply in a mass of papers, never had a regular appointment at Harvard. He seems to have been disliked and was thought socially unacceptable (he lived for some time with a woman who was not his wife, but he later married, was divorced and then remarried). He was appointed as a part-time lecturer in logic at Johns Hopkins in 1879, but was sacked for reasons which are obscure, although James implied that Peirce had been difficult and irresponsible. He had 'dished himself', he said. For a while Peirce had a job with the Coast Survey, which he inherited from his father, as did J.S. Mill *his* post. But at the end of his life, apart from occasional lectures at Harvard, he existed on charity. Peirce was a great logician and philosopher of science. He also had metaphysical views which were more of an object of curiosity, although today they may well be thought no more so than those of the other main philosopher at Harvard, Josiah Royce, one of the Hegelian idealists previously referred to. Royce was something of a counter to James for whom idealism was the great bête-noire. Royce's reputation has not persisted, while that of Peirce has, if anything, increased. It is remarkable that someone of Peirce's standing was forced to remain outside the institutional context of philosophy as it became more professionalized. Thereafter, philosophy at Harvard, and everywhere else in the USA, was extremely professional, and technical to boot. But that is a story which belongs to the next century and must be left to the next chapter.

6

THE TWENTIETH CENTURY

THE PROFESSIONALISM OF TWENTIETH-CENTURY PHILOSOPHY

It is impossible, or at least undesirable, to treat the position of philosophy in the twentieth century as I have treated that in the nineteenth century in the previous chapter. I shall not try in this chapter to be at all comprehensive about individuals, although I shall consider some in a certain amount of detail. The views of individual philosophers and details of philosophical schools or movements can easily be discovered by reference to histories of philosophy or surveys of recent philosophy. But as one comes up to date the less one can be sure about the relative importance of individuals, and it is also easy to overlook the nature of the wood because of concentration on the trees. In any case, when considering the practice of philosophy, differences between philosophical doctrines and theoretical approaches pale into insignificance by comparison with the almost universal fact that in this century philosophy has become an academic and professionally managed subject.

I noted in Chapter 5 the rise, towards the end of the nineteenth century, of philosophical journals and of professional philosophical societies concerned with the furtherance of the subject. It is not until the twentieth century that there occurs also the rise of professional unions for philosophers, and similar institutions for the teaching and propagation of philosophy and for the furtherance of the interests of philosophers (the latter sometimes in reaction to the educational and economic policies of governments). All this is an indication, in spite of a very few exceptions, of the thorough professionalization of the subject almost everywhere. This means too that the basis for the practice of philosophy is to be found, again almost universally, in universities and other institutions of higher education recognized by governments, even if the teachers of philosophy in such institutions have their own professional societies and unions.

INSTITUTIONAL ARRANGEMENTS: THE SIGNIFICANCE OF TEACHING

An intimate relationship has also developed between the practice of philosophy and the teaching of philosophy, so much so that many philosophers in Britain would maintain that their own progress in the subject has been helped considerably by having to teach the subject to students of one kind or another. It should be clear from consideration of previous chapters that this has not always been the case, although, with the exceptions noted, nineteenth-century German philosophy was very much linked with university teaching and in pre-seventeenth century periods there were links of other kinds between teaching and philosophical practice. I shall return to these differences and similarities later. It is necessary, however, to note that if the practice of philosophy is linked to teaching it matters what form of teaching is carried out. I indicated, in connection with the late Middle Ages, the effect on at least the presentation of philosophical theses of the practice of disputation. I also mentioned in Chapter 5 the effect of the *baccalauréat* on philosophy in France. So far as concerns nineteenth-century, and probably twentieth-century, German philosophy, the main form of teaching has been the lecture and, at postgraduate level, the seminar. Indeed this is the case in a great many continental European universities today. Students derive their knowledge and enthusiasms from the inspiration provided by lecturers, at whose feet (not always just metaphorically) they sit. The dominance of the lecture as a form of teaching favours the propagation of doctrines and theories, much less the probing and investigation of arguments, although the students who constitute the audience at such lectures are no doubt ever-willing to argue with each other outside the lecture theatre. What happens at a seminar depends very much on the reverence, if any, that the participants feel for whoever is conducting the seminar, and on the manner of that conduct.

The tutorial, especially if it is one to one, has, or can have, a quite different effect, though, once again, much depends on the spirit and attitudes adopted by the teacher, as well as his or her teaching ability. Nevertheless, the aim of the tutorial must be a close examination and critique of a student's work, and of his or her arguments in particular. That is not to say that the aim is always achieved, and many students, where a tutorial system exists, have spoken, sometimes complainingly, of the luck of the draw as to who their tutor happened to be. Even given such reservations, however, the spirit of a tutorial system is quite different from that of a system where the lecture is the dominant form of teaching, and this inevitably has an effect on what is seen as the main concern for the philosopher. Those who have not had experience of a system where the examination and criticism of positions, and of the arguments for them, are such an overriding concern tend to regard the results as nit-picking. That is a common reaction on the part of non-philosophers to Anglo-Saxon philosophy as it is practised today, and it is equally a reaction which is common among philosophers of other traditions, who see in Anglo-Saxon philosophy a lack of concern with large issues. (There may be factors here too which have to do with national temperament, or at least with cultural tradition, but that is not a matter which can be easily assessed.)

I have spoken in this connection of Anglo-Saxon philosophy – philosophy conducted mainly in the medium of English – but in fact the point really applies only where the traditions of the universities of Oxford and Cambridge have been influential; there are other considerations to be noted, particularly as regards the USA, to which I shall come directly. But in England, Oxford and Cambridge, and particularly Oxford, have been dominant in philosophy, since the revival of those universities in the nineteenth century. In the case of Oxford this is in part a result of the numbers studying philosophy. *Literae Humaniores*, 'Greats', with its combination of classical languages and literature, ancient history, and ancient and modern philosophy, came to be regarded towards the end of the last century, whether rightly or not does not matter for our purposes, as the perfect form of liberal education for the prospective government and imperial administrator. It was even seen by some as a kind of education for philosopher kings, in the spirit of Plato's *Republic*. Perhaps this idea now seems rather silly, but later, in this century, when PPE (a joint degree in philosophy, politics and economics) was instituted, it was in conscious imitation of *Literae Humaniores* and was often referred to as 'Modern Greats'. One result of these institutions was that, in addition to chairs in different branches of philosophy (logic, metaphysics and ethics), nearly every college had to have a philosophy tutor. There is still a much greater concentration of philosophers in Oxford than at any other university in Britain. Cambridge philosophers have always been, by comparison, much smaller in numbers, although by no means lesser in distinction.

Elsewhere in Britain the situation has been somewhat different. In Scotland, the practice of compulsory philosophy lectures for all arts students, at least at the beginning of their course, persisted well into this century, but these were lectures which were inevitably delivered to large numbers of students. Those who went on with the subject continued to receive rather similar treatment, although the tutorial had its place too. The situation was similar in the new universities that came into existence in Britain and Northern Ireland, although, in general, these did not make philosophy a compulsory subject. There were, roughly speaking, three stages to their development: first, there was the setting up of the large municipal universities in the late nineteenth century; second, there was the institution of university colleges elsewhere in the first half of the twentieth century, often under the aegis of the University of London (which also played a similar role for colleges in parts of the British Commonwealth), such colleges later becoming independent universities; and finally, there occurred an expansion of higher education and the consequent establishment of new universities after the Second World War. Subsequent to that there was an expansion of philosophy into some of the new polytechnics. All but one of the new universities taught philosophy (and the 'one', Essex, later fell into line), and they have continued to do so until recent government cutbacks have, most regrettably, led to the abolition of some university departments of philosophy and the contraction of others.

Unlike Oxford, however, nearly all the other universities and polytechnics, where philosophy has existed, have had departments of philosophy. (One might argue that Oxford has had one in all but name, since departments usually come under faculties and at Oxford there is a sub-faculty of philosophy – but the organization there is in fact quite different from that in other universities.) Departments tend to be inward-looking, especially when they teach for a degree which is confined to the members' own subject. A joint degree with another subject or subjects may help to obviate that tendency, but it does not necessarily have that result; indeed, at Oxford, where it is still impossible for an undergraduate to study philosophy by itself, it is not obvious that philosophers are more outward-looking than those elsewhere (and they are certainly not outward-looking *from* *Oxford*!) The general consequence may well be an emphasis on the autonomy of philosophy and an increase in its tendency towards specialism. Here much depends upon the size of the department and on the number and kinds of students with which it has to deal. Where the number of students is relatively small, and small relative to the number of staff, a greater possibility exists for close tutorial teaching, and I suspect that most departments of philosophy in Britain would like to put as much emphasis on tutorial teaching as possible. This has the consequences already noted for the practice of philosophy, particularly the concentration on argument and criticism.

There is, however, a limit of another kind which is a result of the size of a department and its staff. When the staff of a department gets beyond a certain number it becomes increasingly difficult to maintain a cohesive approach to the subject. Philosophers being what they are, there is an increasing likelihood of differences in attitude to the subject. In the USA, where departments are often very large indeed, there is sometimes a tendency to recruit 'one of each'. That is to say that there is a tendency to think that many aspects of philosophy and many philosophical approaches should be represented on the staff of a department, on the basis that each aspect and approach is the responsibility of a specialist. Until comparatively recently, philosophy, in Britain at least, has been less beset by specialisms than most other subjects; one reason for that may be that a tutor, particularly at Oxford which is not organized on a departmental basis, may be held responsible for giving tutorials over a wide range of the subjects which undergraduates may have to study. (There are limits to that, of course; someone without knowledge of Greek, for example, is not well equipped to teach ancient philosophy with real authority.) In a department, such responsibility may more easily be shared out, and it is sometimes maintained that in very large departments, of the kind which I have mentioned as existing in the USA, specialism may become so acute that members of the staff are not really capable of arguing with each other on philosophical issues. That may be an exaggeration, but the danger is certainly there. If professionalism entails specialism, that accentuates the danger. The question is whether it does have that implication, and it is not clear that it necessarily does.

It remains the case that in English-speaking countries the department/faculty structure is the norm. Something similar holds good in other countries too. I said earlier that nearly all British universities have had departments of philosophy. In fact, in some of the new universities founded after the Second World War, there was a conscious opposition to a departmental structure when their organization was established. Instead subjects were grouped within 'schools' or their equivalent, presumably in the hope that this might help to break down subject-barriers and cut down specialization at the undergraduate level. In fact, as time has gone on, there has been a gravitation towards the departmental structure in spirit, if not in name, even where joint degrees of one kind or another are the normal pattern. This is almost inevitable because of outside, professional, demands upon individual teachers which presuppose that those individuals recognize that they belong with certain others who have similar concerns, ask similar questions and employ similar methods in attempting to arrive at answers to those questions. In universities which have remained firmly opposed to a departmental structure, philosophers tend to come together and are thought of by outsiders as belonging together because they have these similar concerns; they write for similar journals and other publications; they attend the same conferences, and discuss issues with similar individuals, and so on. Where this is not so, individuals become isolated and indeterminate in their role in learned circles at large. (I would stress, nevertheless, that the word 'similar' should be treated without undue precision; a degree of specialization entails that one philosopher may differ from immediate colleagues in the philosophical circles within which he or she moves. There must, all the same, be some recognition of who one's philosophical colleagues are.)

At least one qualification must be made to this last point. Some philosophers are intimately concerned with the thought and procedures of other disciplines; they may be concerned with the philosophy of physics, law or sociology, for example. They may find it natural to have connections with colleagues in the other disciplines with which they are concerned; indeed the need to have at least a modicum of expertise in those disciplines may necessitate such connections. In one particular case, that of psychology, there is a special consideration to note. The pursuit of what was called 'psychology' once fell within the province of philosophy. Psychology later attained independence as a branch of science, and psychologists became almost fiercely insistent on that independence, wanting to have having nothing to do with philosophy. This has of course been a gradual process, with some pockets of resistance remaining well into this century. (Oxford did not recognize psychology as a subject suitable for a degree until after the Second World War!) Recently there has been some reversal of this trend, in part because of the recognition by psychologists in some branches of the subject that philosophical questions relevant to them still demanded an answer. (Jean Piaget, who has been such a dominant figure in developmental psychology, had something of a philosophical upbringing as well as one in other disciplines, and, partly through him, it is accepted by many that philosophical questions remain to be answered in that field.)

Another factor is the belief held by some American philosophers – on doctrinal grounds connected with the supposed untenability of the distinction, formalized by Kant, between analytic and synthetic judgments or propositions – that there is no clear distinction between philosophical questions and questions of empirical science, particularly psychology. As a result of this, there are now some people, officially philosophers, who raise questions which might be thought to belong to psychology and who employ methods and considerations, in attempting to answer them, which would have been thought by an older generation of philosophers to be non-philosophical. Argument continues about the justification for, and fruitfulness of, such practices. Nevertheless an interdisciplinary subject has come into existence – cognitive science – to which psychologists, physiologists, computer scientists, linguists and philosophers make contributions. Opinions on the validity of this are still varied at present. It should be emphasized, however, that the possibility of interdisciplinary inquiries is not in dispute; the issue is whether the participants should contribute to them on the same level and in the same way, without specific differentiation as to expertise.

It may well be argued that it is all to the good that philosophers should not be too introverted. But some part of philosophy has always been second-order, concerned with philosophical questions arising from the theorizing and practice of other disciplines. As I said earlier, for this purpose philosophers may need at least a modicum of expertise in the first-order discipline, if their questions about it are to have pertinence. Normally, however, this does not require the backing of any institutional arrangements or any transcending of departmental barriers. The existence of a subject like cognitive science may have an opposite tendency, however. William James was, as a psychologist, a member of a philosophy department. More recently such an arrangement or its converse (a philosopher being a member of a psychology department) has rarely existed, except perhaps for very special reasons. Now, with the growing influence of cognitive science, it is not unknown for someone to be a member both of a philosophy and of a psychology department. So, for such special reasons, the strict departmental separation of subjects can break down. Such departmental interrelationship is not, however the rule as yet.

The norm in Britain, outside Oxford, is for philosophers to belong to philosophy departments, which provide, at the undergraduate level, courses in various branches and parts of philosophy, some of which are thought indispensable for anyone educated in the subject, and others of which may be regarded as a matter of choice on the student's part. The relationship between these two elements is extremely variable and there are some places, though probably a small minority, where the structure of an undergraduate course in philosophy is almost all a matter of the student's choice, within the limits set by what the department can provide. (Some might well argue that, whatever limits of this kind are officially recognized, it is almost bound to be uneconomical with staff time and resources.) Such an arrangement is more common in North America, where departments tend to be bigger. There it is frequently the case that students can simply choose which courses to 'audit', with, it is to be hoped, some advice on the part of the teachers.

As well as undergraduate courses there may be postgraduate classes or seminars, at any rate where the department is able to recruit a sufficient number of postgraduates to make classes, as distinct from individual supervision, justifiable. Courses for master's degrees tend to be taught by means of classes, in part at least. Wherever there are research students, all or some members of the department are likely to be involved in thesis supervision. University teachers are also expected to undertake research – something that is becoming increasingly subject to the supervision of university research committees and the like (which has been the practice on the continent of Europe for some time). But research in philosophy is difficult to specify, and is not very like research in other subjects. It may be a matter, as in the case of the history of philosophy, of the individual's marshalling in a critical way facts about philosophical ideas and theorizing; it may be, on the other hand, a matter of attempting to substantiate by argument some first-order philosophical thesis, and success at this is likely to depend heavily upon arguing with colleagues and meeting their criticisms. In this latter respect philosophical research can be much more dependent on discussion with others than is the case with other kinds of research. That way of pursuing philosophy goes back, of course, at least as far as Socrates.

There are still, unfortunately, practices followed by some philosophers, and indeed by some philosophical departments, the source of which lies in extra-philosophical considerations, as indeed was the case in the Middle Ages. The constraints may be religious or indeed political, as was long the case in communist countries. Even where this is not explicitly the case, ideological considerations may sometimes determine what is thought acceptable in a philosopher's argument at a given time. Materialism, for example, is taken almost as a datum in large sections of American analytical philosophy. (For one who has been involved in philosophy for a long time the changing effects of fashion over what is taken as acceptable can seem rather depressing.) Even where there are no extra-philosophical constraints, there can be great differences among philosophers over the aims of the subject or the methods to be pursued, and the experience of not being able to talk to another philosopher with any understanding, when those concerned come from different philosophical traditions (especially perhaps where the traditions are those of analytical and non-analytical philosophy respectively), is quite common.

I have emphasized these points to bring out the fact that, while the kind of organization on which philosophical practice now depends has a fairly commonly accepted basis, many differences still exist, among its practitioners, over the nature and aims of philosophy. Nevertheless, the degree of importance which is attached to the minutiae of argument does have a considerable correlation with the forms of teaching undertaken, and how those who receive that teaching therefore regard the subject. The enthusiasms of students for what they see as the most important thing going on in the subject can both impress and depress a teacher of long standing in philosophy. At the same time, opinions on what is relevant to an issue, how it is to be treated, and what counts as argument in favour of a position, can vary considerably. The cynic might even say that one man's argument is another man's assertion, although one should not exaggerate this to the point of claiming that objectivity in philosophy is impossible. It is just that the complexities of the subject make its attainment difficult; philosophy is indeed, as is often said, a difficult subject. Moreover, in non-analytic traditions, it may be that a certain kind of vision or even a way of presenting such a vision in words is the thing that is deemed important. Style of philosophizing is not to be ignored as a factor in its pursuit, and things may look very different outside a movement from how they look inside. In the heyday of linguistic philosophy, it was common for those outside Oxford to speak of Oxford philosophers as providing a more or less unified front, while it looked very different inside Oxford; what seemed to Oxonians to be large differences were thought of as mere incidentals outside Oxford. That kind of phenomenon still exists, and is likely to continue to do so wherever there is an organization with a large number of philosophers belonging to it. For example, for a long time continental philosophers tended to be regarded by British philosophers as all of a piece.

The expansion of universities in recent times has brought about an increase in the number of philosophers, both teachers and students. Philosophical conferences have in consequence become very large too, and the idea of a symposium (still used by the Mind Association and Aristotelian Society in connection with their annual joint conference) has tended to become a matter of form rather than spirit. The spirit, it is sometimes argued, continues in the way that philosophers get together and discuss what they want to discuss outside formal sessions. It is not altogether true in this context that 'more has meant less' (to use the slogan used by Kingsley Amis to deplore the expansion of the universities in general), but the popularity of a subject does bring its own dangers. There is also the danger of the organization of the subject taking precedence. The meetings of the various American Philosophical Associations have tended to become dominated by the need of university departments to recruit staff, and by the fact that central conferences provide an opportunity for seeing possible new members of staff, when the geographical size of the USA makes it difficult to bring people together otherwise.

Most of what I have said so far is derived from experience of universities where philosophy is carried on in the Anglo-Saxon tradition. Much of it applies also to universities on the continent of Europe and elsewhere, where that tradition does not exist. But there may be variations there in the general pattern, derived from such things as differing conceptions of philosophy itself, a preoccupation in some places with doctorates, as against other forms of philosophy degree, and, again in some places, a persistent maintenance of the power and influence of professors. Moreover, there have been the interruptions caused by two world wars in Europe, something which has had a very considerable effect on things in Germany in particular, as did the political ideologies of the dominant powers and reactions to them. Nazism had such an effect that there was a gap of many years in the serious pursuit of philosophy in Germany. As far as concerns reaction, it is perhaps relevant to point to the influence of Marxism in many European countries, and not just communist countries. But, with some exceptions, to which I shall come, the restriction of philosophy to universities and other organizations of higher education, with all the consequences for the subject that such organization brings, is the rule on the continent of Europe too.

In most contexts, both there and elsewhere, the experience and thinking of a philosopher may be enlarged by contact with philosophers in other universities, but much less commonly by other forms of contact. Indeed, for a long time, partly as a function of differences in philosophical doctrine and method, but for other reasons too, including linguistic ones, contact between British and European philosophers was negligible. Things are a little better now, but there is a long way to go before free interchange of argument and ideas among all philosophers becomes the norm, and it is questionable whether that goal will ever be attained.

THE EXCEPTIONS IN BRITAIN: RUSSELL AND WITTGENSTEIN

We need now to consider some of the exceptions to the rule which I have outlined in the general context of the major trends. It may be salutary for those who hold that the history of English-speaking philosophy in the twentieth century is the history of university philosophy, to remember the cases of Bertrand Russell (1872–1970) and Ludwig Wittgenstein (1889–1951), who are perhaps the two greatest philosophers in Britain in this century (although, of course, Wittgenstein was Austrian and wrote primarily in the medium of German).[1]

Russell was, it is true, a university don at Cambridge on and off for some part of his life, in spite of various forms of heterodoxy which got him into trouble. He was fellow of Trinity College without teaching obligations from 1894 until 1901, and lecturer from 1910 until 1916, when he was not reappointed because of his pacifist activities. He accepted the offer of a fellowship at Trinity again in 1919, but resigned after a year's leave of absence to visit China. He returned to Trinity as fellow and lecturer in 1944 and gave lectures there which were published as his *Human Knowledge, its Scope and Limits* (1948), and in 1948 the fellowship was renewed for life without teaching duties. In between 1919 and 1944 he gave the Tarner Lectures at Cambridge in 1925 and various courses of lectures in the USA, as well as more incidental lecturing. He even had appointments in Chicago and California, resigning from the latter to take up, as he hoped, an appointment at City College, New York, only to find the offer of the post withdrawn because of his 'immorality'. (Russell set out his career on the title-page of the English edition of his *An Inquiry into Meaning and Truth* (1940) and characteristically concluded it with the words 'Judicially pronounced unworthy to be Professor of Philosophy at the College of the City of New York (1940)'.) He was in many ways a typical English aristocrat (becoming the third Earl Russell on his brother's death in 1931), but he gave away most of his inheritance and certainly needed from time to time the money which he derived from academic employment, from writings (particularly his *History of Western Philosophy*, published in 1946) and from journalism. Russell's career was a somewhat tempestuous one, but nevertheless extremely distinguished. It was not, however, a career typical of an academic philosopher.

Philosophically, Russell began life as an absolute idealist, this being the dominant philosophical movement in Britain at the end of the nineteenth century. He was converted to realism by his somewhat younger contemporary, G.E. Moore. Apart from his book on Leibniz (1900), a product of lectures given without obligation at Cambridge during his first fellowship, his earliest and arguably finest works were on logic and the foundations of mathematics, particularly the monumental *Principia Mathematica* written in collaboration with A.N. Whitehead (1910–13). He soon became involved, however, in issues in epistemology and metaphysics, as is evident from his incomparable introduction to philosophy, *The Problems of Philosophy*, published in 1912. (It is incomparable because, more than any other introduction to philosophy, it is the work of a first-class philosopher who manages to be relatively simple without talking down to his readers.) This was followed by works on other aspects of philosophy. It is arguable that in his later writings in particular, Russell was, with qualifications, very much in the tradition of British Empiricism.

Before taking to philosophy, however, he was a mathematician, and became interested in the foundations of mathematics from a philosophical point of view. This brought him into contact with Frege and others who had similar interests. It also introduced Wittgenstein to Russell, as I shall indicate later in connection with that philosopher. The influence in this respect was certainly two-way, and the lectures which Russell published in *The Monist* in 1918, under the heading 'The Philosophy of Logical Atomism' (arguably Russell's greatest work outside the philosophy of mathematics) are very much a reflection of Wittgenstein's thinking, as Russell acknowledged. (In 1918 Russell spent six months in prison because of a pacifist article he had written which was judged defamatory of the armed forces; he wrote his *Introduction to Mathematical Philosophy* there. At the time, Wittgenstein was serving in the Austrian forces in Italy, where he was captured by the Italians in November 1918; he had completed his *Tractatus Logico-Philosophicus* in August of that year, took it with him into a prisoner-of-war camp at Monte Cassino, from where, with the help of J.M. Keynes, it was eventually sent to Russell for comment.)

Russell went on publishing books and articles of various kinds throughout his life, but he gradually grew out of sympathy with the way in which philosophy was going, and in his philosophical autobiography, *My Philosophical Development* (1959), he expressed his dissatisfaction with his philosophical critics (of which there were many by this time) somewhat peevishly; he clearly did not appreciate the force of the criticisms. At other times, especially in works derived from lectures, he frequently exhibited a somewhat puckish sense of humour. But the list of published works is very long; among them there appear many works which philosophers may prefer to ignore – pamphlets and occasional works on issues of contemporary political and social interest, for example. Towards the end of his life he was very much taken up with the work of the Campaign for Nuclear Disarmament, as the result of which, at the age of 89, he was sentenced to another two months in prison, of which, for medical reasons, he served only one week. This was followed by further campaigning over the Vietnam war. Russell, it is clear, did not at all conform to the stereotype of the academic philosopher; indeed, his political and social involvements invite comparisons between him and Plato, even if his political concerns were much more fundamental than Plato's. Nevertheless, the works written by him which posterity has decided to recognize as truly philosophical are those which derived from some academic context – often enough lectures.

Russell is, therefore, only a partial exception to the principle that by the twentieth century philosophy had become firmly entrenched as a function of the university system. He was dependent on that system in general, even if his contributions to it as a teacher, and then mainly as a lecturer, were somewhat intermittent. But it is arguable that he represents a phenomenon which no longer exists. For he was a member of a progressive, even radical, aristocratic family (his grandfather, by whom he was brought up after his parents died when he was a baby, was Lord John Russell, twice Prime Minister). He did not go to school until he was 16, being taught by private tutors before that, and was then sent to an army crammer in order to prepare for the examination for a scholarship at Trinity College, Cambridge, which he got. It is clear that he was a man of exceptional intelligence who benefited from all the contacts, both intellectual and political, that living with his grandparents in Pembroke Lodge, Richmond Park made possible. There is a certain similarity in that respect between him and J.S. Mill (whom his parents knew). But, unlike Mill, Russell was, and showed in many ways that he was, a member, even if a very rogue member, of the aristocracy. It is unlikely that the circumstances which made him what he was are repeatable today. Russell is, in that respect, a unique case.

The case of Wittgenstein in unique too, but in a very different way. The story of his personal life has been told, and argued over, often enough and there would be little point in trying to reproduce all the details yet again (although some are inevitable). Wittgenstein's family background was very different from Russell's, but he too came from a family of wealth, and later gave all his fortune away, although this time to other members of his family who were rich enough, he thought, for the additional wealth not to corrupt them. He was three-quarters Jewish, and his father was a leading figure in the Austrian iron and steel industry. Three of his brothers committed suicide and he often, during his life, contemplated that himself. The remaining brother, Paul Wittgenstein, who lost an arm in the First World War, was a celebrated pianist, even with the remaining left hand, for whom Ravel wrote his 'Concerto for the Left Hand', and for whom the

Austrian composer, Franz Schmidt, also wrote. The Wittgenstein family was a musical and cultured one at a time which saw the amazing flowering of artistic, cultural and intellectual activity which took place in Vienna at the beginning of this century. Ludwig Wittgenstein had all the appearance (with penetrating blue eyes) and manner of the genius, and it is clear that he actually was a genius. (The art of genius-spotting is a curious one, but one can have no doubt that Wittgenstein was one, although the same cannot perhaps be said of Russell; a similar situation, it might be argued, exists over Plato and Aristotle.)

Like Russell, Wittgenstein was educated at home at first (in his case until the age of 14). He then attended school at Linz, and studied engineering at Berlin. He came to Manchester in 1908 to be a research student in aeronautical engineering, became interested in mathematics and its foundations, and read Russell's *Principles of Mathematics* (1903). Through that he came to know of Frege whom he visited in 1911. Frege advised him to study with Russell at Cambridge, which he did for five terms, during which time he also became friendly with G.E. Moore and J.M. Keynes. After a period in which he lived in isolation in Norway, where he was visited by Moore, to whom he dictated notes on logical matters, there came the war, during which he served in the Austrian forces. Out of this emerged the only book that he published in his lifetime, his *Tractatus Logico-Philosophicus*. It was put together out of previously written notes, in paragraphs numbered according to a decimal system which was supposed to indicate the importance of the statements. (Few of Wittgenstein's other writings ever reach the state of being discursive; that was not how he thought philosophy should be pursued. The one work that more or less answers to that criterion, the *Blue and Brown Books*, was in fact composed of dictated lectures.) The notes which he wrote before the final composition of the *Tractatus* show that he had had an early interest in the philosophy of Schopenhauer, through which was filtered what detailed knowledge he had, which was not much, of the history of philosophy; a little of that is evident in the *Tractatus* itself.

This is not the place for an exegesis of that remarkable work, which, starting from the proposition that the world is all that is the case, presents an account of propositions, of meaning in general, of the structure of language and thought, of logic, and of the world, as logic and thought reveal it to us. After some remarks on the impossibility of aesthetics and ethics, and others on life, death and mysticism, it ends with the statement that 'What we cannot speak about we must consign to silence'. It is an immensely difficult work, but it has fascinated whole hosts of philosophers and has been extremely influential. Wittgenstein thought that with it he had dealt with the issues of philosophy to the extent that they could be dealt with, and gave up philosophy for a time, becoming a teacher in various Austrian schools, then a gardener at a monastery, and finally the architect of an austere house for his sister in Vienna. He was, in fact, recalled to philosophy by contact with Moritz Schlick (1882–1936), founder of the so-called 'Vienna Circle' of logical positivists, who had taken up the chair previously occupied by Ernst Mach in Vienna, and who was eventually assassinated by a student. Schlick met Wittgenstein in 1927 to discuss philosophical issues along with Rudolf Carnap (1891–1970) and Friedrich Waismann (1896–1959), who were members of the Circle, Wittgenstein himself having refused to become a member. The discussions broke up in 1929, although Wittgenstein remained friendly with Schlick and particularly with Waismann. (It was thus especially sad that when Waismann left Austria in 1938 as a refugee he was not welcomed by Wittgenstein in Cambridge, probably because Wittgenstein thought that Waismann had taken over his ideas. Waismann, who was a gentle and kindly man, and who had fully acknowledged Wittgenstein's influence, was extremely hurt, quite justifiably.)

At all events, in 1929 Wittgenstein was persuaded to return to Cambridge, where he submitted the *Tractatus* for a Ph.D., which was examined by Russell and Moore, in spite of its unorthodox character as a thesis. He was then elected to a research fellowship at Trinity College. He lectured to small classes from 1930, and from these lectures, which Moore attended and later reported on, emerged by way of dictation the *Blue and Brown Books*. These were meant for very private perusal by 'close friends and students', but they gradually came into much wider circulation, even at Oxford, which Wittgenstein thought a philosophical desert. He wrote his *Philosophische Bemerkungen* and *Philosophische Grammatik*, both in German, at this period, but they remained unpublished until long after his death. His only other publication was a paper 'Some remarks on logical form', meant to be delivered to a symposium of a conference, the Joint Session of the Aristotelian Society and Mind Association, in 1929; in fact he spoke about something else, mathematical infinity. In any case, he despised the journal *Mind* and what it stood for in philosophy, and he never attended any other philosophical conference.[2]

When his fellowship at Trinity expired in 1935, Wittgenstein returned to his hut in Norway and worked on his *Philosophische Untersuchungen*, the book which was nearest to completion when he died, and which was published in 1953, two years after his death, with a parallel translation into English by Elizabeth Anscombe, under the title *Philosophical Investigations*. He returned to Cambridge in 1937, and lectured there to small classes under austere conditions, his speaking being interspersed with long periods of silence which nobody dared to interrupt.[3] He was appointed to the chair at Cambridge when Moore retired in 1939, but the war intervened, and during it Wittgenstein served as a medical orderly at Guy's Hospital, London, and later as an assistant at a Clinical Research Laboratory in Newcastle-upon-Tyne, without ever revealing who he really was. He returned to Cambridge in late 1944, but disliked the role of a professor, describing it as 'a kind of living death'. In 1947 he resigned the chair, and went to live in Ireland. After a visit to Norman Malcolm at Cornell University in the USA in 1949, his health began to deteriorate, and after periods in Vienna, Norway (briefly) and Oxford (at the house of Elizabeth Anscombe), he died of cancer in Cambridge in 1951.

As I said earlier, Wittgenstein had all the marks of a genius – he was awkward, arrogant, intolerant, and unkind to those whom he thought not really serious about philosophy, but he had an amazing philosophical insight. In those respects at least he was very like Schopenhauer, who was, in many ways, the source of his philosophical interest, although, arguably, Wittgenstein was a much greater philospher. Certainly he has had far more influence on philosophy, by contrast with Schopenhauer's almost total lack of such influence (except of course on Wittgenstein himself). During Wittgenstein's lifetime, except for the *Tractatus* and its influence on the Vienna Circle and logical positivism, he was comparatively unknown outside Cambridge. There were, of course, the few disciples who came there from outside, for example, Norman Malcolm from Cornell University in the USA and Georg von Wright from Finland, who succeeded him in the chair at Cambridge in 1948, but who returned to Finland in 1951. (The chair then passed to John Wisdom (b.1904), another disciple and a propagandist of his own version of Wittgenstein's philosophy.)

In Oxford, following the publication of the *Tractatus*, Wittgenstein's philosophical thinking was known to one degree or another to some philosophers there, particularly Gilbert Ryle (1900–1976), who became in the years after the war the dominant figure there. (Ryle had a great influence over the British philosophical scene in general after the war, partly because of the importance of his own philosophical views but also because of the authority that he exercised in connection with university appointments in philosophy.) Some typewritten copies of Wittgenstein's *Blue and Brown Books* and of some of his lectures on the philosophy of mathematics came into rather limited circulation, as indicated earlier. Otherwise it tended to be a matter of rumour and indirect report. Elizabeth Anscombe, who, along with von Wright and Rush Rhees, was Wittgenstein's literary editor, knew him more intimately, and Wittgenstein stayed in her house for nearly a year in 1950–1.[4] After Wittgenstein had died, and his *Philosophical Investigations* was published in 1953, there started a great flowering of 'Wittgensteinianism' (if one can use that rather horrid word), both in Oxford and elsewhere, including Cambridge, where Wisdom had carried on his version of the tradition.

It is impossible to do more than give a hint here of the later philosophy of Wittgenstein; it has been seen both as a complete rejection of the *Tractatus*, to the extent that one can almost speak of two Wittgensteins, and as a very subtle continuation in modified form of that earlier thinking. The *Philosophical Investigations* consists mainly of a series of remarks on various themes, about, for example, language (including the idea of an intrinsically private language, which was espoused by Russell, although Wittgenstein makes no mention of that fact), and about a whole host of concepts which have to do with the philosophy of mind. There is an opposition to general theories, and an emphasis on practices (an idea which is given even greater weight in other late works), and on the idea of agreement in forms of life. A late unfinished work, *On Certainty*, seems to insist on the idea that certain things have to be taken as true if other things are to be even intelligible. One can see in this a complete opposition to the kind of epistemology and philosophy of mind which was the main tradition of western philosophy as initiated by Descartes. The so-called 'private language argument' set out, although without total clarity, in the *Philosophical Investigations*, is of fundamental importance in that respect. There can be no doubt that Wittgenstein's later philosophy presents a radical critique of the previous tradition of philosophy, of a kind which no previous thinker, however similar superficially, had produced.

The dominance of the Wittgensteinian approach to philosophy in academic circles, both in Britain and, perhaps to a more limited extent, in the USA, lasted about twenty years. (Russell's philosophy never had that kind of following after his death, although during his lifetime he was certainly much better known than Wittgenstein was during his.) There followed the inevitable slackening of interest as other philosophical fashions in Anglo-Saxon philosophy, deriving mainly from the USA, took over. But there has begun more recently a kind of second-generation set of approaches to Wittgenstein's philosophy, which treat it more as something of importance in the history of philosophy, something to be set alongside the philosophical 'greats', such as Hume and Kant, and which use his thought to make philosophical points, as one might use the thought of those other philosophers. I suspect that Wittgenstein himself would have been horrified with this, as with any attempt to do philosophy except in his way, with all his loathing of the academic apparatus.

In different ways, and for different reasons, the philosophies of Russell and Wittgenstein have both really become part of the history of philosophy, although in Wittgenstein's case, if not in Russell's, there have been attempts to continue the spirit of his philosophical approach. Even where that is the case, however, the spirit is moulded to a body given its form by academic institutions, with, for example, lectures on the published works (which have appeared almost in profusion as editions and translations of remaining manuscripts have been produced by his literary editors). Perhaps the ultimate thing of this kind, which would particularly have horrified Wittgenstein, is the publication of large-scale commentaries on those works, with all the apparatus of scholarship. I make no judgment on the usefulness of this, one way or the other. But it is a very good indication of the way in which the institution or institutions in which philosophy is pursued now determine its nature. Compared with some other subjects, philosophy is a subject where the *paraphernalia* of academic scholarship still has only a moderate importance, but it is now impossible to do without it altogether, as Wittgenstein would no doubt have wished.

OTHER INSTITUTIONAL FACTORS IN BRITAIN AND THE USA

Wittgenstein was far from being a typical philosopher. As I have tried to indicate, he was someone who depended on academic institutions without really wanting to be part of them. He did lecture, although not perhaps in the way that this was generally done. But he took no part in such things as conferences or the publication of articles in journals as others at Oxford and Cambridge in his time did. (In those universities, particularly in Oxford, it is still possible to be the 'good college man', carrying out one's teaching and entering into a certain amount of local philosophical discussion without feeling the need to present oneself and one's ideas before the wider philosophical community. It is not an exaggeration to say that many philosophers in other British universities have long felt a certain resentment about what they see as the self-centred character of Oxford philosophy.)

The increasing dependence of British universities on government financing has, in more recent times, produced pressures to conform to what is taken to be the stereotype of the university don, with institutions undertaking forms of assessment of teaching and research. As a counterpart a 'National Committee for Philosophy' has been set up in order to try and safeguard the pursuit of philosophy in academic contexts, in the face of government and other pressures. This is one role which has been adopted to some extent by the American Philosophical Association, as well as that of facilitating the hiring of philosophical teachers by university departments and the organization of philosophical conferences. The main gathering of philosophers in Britain – the Joint Session of the Aristotelian Society and Mind Association – has never combined such roles, confining itself to the organization of philosophical symposia (so-called), although it may play host to such things as the 'Standing Conference of Philosophers' to which the National Committee reports.

Otherwise, the pursuit of philosophy in Britain has been, since the Second World War, almost entirely a function of academia (and the same applies to North America and other English-speaking countries, especially those with universities initially set up under the aegis of British universities, particularly London, as is the case with many of those in the British Commonwealth). The expansion of universities in Britain in this period greatly enlarged the scope for the study of philosophy, either by itself or in combination with some other subject or subjects (as is still the rule at Oxford). As I pointed out earlier, all the new universities, except one, were set up with philosophy departments, and the exception, Essex, eventually followed suit. More recently, as a result of economic pressures, mostly government determined, some universities have closed their philosophy departments (one thing that led to the setting up of the National Committee for Philosophy).

Oxford remains the largest centre for the study of philosophy, followed by Cambridge and London (the 'golden triangle' as it is sometimes referred to). Most other departments are relatively small, although some of those in the 'new universities' were initially quite large. Most of them too put the emphasis on undergraduate teaching (later to be supplemented by MA courses), the bulk of research postgraduates being at Oxford, Cambridge and London. With the expansion in the number of philosophy departments after the war and the consequent demand for more teachers of philosophy in them and also in the new polytechnics, Gilbert Ryle (who, as has already been mentioned, was one of the leading British philosophers in the 1950s) promoted the idea of a new kind of postgraduate degree at Oxford. The aim of B.Phil., as it was called, was to broaden as well as deepen a philosopher's knowledge and expertise from what could be expected from an undergraduate degree, so as to make him or her better qualified as a teacher in higher education. The B.Phil. thus involved the passing of a number of examination papers at a very high level, as well as a shortish thesis. Seminars were organized as a preparation for such examinations. This pattern has been copied to some extent elsewhere, although not necessarily with the same expectations, and sometimes against the opposition of those from other subjects who see in it a watering down of the purely thesis higher degree. (It also has to be said that some philosophers have come to doubt the efficacy of question-paper examinations at this level.)

The only institution concerned with the propagation of philosophy outside this academic context is the Royal Institute for Philosophy, set up in 1925, with a journal, eventually to be called *Philosophy*, being published by it from 1926. The aim of the Institute has always been to promote the study of philosophy by a wider stratum of the public than those taking or having taken university courses. In that sense it has had a somewhat popularizing role, without any wish to lower standards. It has organized courses of lectures in London, given weekly, on specific themes, and has concerned itself with the spreading of interest in philosophy, including the setting up of some branches elsewhere in Britain, as well as publishing *Philosophy*, which has a wider philosophical remit than some other journals. For some time its director was non-academic, as indeed was the secretary of the Aristotelian Society, which also meets in London. But the president of the Aristotelian Society is normally a distinguished academic philosopher holding office for one year. The president of the Royal Institute of Philosophy has tended to be a member of the House of Lords with philosophical interests, and for some time this was Lord Samuel, who had very definite philosophical aspirations. Gradually, however, the running of these institutions has come under the aegis of academics, and the current president of the Royal Institute of Philosophy is both an academic philosopher (although he has now officially retired) and a member of the House of Lords – Lord Quinton. While, however, the Aristotelian Society is very much a forum for professional philosophical discussion (even if not, in general, very well-attended discussion these days) the Institute retains its more generalist image. Latterly it has undertaken the role of promoting the study of philosophy in schools, something in which, in a rather different way, the National Committee for Philosophy has an interest.

As I remarked in the previous chapter, there is a tradition in France and Germany of teaching philosophy in schools, so that philosophy forms, for example, part of the 'baccalauréat' in France. Nothing of this kind has been the rule in Britain, except where certain dedicated teachers with philosophical interests and expertise could persuade head-teachers to allow some periods of philosophy teaching as a minority interest for sixth-formers. Indeed, some university teachers of philosophy have positively discouraged schools from dabbling, as they would have it, in philosophy, except perhaps in logic.[5] Quite recently, there have been set up A-Level syllabuses in philosophy, so that some philosophy teaching does have an official place in schools (and certainly in further education colleges), although still in a rather small way. What effect this is likely to have on the general pursuit of philosophy it is too early to say, although it is clear that philosophy is a subject which can raise great enthusiasms in young people, if only because its methods and concerns are so different from those of most other academic subjects. The Royal Institute of Philosophy has shown a distinct interest in these matters, particularly in trying to raise and promote an interest in philosophy on the part of school-teachers. In addition, the National Committee for Philosophy has been trying to promote philosophy in schools more directly. Nevertheless, apart from extra-mural courses and the like, philosophy can, in the end, be pursued in a substantial way only in or through institutions of higher education.

In the USA there is perhaps an even greater tendency to reserve philosophy for university courses, as opposed to schools, because of the fact that with four-year BA courses some of what takes place in sixth-forms in British schools is carried on in universities there. There have been attempts in some places in the USA to institute school courses of philosophy for children, but such courses do not ape what takes place at university; they are specially designed courses aimed at getting children to think philosophically in a manner appropriate for their age. But because university courses in the USA are built up on a credit system, it is possible there, in a way which is not generally the case in Britain, for students to select certain courses in philosophy, on the principle of 'taste and see', and then to go on to other courses if that suits them. As far as university teachers are concerned, the tenure system ensures that at least lip-service is paid to research and the promotion of the subject. Such teachers are in any case much more mobile than university teachers are in Britain, and they move around from one department to another as their career and other considerations determine. Hence, the system within which philosophy is pursued in the USA is in some respects less structured than it is in Britain. (Whether that is an advantage or disadvantage is a matter for argument.)

There is one institution in North America which is in one way a relic from an older way of doing things but which also provides a partial exception to the rule that it is in universities that philosophy is carried on. This is the summer-school, whereby courses are given, again mainly by university teachers, during the summer vacation, to interested individuals. In Britain, extra-mural departments sometimes arrange summer-schools, which provide more concentrated courses of study for those who would otherwise follow weekly courses more sporadically. The Open University also organizes similar summer-schools which are obligatory for those taking its courses. But the phenomenon of the summer-school in North America is both more widespread and more entrenched. Once again, however, while those attending such courses may not be regular university students, the courses are generally organized by universities. Hence, they depend on the university system even if they are not, strictly, part of it.

There are no figures in North American philosophy, this century, who have the kind of 'eccentricity' in relation to the university system which Russell and Wittgenstein had in Britain. I have previously referred to the book by Bruce Kuklick, *The Rise of American Philosophy*, which is an account of the development of the philosophy department at Harvard University. The book acknowledges the existence of philosophy at other universities, even at the turn of the century. It was still, in Kuklick's view, reasonable to see the rise of American philosophy as having Harvard as its centre. Certainly the best-known American philosophers in the first half of this century came from there, particularly C.I. Lewis (1883–1964) and W.V. Quine (b.1908). They were initially perhaps best known for their work in logic, although they both wrote on other things. This in a way set the tone for subsequent American philosophy, which has often tended to be technical in a way which happens to fit the scientific culture typical of the USA. (In recent years, as I mentioned earlier, materialism has become almost *de rigueur* there, as it has also done, incidentally, in Australia; one might speculate about the reasons for this.) Kucklick emphasizes the growing technicality of philosophy at Harvard, its emphasis on the Ph.D., and the tendency of the professionals there to be contemptuous of their less professional predecessors, whom they do not even bother to read. But that last tendency has, by now, become the rule almost everywhere, at least among Anglo-Saxon philosophers.

Some of that tendency towards technicality was reinforced by the fact that several notable members of the Vienna Circle, with their preoccupation with logic and the philosophy of science, came to the USA before the Second World War as refugees (as Waismann did in coming to England, and as did that very distinguished philosopher of science, Karl Popper (b.1902), in going to New Zealand and from there to England after the war, although he was never a member of the Vienna Circle as such). Carnap, for example, established himself at Chicago, and was very influential in setting the tone of American philosophy. After the Second World War there was a great expansion of universities in America too, and philosophy in all sorts of forms, some analytical, some owing more to the European continental tradition, others in one sense or another indigenous – particularly in their leanings towards pragmatism – spread widely through the university system. Even in the analytical tradition the centre of activity has moved from Britain to the USA. (When I was beginning my own philosophical career in 1950, Oxford was a sort of philosophical Mecca, to which philosophers came from all over the English-speaking world, particularly North America and Australia. Whatever the contemporary philosophical importance of Oxford, it is not like that, and it cannot be denied that, in general, American philosophers are dominant in the analytical field. Apart from other considerations, here, as in other areas of competition, numbers tell.)

I doubt that what I said in my Introduction about the lack of respect given at present to philosophy and philosophers in Britain applies equally to the USA. This is not so much because philosophers still tend to be seen there, as they do in continental Europe, as intellectual leaders, but because the style of American philosophy in general fits well with the dominant culture. Industry there, for example, sometimes appeals to philosophers for help or advice in a way that almost never happens in Britain. That may be in part due to the fact that much of American philosophy has an emphasis on logic and the philosophy of science (although the scale of university philosophy in the USA is such that nearly every aspect of the subject is represented somewhere, and many aspects can be found in any one place); it is also due to the fact that there is more respect there for the kind of thinking that typifies philosophy and the way in which that can be given application. Although medical ethics, for example, does flourish now in Britain, in the USA, in the form of so-called bioethics, it is no less than a growth industry. That this sort of thing holds good of Britain to a much less extent is no doubt partly due to the conservatism and élitism of our system of education and social system generally.

THE SITUATION IN EUROPE: GERMANY AND ELSEWHERE

On the position in continental Europe I can speak much less authoritatively, but one thing is very obvious – the effect of two world wars. As far as Germany is concerned, there are also the consequences of Nazism, although that affected the occupied countries too during the Second World War. One major feature of Nazism was of course its anti-semitism; I have already referred to the fact that several German and Austrian philosophers had to leave their own countries as refugees. Those who remained, on the whole, temporized with the Nazis. Moreover, the philosopher who has come to be thought of as the leading German philosopher in the 1930s and afterwards, Martin Heidegger (1889–1976), became a member of the Nazi party in May 1933, subsequently becoming Rector of the University of Freiburg. Heidegger's followers, who are many and, frequently, eminent, have tried hard to excuse him for this – he was a German nationalist, he saw in the Nazis support for his defence of culture against the inroads of technology, he was a romantic, and so on. It is claimed that he resigned from the Nazi party in 1934, when he also gave up the post of Rector at Freiburg, but this claim has recently been refuted. In any case, the period in which he was Rector of the University was one in which book-burning took place and Jewish professors had their licences to teach removed. Moreover, he deleted his dedication to his teacher Edmund Husserl, who was Jewish, from what is perhaps his main work, *Sein und Zeit* (*Being and Time*). This work was published originally in 1927, but there are still echoes of the idea of a German mission in later works. After the war he was forbidden to lecture until 1951. In the face of all this, the adulation which he has received in certain quarters as a philosopher, teacher and man of almost religious missionary zeal, is surprising.

I shall return to Heidegger later. As far as concerns the first part of this century the leading German philosopher outside the positivist movement was Edmund Husserl (1859–1938), referred to above. Husserl began academic life as a mathematician before becoming a philosopher, but came under the influence of Brentano in Vienna. As I suggested towards the end of the previous chapter (see p. 121), Brentano's emphasis on intentional acts of mind with their immanent or intentional objects led Alexius von Meinong (1853–1920) to produce a theory of such objects of thought (a theory which emphasized, as against Brentano, a distinction between objects and the contents of thought, and which, incidentally, affected Russell at least to the extent of providing an ontological 'aunt Sally'); it also led Husserl to produce a theory of how such objects presented themselves to consciousness, a theory which he designated as 'phenomenology'.

Initially Husserl applied this idea to logical and similar matters in his *Logische Untersuchungen* (1900–1), but the theory gradually became wider in scope. He took as his project that of attempting to arrive at the essence of things by a bracketing-off of all presuppositions (an idea for which he adopted the term *'epochē'*, derived from its use by the Greek Sceptics for suspension of belief). This was first set out in his *Ideas* (1913). Some have seen in his later thinking, particularly in his *Cartesian Meditations* (1931), a return to a form of idealism, and this alienated some followers. In other works written at about the same time, however, he makes use of the idea of a 'life world' which is a presupposition of perception, and thereby knowledge, in a way which has suggested a similarity to Wittgenstein's idea of forms of life. But the life world is still said to be derived somehow from 'subjective operations', so that the accusation of idealism perhaps still sticks. Nevertheless, Husserl's phenomenology has been immensely influential, affecting not only other German thinkers but French ones too, including Sartre and, particularly, Merleau-Ponty.

Husserl was, however, the complete university professor in the German tradition, holding posts first at Halle and Göttingen and finally at Freiburg from 1916 to 1928, where Heidegger, his pupil, succeeded him, having had a brief, five-year spell away at Marburg. Heidegger came from a Catholic family and had originally intended to enter the Jesuit order. It may be the incipient religiosity which remains in his writings that enables some to regard them, especially *Being and Time*, as having something of the character of a religious text. He was bitterly opposed, as I have already said, to a technological and industrial society, and, as his inaugural lecture at Freiburg made explicit, he saw Hitler's new regime as an opportunity for German universities to stand up for true culture. It was all a great mistake, and one wonders how someone who could make that kind of mistake could be as great a thinker as many have suggested.

Being and Time was, of course, published before all this in 1927; it is an attempt to set out an account of human existence, what Heidegger calls *Dasein* (meaning 'presence there' or 'presence in the world'). Time is the horizon of that existence, in that it must end in death, a fact which authentic being must recognize. The work is immensely difficult, with a plethora of what many think of as unnecessary technical terms. The book was meant to be the first half of a systematic treatment of being, but only the part on *Dasein* was written, so that for Heidegger's thoughts on being in general we have to turn to later, more fragmentary, essays and lectures. In them, Heidegger has a tendency to go back to the beginnings of Greek thought, almost on the principle of 'the earlier, the more likely to be true', and he engages in much dubious etymologizing and reliance on neologisms. It is a bad habit which has unfortunately infected many of those whom he has influenced, particularly some French philosophers. Disciples have seen it as marvellous, the profound words of a prophet and seer; some critics have seen it, perhaps more plausibly, as a fraud.

In general, however, Heidegger is a late example of German romanticism, as his own acknowledgements of the influence and importance of Nietzsche makes clear. His opposition to the effects of technology, science and industry on society and culture puts him in clear opposition to what I have described as the dominant ethos of contemporary American philosophy. Heidegger's views are also quite opposed to Marxism, and in his *Introduction to Metaphysics*,[6] he speaks of Europe lying in the great pincers 'squeezed between Russia on one side and America on the other'. 'From the metaphysical point of view', he says, 'they are the same; the same dreary technological frenzy, the same unrestricted organization of the average man'. This may seem inspirational to some (although the terms of reference have now become somewhat outmoded), but it is less clear what one is to think of his subsequent call upon Germany, as the most metaphysical of nations, to 'move itself and thereby the history of the west beyond the centre of their future "happening" and into the primordial realm of the powers of being'. (And there is a good deal more of the same.)

It should perhaps be added that fascist Italy had its own philosopher propagandist, of a rather cruder and less distinguished kind, in Giovanni Gentile (1875–1944). He was an Hegelian idealist of a certain sort who preached the doctrine of the state overriding the individual. He became a minister in Mussolini's government and then president of the National Fascist Institute of Culture, having earlier held chairs in various Italian universities. He was assassinated by communist partisans when Mussolini was overthrown. But the most distinguished philosopher during this period was Benedetto Croce (1866–1952). He too held ministerial office, but in the government which existed before Mussolini became dictator, and he was later firmly opposed to the fascist regime. Interestingly enough, for our purposes, he too is an exception to the general rule of philosophy being the province of the universities; he belonged to a wealthy family and was able to live as a private scholar, like Schopenhauer. He too was an idealist of a kind, but, like R.G. Collingwood (1889–1943) in England, another recalcitrant idealist influenced by Croce, he is best known for his contributions to the philosophy of history and aesthetics. For our present purposes, there is not much to be said about Italian philosophy since his death; what there is is certainly a function of the university system.

In Germany, since the Second World War, philosophy has continued to be a function of the university system too. In that system much of the old way of doing things remains, with the concentration on the doctorate and the seminar. It is less open than it was, with restriction on numbers of students (the so-called '*numerus clausus*') in certain places and in some subjects. It has been argued that the general ethos of the universities is utilitarian in character, by comparison with the nineteenth-century emphasis on *Wissenschaft*,[7] although that is far from being a particularly German disease. How that affects the place of philosophy in particular is less clear, except that that place is obviously and inevitably less general than it was in, say, Hegel's time. What are perhaps the two main movements are represented by Hans-Georg Gadamer (b.1900) and Jürgen Habermas (b.1929) respectively.

Gadamer was a pupil and friend of Heidegger. He was Rector of the University of Leipzig after the war and was involved in the rebuilding of that university. During the last nineteen years of his academic life, until his retirement in 1968, he held the chair in Heidelberg, and was notable for his contributions to the hermeneutic movement which is concerned with the nature and conditions of understanding (something that goes back to the theory of '*Verstehen*' put forward by the earlier Wilhelm Dilthey (1833–1911). Gadamer stresses the part that the individual's history has in that process of understanding, something that makes understanding a relative matter to some extent. Habermas, by contrast, is a member of the so-called 'Frankfurt School' set up earlier by Theodor Adorno (1903–1969) on his return from the New School for Social Research in New York, where he went in 1934 as a refugee. Adorno had contributions to make to the theory of music but the main emphasis of the school has always been on social philosophy. Habermas, like nearly all philosophers on the continent of Europe, was influenced by Husserl and phenomenology, but he has attached importance also to the idea of praxis, after the thinking of the young Marx. Indeed, there is a great deal of Marxism in the thinking of the Frankfurt School, Marxism being the other great strand in recent European philosophy. Nevertheless, Habermas has done a certain amount of bridge-building between that and elements of Anglo-Saxon philosophy of science and philosophy of language. He has recently been director of the Max Planck Institute at Starnberg.

I shall have next to nothing to say about things in eastern Europe. Apart from the inevitable Marxism that has held sway there, phenomenology has had its influence in Poland and Czechoslovakia, to mention only two countries. Poland was earlier a great source of logicians, but many of them left the country to go elsewhere. In the Soviet Union, and most of the countries under its hegemony, there were, for a long time, compulsory lectures on dialectical materialism, which some philosophers no doubt resented. But in spite of some such individual exhibitions of independence, the official front of philosophy, as reflected in appointments and publications, was overbearingly in conformity with the system. No doubt the situation will change as a result of the second 'revolution'. In Poland things have been a little more free for some time, while in Czechoslovakia, after the repression of the 'Czech spring' and before the restoration of democracy, there were attempts, often repressed by the authorities, to set up pockets of independent philosophy outside the universities, with private classes on aspects of the subjects. Of these, that organized by Julius Tomin attracted most notice outside Czechoslovakia, and he and others received the support of some British philosophers who went to lecture to such classes; there have also been connections between some British and Polish philosophers. Tomin himself was eventually expelled from Czechoslovakia, and he tried, rather unsuccessfully, to obtain a place in the British university system. Others continued their work there.

The political changes in eastern Europe must inevitably entail a reversion to the pattern which holds good elsewhere. But none of what I have said affects the general point that philosophy today is in nearly all cases a university matter. Even those who, in the period under communism, sought to practise philosophy outside the universities would have liked to be in them. For similar reasons, there is little point in going into any detail about other countries in western Europe, where there are no big figures or exceptions to the rule – except in France.[8]

FRANCE

Bergson, whom I mentioned in the previous chapter, taught at the Collège de France until he retired because of ill-health at the end of the First World War. While there, he was a fashionable figure and attracted large crowds to his lectures. He went on writing after retirement, was elected to the French Academy and in 1927 was awarded the Nobel Prize for literature. He had a considerable influence on Marcel Proust and on Italo Svevo, the Italian novelist. He also tried between the two world wars to encourage movements aiming at peace and international understanding, but he was caught by the Second World War, and when he died France was occupied by the German forces. His father was Jewish, but Bergson refused the offer of the Vichy Government to exempt him from the force of anti-Jewish laws. No doubt his death came, in a sense, in good time. But during his lifetime he was regarded as a leading French intellectual.

Certainly, there is no one else of philosophical note in the period up to the Second World War, apart from Simone Weil (1909–1943), whom I mentioned in the last chapter in connection with her teaching philosophy at a lycée for girls in 1933–4. She wrote on a number of religious and social issues, emphasizing the place of human beings and their freedom in an over-socialized and over-industrialized world. She fits no obvious stereotype of the philosopher and belongs to no recognizable philosophical movement of a wider kind. She is also what was, up to her time, a unique example of a notable female philosopher. It is generally suggested that she could have had a distinguished academic career, but she did not aim at that, preferring to work for a time as a manual labourer, apart from the lycée teaching. But she adopted an attitude of total commitment to what she believed in, including the position of the left in the Spanish Civil War and the Resistance in France during the Second World War. She died of starvation in England, refusing to eat what the suffering people of Europe during the war could not.

From that war there emerged Jean-Paul Sartre (1905–1980), who is the greatest exception, among more or less straightforward philosophers of the twentieth century (which Simone Weil is not), to the rule of the dominance of philosophy by the universities. He is an exception which, perhaps, only France could produce, partly because of the special character of its institutions of higher education (for example, the École Normale Supérieure and the Collège de France) to which reference has already been made (see pp. 122–3), and also because of the fashion of lionizing leading intellectuals in Paris. (Albert Camus (1913–1960) is another example of such an intellectual, who is sometimes classified with Sartre as an existentialist, stressing the absurdity of things. It is not obvious, however, that he really belongs seriously to the history of philosophy, and I shall not consider him further here. He is not alone, however, in being the sort of propagator of ideas that French intellectuals often are.)

Sartre is an exception to the normal pattern of the philosopher in another way too, in that he was a literary, as well as a philosophical, figure. Between 1931 and 1945, apart from the time during the war when he served in the forces and was made a prisoner of war, he worked as a teacher in a lycée. His first novel, *La Nausée*, was published in 1938 and was already an expression of some of the philosophical attitudes which made up his existentialism – the emphasis on freedom, on bad faith, and on the dread produced by the recognition of the sheer contingency of things. Some of it is an echo of Heidegger's emphasis on the finiteness of *Dasein* and the anxiety or dread that the thought of this produces. But round about the same time Sartre also published monographs on the emotions and on the imagination, which perhaps owe more to Husserl.

The book which is perhaps his main work *L'Être et le néant* (translated as *Being and Nothingness*), published during the war in 1943, is very much a French version of Heidegger, although there are echoes of Hegel too. (The cynic might say that it is Heidegger seen through the eyes of a Parisian café-loving intellectual.) It became the Bible of French existentialism, and was complemented by subsequent novels and plays that he wrote, particularly the trilogy *Les Chemins de la liberté* which appeared after the war. It is possible to argue about how far the literary works which give flesh to the philosophical ideas are something of a cheat, if considered as giving support to those ideas. But Sartre is unique (apart from Plato?) in writing literature and philosophy in close relation to each other. The early Sartre is very much the individualist, but later he became concerned with social considerations and in the end, perhaps surprisingly, embraced Marxism. In this, once again, the philosophical and literary works go hand in hand.

Sartre never held an academic post in an institution of higher education. Apart from producing his own philosophical and literary works, he was editor for some time of the review, *Les Temps Modernes*. He has come to be thought of, however, as the epitome of the cigarette-smoking café-frequenter of the period. For some time Anglo-Saxon philosophers would have nothing to do with him, suggesting that it was all nonsense (just as Carnap and A.J. Ayer (1910–1989), the British representative of the Vienna Circle, as positivists, quoted Heidegger's remark 'Das Nichts selbst nichtet' as the supreme example of metaphysical nonsense). He is now fully accepted, however, as a figure to be reckoned with in the history of philosophy, even if things have moved on somewhat in France. *Being and Nothingness* presents a metaphysical system based on the contrast between the two ultimate categories of the *en soi* (things/being) and the *pour soi* (consciousness), the latter constituting the nothingness of the title of his main work. This dichotomy also presents the contrast between human freedom and the so-called facticity of things. The *pour soi* has in effect a free choice of a world, and this entails an inevitable clash between consciousnesses, each of which is trying to encapsulate things, including other people, in itself. Hell is thus other people, as it is put in Sartre's play *Huis Clos*. There are in this echoes of Hegel's famous account in his *Phenomenology* of the necessary clash between master and slave. Other aspects, including the idea of nothingness, are echoes of Heidegger, although there is nothing in Sartre's existentialism that could conceivably be thought of as having a religious character.

The other main French philosopher of the same period was Maurice Merleau-Ponty (1908–1961), who was associated with Sartre for a time, until he broke with him in disillusionment with the Communist Party. But Merleau-Ponty is closer to Husserl than Sartre ever was. His first book, a rather austere and dry work, *La Structure du comportement* (1942), was a critique of behaviourism, in many ways ahead of its time. The second, *La Phénoménologie de la perception* (1945), was not only a critique of empiricist views on perception but a fairly systematic presentation of his philosophy, based on the idea of the subject's presence in the world through his or her living body. It contains an interesting, but in many ways misguided, thesis about temporality, and what may well be regarded as the obligatory (from the French point of view) defence of human freedom, based on the idea that there is no causal relation between the subject and his body. Later works are more fragmentary, though some regard them as more prophetic. He is regarded by many as the best French philosopher this century. Like Sartre he was initially a lycée teacher, but after the war he became a university professor at Lyons, then at the Sorbonne, and finally at the Collège de France. Towards the end of his life he had, in some ways, the status of a member of the French establishment.

More recent French philosophers have mostly taken their inspiration either from some member of the phenomenological or hermeneutic movement or from Marx, though this has often produced a heady mixture of ideas, sometimes blended with those of psychoanalysis, which has not always found acceptance, or even understanding, among other philosophers, or at any rate among Anglo-Saxon philosophers. All of these figures – the Marxist, Louis Althusser (1918–1990), who was committed to a mental asylum in 1981 after murdering his wife, Michel Foucault (1926–1984) who combined hermeneutics with a social and cultural relativism, and Jacques Derrida (b.1930) the high-priest of 'deconstructionism', whose theory owes something to the etymologizing of the late Heidegger and has been much taken up by literary critics – are or were university professors. The same applies to others who might be mentioned, although one cannot disregard the French tendency to lionize their leading intellectuals and to take up their thought as the latest intellectual fashion.

The situation in France, therefore, is somewhat unusual. Hence, if one says that there too philosophy has become an academic matter, that assertion has to be made with considerable qualification. Where, as in Britain, intellectuals as such are not well regarded, the confinement of philosophers to academia is almost inevitable, even if university professors have no great standing in society at large either. It is not perhaps too distorted a judgment to maintain that Germany respects, still respects, the scholar, France respects, indeed worships, the intellectual, whereas in Britain both these things are distrusted, and it is the amateur who makes a successful coup who gets the regard. That certainly affects the position of the philosopher in these different countries. I have already said something of the different situation that exists in the USA.

7

CONCLUSION

It may be thought by some that the sentiments expressed in the concluding lines of the previous chapter smack of sour grapes. Some may indeed regard them as politically motivated – a comment on the recent state of Thatcherite Britain, and the inheritance of that. The tendency in England, if not in Britain at large, to depreciate the role of the university academic is no new phenomenon, however, even if that tendency has been aggravated both by the policies espoused by recent governments and by the social values and attitudes that have come about, at least in part, as a result of those policies. The BBC, for example, appeals to a relevant academic when a special need arises, but that is no indication of any permanent regard for the scholar. On the other hand, intellectuals, as such, are certainly distrusted, at any rate, by the English, and, in spite of attempts to bring business into the universities, there still remains a gap between academia and industry in a way that does not hold good in, for example, the USA.

Some of this may be due to the social and educational system which we have inherited. It is no coincidence that before the 1830s there were only two universities in England; they were only just then recovering from being in a moribund state, and they existed to a large extent only for an élite. Although they acquired a pre-eminent status in the years that followed, when other universities were founded, this was at a cost, in that they then tended to look down on the rest of the university system, a tendency which has been perpetuated by many of their graduates who have acquired political and social status. If one's regard is restricted to the position of philosophy in all this, it may well seem to some, and not altogether without justice, that the history of recent philosophy in this country is, especially if one ignores Scotland, the history of what has gone on in Oxford and Cambridge. It is not altogether without justice simply because Oxford and Cambridge, as universities, have had a dominant role in the English educational system, and this carries over to at least the more traditional subjects taught and pursued there.

It might be objected that most countries have what some would call 'centres of excellence' and others might call 'institutions of privilege'. France, after all, has the Collège de France, the École Normale Supérieure, and so on; there are the Ivy League universities in the USA. In those countries, however, there is not in addition the kind of cult of the amateur and distrust of the expert that exists in England. A natural reaction to such attitudes is for the 'experts' to turn in on themselves, and to represent what they do as something exclusive, something in which outsiders can have no place. In a subject like philosophy, where the nature of the relevant expertise may well not be clear to those outside it, there can be a tendency on the part of its practitioners to seek a kind of technicality (or alternatively, some might say, a kind of obscurantism) which, it is hoped, may impress outsiders without necessarily producing in them a wish to join in.

Whether for that reason or not, there has certainly been a great increase in technicality in recent British philosophy, in spite of some pockets of resistance. (The similar increase in technicality in American philosophy may be for different reasons, which I have previously mentioned, connected with the character of American culture; but the type of technicality which is characteristic of the USA has infected British philosophy too, constituting an additional factor in the situation in Britain.) Although the enthusiasm with which newcomers to the subject often respond to it is evident enough (particularly, as I have discovered in my years at Birkbeck College, when those newcomers are so-called mature students), comparatively few such philosophers show much inclination to approach the general public with their subject, and 'popularizer' is still a word of abuse. It is not entirely clear what the modern counterpart of Socrates in contemporary society would be, but there are few obvious attempts to fulfil such a role. The result is the accusation that philosophers occupy an ivory tower.

I present this last accusation simply as something that is often suggested, whether justly or injustly. If the other side of this particular coin is the academicization and professionalism of philosophy, which, as I have tried to show, are rife everywhere, it matters for the importance of that phenomenon what the social and intellectual milieu is in which it all takes place. Professionalism is fine if the subject-matter demands it; but it is another thing altogether if it is simply a response to a popular disregard of the subject, a defence-mechanism against such disregard. The question therefore arises as to whether the subject-matter of philosophy demands for its practice a form of professionalism.

One thing that my history should have shown is that there was certainly one period, that of the seventeenth and eighteenth centuries, when philosophy, or at least philosophical progress, did not depend upon its practice within academic institutions. (I make this qualification only to indicate a recognition of the fact that universities did exist during the period in question, although what deserved the name of progress in the subject took place, in general, elsewhere.) This is not to say that the practice of philosophy during this period observed no professional standards. Those standards were a function of the conventions followed by philosophical scholars and intellectuals, and standards were maintained through mutual criticism carried out in correspondence and in response to publications. But to make progress in accordance with such intellectual standards involved, in general, a flouting of what went on in the universities. Apart from the seventeenth and eighteenth centuries, it might equally be suggested that the exceptions to the general rule of involvement in academia, which I have pointed out as occurring in later periods, indicate that real excellence will emerge whatever the system.

These things may be so, but to point to them does not deal with the question of whether the current kind of professionalism in the university context is necessary to, or desirable for, the progress of philosophy *given our present circumstances*. It might indeed be said that what happens now is in one way simply an extension and elaboration of what I have suggested as the seventeenth- and eighteenth-century pattern. The present-day apparatus of philosophical interchange and communication, such as publication in journals and books, and conferences and the like, is, it might be suggested, just something that increases the possibilities which were already there in the seventeenth and eighteenth centuries. To be content with that, however, would be to ignore the connection between the practice and teaching of philosophy which I have emphasized as being true of present-day practice of philosophy in universities and other institutions of higher education, and which was not so in the seventeenth and eighteenth centuries. The question is whether that connection is either necessary to, or desirable for, the fruitful practice of philosophy as things now are. One way of approaching that question is to ask (speculatively of course) how those who started western philosophy would regard the practice of the subject if they were reborn into the contemporary world.

The most likely answer to that question is that they would be completely bewildered, so great are the cultural, social and other changes that have taken place. For one thing, the number of people involved in the subject today is so great. Let us, nevertheless, persist with the question imaginatively and waiving possible doubts about the whole issue as put in these terms. How, for example, might one expect Aristotle to regard the present state of things in philosophy? He might deplore the narrowness of many present-day conceptions of the subject and the separation of philosophy from the pursuit of the natural sciences. But he might be persuaded that the changes that have taken place in the natural sciences necessitate that, and he might admit on reflection that his own conception of philosophy as dialectical would put philosophy in a different category from that of the empirical sciences as now conceived. One thing that he might welcome, however, is the fact that philosophy is generally pursued in institutions which have a recognizable connection with his own school, the Lyceum, and that people come to study and teach philosophy in such institutions.

If, on the other hand, he were to become acquainted with some of the ways in which philosophy has been practised in the interval between his time and now, there are many things over which he might well be puzzled. Why, even given his own, admittedly somewhat qualified, view of the status of theology as 'first philosophy', should philosophy be subservient to theology, as it was in the Middle Ages? And why should the institutions concerned with the pursuit of philosophy be restricted in their aims and methods, as they then were? Aristotle might well, indeed, wonder about the use that was made then of his own views. On the other hand, he might justly think that when the Church lost its position in the intellectual world, as it did at the Renaissance and in the pre-Cartesian world, the immediate effect on philosophy, whatever was the case with humanism in general, was a drop in standards and a dimunition of philosophical rigour. But what Aristotle would surely be puzzled about, above all else, is the position of philosophy in the seventeenth and eighteenth centuries. Why was it pursued simply by individuals, whatever were the means of intercommunication possible for them and what were the universities doing in not being concerned with the development of new knowledge and new ways of thinking? How could those individuals think of the pursuit of philosophy without being concerned with the propagation of the subject through teaching and the forms of joint research that an institution such as a school can make possible?

A question such as the last, however, reflects a view which represents only one aspect of the issue. Given the complexity of modern universities and their curricula, it needs to be asked, not merely whether the existence of such institutions is necessary or at least useful for the furtherance of philosophy, but also whether the practice of philosophy within them is necessary to or at least desirable for those institutions. What does the practice of philosophy do, if anything, for an institution concerned with the pursuit and communication of knowledge in general? In times like the present, when utilitarian conceptions of education loom large, and when there is a tendency for universities and university administrators to respond to financial and other pressures from outside by concentrating on what brings in money and support from outside sources, there is almost inevitably a tendency to depreciate subjects like philosophy. I say 'subjects like philosophy' (part of what the eighteenth- and nineteenth-century German universities termed the 'philosophical faculty' and what we now call 'arts'), rather than just 'philosophy', but philosophy itself occupies a particularly dangerous position in this respect. Its utilitarian aspects are not obvious even when they exist, and the more critical aspects of the subject are sometimes regarded merely as presenting obstacles to the pursuit of knowledge, or even as destructive. Above all, however, non-philosophers often fail altogether to see the point of the subject.

This is not the place to try to make that point clear in any detail; to attempt to do so would be to try to provide an introduction to philosophy itself, and my brief remarks about the thoughts of the philosophers whom I have mentioned in preceding chapters have been meant only to indicate the place of those philosophers in the tradition of the practice to which they belong. Something must be said, however, on this issue, if only in the briefest of ways. The following remarks have that aim and purpose.

Much of philosophy is second-order in character; that is indicated by the extent to which different branches of philosophy are described as 'the philosophy of . . .'. There is, for example, philosophy of science, philosophy of mind, philosophy of art, philosophy of language, and philosophy of conduct (or ethics). Epistemology is the philosophy of knowledge. Some of these branches of philosophy have a critical concern with other disciplines, seeking to sort out the concepts presupposed in them and above all to make clear how what is done in the name of that discipline is possible. The same applies to epistemology, which is concerned with how knowledge is possible and what exactly is presupposed in that possibility. Many, if not all, of these concerns with the possibility of this and that set themselves against forms of scepticism about that possibility. There have been philosophers who were sceptics in a positive sense, and who thought that scepticism was the rational attitude to adopt to things. But sceptics are sometimes also invoked in a form which is, in effect, that of a mythical being; they are set up as representing a position which has to be countered if the possibility of this and that is to be demonstrated.

In addition to these philosophical concerns, which stem, or partly stem, from ideas and forms of thought outside philosophy itself, however much the philosophical treatment of those concerns has its own special character, there are issues which philosophers have raised in their own right. The prime example of that is metaphysics, a term which has come to suggest in the popular mind something abstruse and even airy-fairy. What it in fact consists of is actually a philosophical issue in its own right (that is to say that the nature of metaphysics is not something agreed about by philosophers); but one conception of it, which goes back at least to Aristotle, is that it is concerned with what basically exists and why this, whatever it is, must exist if other things are to exist. It is thus concerned with concepts which are fundamental to the very possibility of our being able to think about a reality in which we too exist.[1]

Why should it be thought either desirable or necessary that university students, or some of them, should be confronted with these sorts of issues? It might be suggested, by way of some sort of an answer, that it cannot be denied that these issues are in some sense fundamental, that getting clear about them is desirable, and that some students at least should be enabled to think about them, if only as a training for the mind (though that is certainly putting it at its lowest level). This is not to say that all

CONCLUSION

students should have to study philosophy; it is, arguably, not suited to all. Aristotle thought that ethics, for example, was not a subject suitable for young people; they needed more experience of life if a consideration of ethical issues was to be profitable. Analogously, those branches of philosophy which are second-order to some other discipline seem to presuppose for their successful pursuit some acquaintance with the first-order discipline. For this reason, it is sometimes argued that joint degrees including philosophy are better for students of the ordinary undergraduate age than a degree involving philosophy alone (although of course, such students may well have some experience of other disciplines from school studies, whatever experience they have of life).

These are matters of debate, and will no doubt continue to be so. What is clear is that, just as young men came to Aristotle's Lyceum to study, and others later came to sit at the feet of Abelard, many young people who get a taste of philosophy today want more of it. It cannot be said that the numbers involved are as great as those wanting to study English, for example, although they are by no means negligible. Many people have doubts as to where it all leads in practical terms, especially as regards future employment (although surveys on that score, such as one carried out by the Royal Institute of Philosophy, indicate that philosophy graduates do gain employment and that they are welcomed in certain areas, for example, computing). In any case, career issues should not, surely, be overriding in a university context. If universities were to give up the idea of the pursuit of knowledge *per se*, whatever else they did, they would not be worth the name.

There are other large issues at stake here, however. What does the study of philosophy do for society and its intellectual well-being? That is not a question that can be answered simply, without regard to the kind of society that exists; that at least should be clear from my historical survey. It will not do, on the other hand, to appeal to the Greek idea of philosophy as the pursuit of wisdom, since philosophical wisdom, if it exists, is wisdom of a special kind, and no philosopher nowadays can claim to have a view of things which covers all time and eternity. Philosophers today generally find it very difficult to say what their special expertise consists in, and if called upon to explain their subject may well prefer to have recourse to certain paradigms, such as Plato's dialogues or Descartes' *Meditations*. Certainly, however, philosophical thought involves an ability to sort out abstract concepts and to make clear what is a presupposition of what. That is not all there is to it, but it involves at least that. Surely it is desirable that there should exist in an intellectual society people who can do that sort of thing, who can approach those issues which are a particular challenge to the understanding, and who can provide criticism, from a relatively detached point of view, of those who cannot, because of their first-order preoccupations, so stand back from their subjects? At one extreme, philosophers could try to play the Socratic role of the gadfly, more perhaps than they do at the moment. If others, like those who were confronted by Socrates, find this irritating, it may still be for their, or their society's, intellectual good.

Apart from the role that philosophers may have in society at large, there really ought to exist in a body such as a university those who are capable of the kind of thought that makes a philosopher. But it is also clear that philosophers, too, ought to recognize their role in that respect and not bury themselves in their own technical preoccupations to the exclusion of all else. This does not mean that they should continually be criticizing their colleagues in other subjects or even demanding some form of co-operation with them, although there are some areas, like that of cognitive science, where such co-operation can only be beneficial. One role of a philosopher should be to contribute to the general intellectual atmosphere of the institution by way of the particular cast of mind that a philosopher acquires. That entails some ability to add clarity to whatever questions are at issue and perhaps an ability to get behind the questions being asked so that things are not taken for granted. It is even possible for philosophers to add something to the administration and running of the institutions in which they find themselves.[2] This indeed happens more than is always recognized.

Whether or not philosophers do take part in administration, they ought to present themselves to their institutions, and indeed to society at large, as people who can offer a challenge, where it seems to them desirable, to accepted beliefs and ways of thinking. The Socratic role of the gadfly must not be forgotten, however it is to be fulfilled. It is important also, however, not to forget what may well be regarded by philosophers as their main positive role – that of attempting to provide an understanding of those abstract concepts which are presupposed in our relations to the world and to other people, and which are thus presupposed by the sciences, by theories of conduct, art and so on. But the life-blood of philosophy is, or ought to be, the argument by means of which positions are justified or are challenged. Philosophy is not a history of ideas nor the presentation of systems of attractive or fascinating concepts. Wherever argument in philosophy may lead (and it is arguable that its aim, as good argument, should be to produce conviction, not self-evident truth), philosophy is nothing without that argument. Hence the importance of logic within philosophy. One might, therefore, justifiably expect from philosophers a keen sense of the nuances of argument. The non-philosopher may sometimes think of this as nit-picking, but the intellectual fabric of our society would have less integrity without it. Exactly the same applies to universities. They ought to contain philosophers who are encouraged to respond to the kind of thinking that goes on in them at all levels, with the aim of getting behind the more obvious elements of that thinking in a way that ensures its foundations.

Much of this may seem like rhetoric, but let us, in the light of it, return to my earlier question of whether philosophy, as it now exists, essentially depends for its well-being on its taking place in institutions like universities. It may be that the positive answer to that question gains a depth that it did not previously have. We have seen that in the seventeenth and eighteenth centuries, when the progress of philosophy was not an institutional matter in the obvious sense, individuals had, in effect, to manufacture their own 'institutions' by way of correspondence and publication. What may not be obvious from the account which I have given is the number of philosophical, or quasi-philosophical, works which were published during this period – works often with a theological theme or connection written by, for example, clerics. (Lists and catalogues produced by antiquarian booksellers make that clear.) These people had mostly attended a university at some time, but had then gone on to occupy a 'living' (often a living in the ecclesiastical sense) with enough money to make the publication of their works possible. This is a phenomenon which has more or less ceased to exist; professionalism has taken over publishing too, and a changed economic situation makes publication by authors themselves almost impossible if there is to be any hope of reaching a wide range of readers. In the seventeenth and eighteenth centuries, however, things were different, and behind both the philosophical giants of the period and the ossified teaching of the universities and academies there existed various manifestations of intellectual curiosity and enterprise in a more or less philosophical form.

The trouble with that enterprise was that it lacked standards and, equally, lacked life. These two things go together in philosophy. Both depend upon the existence of a context of criticism which provides a steel on which philosophical argument can be honed. That may be provided by colleagues as peers, but there is in fact no better source for it than the response of students to the teaching which they receive, especially if that teaching takes the form of the tutorial or seminar. (Lectures are fine for the presentation of ideas and existing knowledge, or even for the initial presentation of an argument, but they lack much if there is no feedback.) Philosophical research, like other forms of research, certainly requires the response of colleagues by way of whatever institutions exist to that end; but there is perhaps something unique about what can be achieved, philosophically, in the effort to produce conviction in intelligent, enthusiastic and critical students. (And of course students who are less bright present yet another kind of challenge.) For the understanding which philosophy should produce is not all confined to technically equipped experts. All this underlines the point about the importance of teaching for the well-being of philosophy, and therefore the importance of there being institutions which make such teaching possible.

It may be objected that the seventeenth and eighteenth centuries, where this was not the case, also saw what many consider the 'classical' period of philosophy. The reply to this is that this picture results from a concentration, almost inevitable for the historian of philosophy who is anxious to chart the progress of philosophical thought, as distinct from philosophical activity, on a few high peaks in a terrain of general mediocrity. It is not to be denied that those who occupied the 'high peaks' were such that the attribution of the description 'classical' to the period is justified. It might be argued, however, that this status came about in spite of, not because of, the character of the system. It would not have done for things to have gone on like that. Although the big names of the time are indeed very notable, the confinement of good philosophy to a few cannot be to the good of the subject in the long run.

The great seventeenth- and eighteenth-century philosophers were part of an intellectual movement which embraced men of science as well as distinguished men in other fields, including theology. In a way they formed a society within a society, even if many of them were dependent on elements in the wider society, including royal and aristocratic patronage, for their well-being. The clerics and others who, as I have said, published what they saw as contributions to philosophy or theology were not really part of that society within a society. However that may be, things are not like that now. We do not today have this contrast between a select intellectual movement and a host of intellectual amateurs – or not in the same way. There still exists, of course, the contrast between those who have made contact with university philosophy and those who have not, but who are to some extent philosophically literate; but the second set of people is not very large. Moreover, as we have seen, there is little scope for this second set, or indeed for those in general who have no academic position, to continue an active philosophical role.

The situation today is also unlike that which existed in eighteenth-century Scotland. It is sometimes said, in tones of regret, that there no longer exists an educated public, such as that on which the Scottish philosophers of the eighteenth century depended.[3] The question is whether that ever really existed in terms which have any application to today. The Scottish 'educated public' of the eighteenth century was simply an extension of that intellectual sub-society to which I have made reference, an extension which was made possible by the cultural forces of the time and place. The number of people who have had contact with university philosophy today is much greater than any public which was philosophically educated in the eighteenth century, simply because of the growth of university education generally. Nevertheless, it is now extremely difficult, to say the least, to carry on philosophy outside the universities, because of the amount of philosophical scholarship and the apparatus necessary for that which is presupposed in philosophical activity, and because the apparatus necessary for philosophical scholarship entails an involvement in the teaching of the subject.

It is this last point which is the really important one, and I make no apologies for emphasizing it yet again. It implies a certain continuity, as we have seen, between the position of philosophy in Aristotle's time and the position that it has now. It is highly improbable, however, that today there would be any vast turn-out of the general public for the funeral of a philosopher, as there was reported to have been at the death of Theophrastus.[4] Our present social, cultural and political situation is too different from that of ancient Athens for it to be at all plausible. But respect for the role of the philosopher is surprisingly lacking in England, by contrast with Germany, where such respect for the scholar has been traditional, or

France, where there is a tradition, as we have seen, of respect, and indeed more than respect, for leading intellectuals. Contemporary utilitarian attitudes to education in this country tend to underline that lack of respect.

I was once present at a social gathering after a meeting of the Senate of the University of London. I was talking to the Dean of the Faculty of Arts, a scholar in English literature, when we were approached by the press-officer of the Committee of Vice-Chancellors and Principals, who asked, among other things, how we should justify our subjects. I spoke about the way in which philosophical thinking can have a long-term effect, if only a long-term effect, both upon the other subjects to which philosophical criticism is applied and upon the thinking which permeates society in general and influences its practices. I mentioned the case of Jeremy Bentham and how long it had taken for his ideas to affect the practice of the law, emphasizing the point that it nevertheless did affect it in the end. I realized afterwards that what I should have said was that it was a sign of the corruption of our times that the question was asked at all. But it would not have been asked in some other countries, even where there are similar political attitudes to those which have been dominant in Britain. For even when utilitarian attitudes to education and culture are generally accepted elsewhere, there may still exist a sense of the usefulness, perhaps in an undefinable way, of what the universities call 'arts' and of philosophy in particular. They may, indeed, be seen as crucial elements in the well-being of intellectual culture.

Given that it is right for philosophy so to be seen, what do philosophers do in that respect and what should they do? I have tried to indicate that what they have done in the past has varied according to the dominant institutions and the dominant intellectual attitudes at any one time. But there has been a continuity, nevertheless, in the philosophical spirit, even if that too has had its ups and downs. It is dominated by a certain scepticism, a certain kind of questioning about the possibility of this and that, underneath which lies, it is to be hoped, a view of the world and the place of human beings in it, together with a willingness to challenge what is accepted. Sometimes the 'gadfly' element in this has loomed largest; sometimes, by contrast, philosophers have tried to give the appearance of presenting that abstract wisdom which the word 'philosophy' suggests and which Plato and Aristotle sometimes laid claim to. If technicality sometimes obscures both these things today, that is inevitable, given the scientific and often utilitarian character of our culture. The nature of the institutions in which philosophy now has its being increases that inevitability. But if some young people can be encouraged to think critically about the sort of issues which I have mentioned, getting behind the presuppositions of other sorts of thinking, this can only be for the good of our intellectual culture. Philosophy certainly has an important role in all this, especially given how far education now reaches in modern society, and in spite of obstacles that are presented by other features of that society.

We are left at the end with a certain paradox. That period which is often represented as the classical period of, at least, modern philosophy presents a pattern which is not likely to be repeated, and, more important, it is not desirable that it should be. For in spite of the role that philosophers then had in the scientific and intellectual framework of the time, their influence did not permeate to the great majority of the, even moderately educated, people of the time. The practice of philosophy was not linked to the educational system current at the time, as it has been at more or less every other period, although with some exceptions. It is now inconceivable that fruitful philosophy should mean anything other than academic philosophy as practised in systems of higher education, even if something of that gets passed on to other educational strata. Systems of higher education maintain standards, but, perhaps above all, they ensure that philosophy is taught and practised within a context of teaching. I have tried to indicate how that can only be to the advantage both of the subject and of the institutions in which it finds itself, and thereby of society too. But the value of philosophy in the end lies in itself and what it does for human thought and life. It lies, that is, in the insights which it produces, whether the questions at issue are raised by philosophers themselves or by others. Nevertheless, philosophers have to ensure that faith in that is justified.

NOTES

I have not attempted in these notes to acknowledge all the sources of the information provided in my text. Such sources are too many and too various to record with any ease. I am nevertheless grateful to a whole host of scholars on whose works I have relied. I might perhaps mention one in particular – F.C. Copleston's truly monumental *A History of Philosophy*, Vols 1–9 (London, Burns, Oates and Washbourne, 1964–75).

INTRODUCTION

1 Diogenes Laertius, *Lives of Eminent Philosophers*, IX.6. Diogenes Laertius is quoting someone else on this point, but his accounts of previous philosophers are often quite unreliable in any case.

1 THE ANCIENT GREEKS

1 See, e.g., my *History of Western Philosophy* (London, Viking/Penguin, 1987), ch.1.
2 The practice of recording the views of previous philosophers goes back, in effect, to Aristotle, who did this as a way of setting off his own views. His follower, Theophrastus, was the first to write a history of philosophy for its own sake. But the practice of arranging philosophers in schools came later, when schools of philosophy were formally established.
3 It is common for those, looking back at them from our present standpoint, to regard the Sophists as the first university professors. See, on the general question of the professionalism of the Sophists, G.B. Kerferd, *The Sophistic Movement* (Cambridge, Cambridge University Press, 1981), ch.4.
4 I owe this observation to my ex-colleague in the classics department at Birkbeck College, the ancient historian, Brian Caven.
5 This is epitomized by the story related in the *Apology* (20eff.) to the effect that the Delphic Oracle declared that Socrates of Athens was the

wisest man in Greece, something that the initially disbelieving Socrates in due course decided was right because he knew that he knew nothing while everyone else thought that they knew all sorts of things.

6 The question of the genuineness of the Platonic letters, which have to do with Plato's political concern with the affairs of Dion in Syracuse, is a complex one. The remark from the *Seventh Letter* referred to here is made in the context of a rebuke to Dionysius – the tyrant of Syracuse, in Sicily, in whom Plato may have seen the possibility of a 'philosopher king' (as the *Republic* puts it) – for laying claim to philosophical expertise which he did not possess. But the letters were no doubt used by partisans of Dion, who was Dionysius' brother-in-law, in support of his campaign against Dionysius. Scholars have varied in their estimate of how many of them, if any, were really written by Plato. But the *Seventh Letter* has a bigger claim to genuiness than most.

7 Gilbert Ryle, *Plato's Progress* (Cambridge, Cambridge University Press, 1966).

8 H.J. Cherniss, *The Riddle of the Early Academy* (Los Angeles, University of California Press, 1945).

9 Felix Grayeff, *Aristotle and his School* (London, Duckworth, 1974), pp.37ff.

10 This is the general view. But the title looks to me like a library classification and this may be the source of Andronicus' categorization. As Grayeff argues, it is implausible to suppose that there were not copies of the works in libraries, to which Andronicus might have had access. The books from Aristotle's own collection which Sulla brought to Rome were, in any case, supposed to be defective because of previous neglect.

11 See D.W. Hamlyn, 'Aristotle on dialectic', *Philosophy* 65, 1990, pp.465–76.

12 W.K.C. Guthrie, *A History of Greek Philosophy*, Vol. 1 (Cambridge, Cambridge University Press, 1962), p.17.

13 Gilbert Murray, *Five Stages of Greek Religion* (London: Watts & Co., 1935), esp. chs 3 and 4.

14 I have heard Myles Burnyeat suggest that what went on was something like psychotherapy!

2 THE MIDDLE AGES AND RENAISSANCE

1 See Richard Sorabji, *Time, Creation and the Continuum* (London, Duckworth, 1983), ch.18.

2 See the brief remarks in D.W. Hamlyn, *A History of Western Philosophy* (London, Viking/Penguin, 1987), p.100, and more particularly the work referred to there, Martin M. Tweedale, *Abailard on Universals* (Amsterdam, New York and London, North Holland, 1976).

3 St Thomas Aquinas, *Commentary on Aristotle's Physics*, translated by R.J. Blackwell, R.J. Spath and W.E. Thirkel, with an Introduction by V.J. Bourke (London, Routledge & Kegan Paul, 1963), p.xxi.

4 Aristotle's *Categories* and *De Interpretatione* had been made available by

Boethius. The rest of the *Organon* was translated into Latin from the Greek in the early twelfth century.
5 The fact that this was for arts, not theology, needs to be noted; it heralds a greater importance being given to arts. This increased still further as a result of the emphasis on humanism brought in by the Renaissance. Most philosophy, nevertheless, was still pursued at the master's level.
6 I owe the details of Scotus' life to the Introduction to the translation of his *Quaestiones Quodlibetales* by Felix Alluntis and Allan B. Wolter, published as *God and Creatures; The Quodlibetal Questions* (Princeton NJ, Princeton University Press, 1975).
7 During the Renaissance it was still mostly Aristotle's philophy that was the subject of courses in philosophy in the universities, though philosophy in that form was given greater emphasis in faculties of arts, and was thus taught at the BA level, not just for the mastership. This was so, for example, in the case of courses given by Zabarella at Padua in the sixteenth century.
8 I shall return to these philosophers and Francis Bacon also in the next chapter.

3 THE SIXTEENTH AND SEVENTEENTH CENTURIES

1 Jonathan Rée, *Descartes* (London, Allen Lane, 1974), pp.124–5.
2 See, for example, Ben-Ami Scharfstein, *The Philosophers* (Oxford, Basil Blackwell, 1980), ch.6.
3 Bertrand Russell, *The Philosophy of Leibniz* (London, Allen & Unwin, 1900).
4 The qualification derives from the work of the Cambridge Platonists at that university. The movement, originated by Benjamin Whichcote, who published nothing, is mainly associated with Ralph Cudworth and Henry More, who corresponded with Descartes. It emphasized reason, was opposed to empiricism, and supported Platonism, or rather Neoplatonism, against scholasticism. Its main impetus was, however, theological.
5 John Locke, *An Essay Concerning Human Understanding*, edited by Peter H. Nidditch (Oxford, Clarendon Press, 1975), pp.xii–xxxiv.
6 Gibbon's description of the fellows of Magdalen as 'decent, easy men who supinely enjoyed the gifts of the founder . . . from the toil of reading, or thinking, or writing, they had absolved their conscience' is well known.

4 THE EIGHTEENTH CENTURY

1 I owe knowledge of this fact to Norman Kemp Smith, *A Commentary to Kant's Critique of Pure Reason* (London, Macmillan, 1918, 2nd edn 1923), pp.6–7. Kemp Smith comments: 'A Minister of Education who thus ranks philosophy above professional studies, and both as

more important than all academic machinery, holds his office by divine right.' By contrast, a recent Secretary of State for Education in this country took the occasion of the death of A.J. Ayer to write to the press disparaging contemporary philosophy and philosophical practice.

2 See, for details of the position of the universities in France in general during this period, L.W.B. Brockliss, *French Higher Education in the 17th and 18th Centuries* (Oxford, Clarendon Press, 1987). I have to thank Professor William Barber for drawing my attention to this book and to other matters about eighteenth-century France.

3 It was the custom of the time to dedicate works to eminent members of the aristocracy, who might or might not be patrons. Locke dedicated his *Essay* to Thomas Herbert, Earl of Pembroke, and Berkeley dedicated his *Principles* similarly. The Earl of Pembroke, who was, among other things, a fellow and president of the Royal Society 1689–90, asked to see Locke's *Essay* ahead of publication and hinted that he would like to be its dedicatee. Berkeley, on the other hand, was quite unknown to the Earl, as he makes clear in the Dedication of the *Principles*.

4 Subsequent philosophers have generally preferred the *Treatise* to later works such as the *Enquiry Concerning Human Understanding* and the *Enquiry Concerning the Principles of Morals*, which appeared in 1748 and 1751 respectively. It is perhaps something of a paradox, considering the faults found in his style by the review, that Hume has sometimes in recent times been congratulated for the supreme clarity of his style.

5 'His face', wrote Lord Charlemont, 'was broad and flat, his mouth wide, and without any other expression than imbecility'; and he goes on in similar terms about both his appearance and his speech. In spite of this Hume was generally known for the affability of his social life.

6 I have an engraving of a portrait of Hume, under which is inscribed 'David Hume Esq. History and Pihlosophy (sic!)' in that order.

7 Butler was brought up as a Presbyterian and as such was sent to the dissenting academy at Tewkesbury, before joining the Church of England and going to Oxford in 1715. The dissenting academies were private institutions for those who, not being members of the Church of England, could not go to Oxford or Cambridge. The Tewkesbury academy was run by a Mr Samuel Jones, and was previously at Gloucester.

8 I owe this observation to the booklet produced by George Davie for the Historical Association – G. Davie, *The Scottish Enlightenment* (London, The Historical Association, 1981). The booklet produces in a very brief compass an interesting, but sometimes puzzling, account of the circumstances of the Scottish Enlightenment in the eighteenth century and the place of philosophy in the social and political setting of the time.

9 Davie maintains that this balance broke down in the nineteenth century because of the difficulty of maintaining the relationship with England that was entailed. See also his *The Democratic Intellect* (Edinburgh, Edinburgh University Press, 1961). It was maintained by H.T. Buckle,

On Scotland and the Scottish Intellect (reprinted by University of Chicago Press, 1970) that the hold of theology on Scotland led to Scottish philosophy being deductive, rather than inductive as was the case with English philosophy. See also Buckle's *Civilization in England*, Vol. 1, 1899 (reprinted, London, Watts, 1930, pp.134–7). This is a caricature of both English and Scottish philosophy, and does not reflect the balance of which Davie speaks.

10 I owe this observation to my wife, Eileen Carlyle Hamlyn.
11 I owe information on the details of this and on other matters affecting German universities to C.E. McClelland, *State, Society and University in Germany, 1700–1914* (Cambridge, Cambridge University Press, 1980).
12 For a brief outline of that philosophy, see my *History of Western Philosophy* (London, Viking/Penguin, 1987), ch.13.
13 One figure whom I have had to omit from this account of the eighteenth century is the Italian, Giambattista Vico (1668–1744). He falls outside the trends of the time in most ways. He was professor of rhetoric at Naples, and for the most part lived in poverty; but in spite of his influence on some later philosophers, particularly Johann Herder in Germany, because of his emphasis on philosophy of history and culture, he is so untypical as not to provide a significant example for any theory of philosophical practice in his time.

5 THE NINETEENTH CENTURY

1 A little of the story of Bain's place in the founding of *Mind* was told in the paper by R.C. Cross, 'Alexander Bain', *Proceedings of the Aristotelian Society, Supplementary Volume*, XLIV, 1970, pp.1–13. More is told in the contributions by Anthony Quinton (on Croom Robertson) and J.A. Passmore (on Stout) to the Centenary Number of *Mind*, LXXXV, January 1976, pp.6–16 and 17–36. I am indebted to these sources. I myself made some observations about philosophical journal publishing and about *Mind* in particular in that Centenary Number (pp.1–5). It may be worth noting that there were only five editors in the hundred years.
2 Bruce Kuklick, *The Rise of American Philosophy. Cambridge, Massachusetts, 1860–1930* (New Haven and London, Yale University Press, 1977). I owe acquaintance with this book to Timothy Sprigge, and I am much indebted to it.
3 Quoted from the foreword by J.N. Findlay to the translation of that part of the *Encyclopaedia* by William Wallace, with a translation of the *Zusätze* by A.V. Miller, under the title *Hegel's Philosophy of Mind* (Oxford, Clarendon Press, 1971), p.vi.
4 C.E. McClelland, *State, Society and University in Germany, 1700–1914* (Cambridge, Cambridge University Press, 1980), p.140.
5 Simone Weil, *Lectures on Philosophy*, translated by Hugh Price with an introduction by Peter Winch (Cambridge, Cambridge University Press, 1978).

NOTES

6 Bruce Kuklick, *The Rise of American Philosophy*, p.xxiii.

6 THE TWENTIETH CENTURY

1 I well remember an occasion in my own department when a colleague, explaining to a prospective student what sort of philosophy we taught, said that we taught mainly Anglo-Saxon philosophy, covering such philosophers as Frege, Russell and Wittgenstein! Wittgenstein did spend a good part of his life in this country and many German-speaking philosophers, especially those who were Jewish, sought refuge here and in America during the 1930s. But the case of Gottlob Frege is inexplicable by reference to such considerations. The ability of Anglo-Saxon philosophers simply to adopt those of other countries who they find sympathetic is notable.
2 I was once told by Karl Britton, who taught at Swansea and met Wittgenstein during visits of the latter to Rush Rhees – his friend and pupil, who was one of his literary executors and who also taught at Swansea from 1940 – that he was severely rebuked by Wittgenstein for attendance of Joint Sessions! No philosophical good came from such things.
3 Some details of all this are given by Norman Malcolm, who was a student of his, in his *Ludwig Wittgenstein: A Memoir*, with a *Biographical Sketch* by G.H. von Wright (Oxford, Oxford University Press, 1958). Malcolm also reports on the exhaustion produced in him by teaching and his habit of going to the cinema afterwards, where he sat in the front row. He preferred American films, particularly comedies, and also had a liking for detective stories, which he compared very favourably with *Mind*!
4 During that year my wife and I went to tea with a friend of my wife's who was living with her husband in Elizabeth Anscombe's house (I did not myself know Elizabeth Anscombe at that time). We were sworn to secrecy about the great man who was staying in the house, whose every word, it was said, was fascinating, even about the plumbing!
5 Years ago, in the context of the institution of A-Level Logic, I once heard A.J. Ayer say, as an objection to philosophy in a more general sense being taught at that level, that the trouble with French philosophy was that it was taught in schools, so that by the time students came to university philosophy they had various doctrines and schools of philosophy firmly compartmentalized. Apart from that, perhaps rather chauvinist, attitude to French philosophy, it is clearly not a necessary truth that philosophy should be taught in schools in such a way as to produce that result. The case of Simone Weil, mentioned in the last chapter, is some indication of that, even if she was something of an exception to the general rule in France at that time.
6 M. Heidegger, *Introduction to Metaphysics*, translated by Ralph Manheim (New Haven and London, Yale University Press, 1959), p.37. This book was published in German in 1953, but as a reworked version of lectures given in Freiburg in 1935.

7 C.E.M. McClelland, *State, Society and University in Germany, 1700–1914* (Cambridge, Cambridge University Press, 1980), p.330.
8 I have said nothing either about philosophy in other parts of the world. Perhaps the situation in India requires a mention. There the universities tended to emerge from the old missionary colleges, and the philosophy taught was for a long time simply western philosophy ossified at about the time in which these colleges were set up. More recently there have been attempts to profit from India's own cultural and philosophical heritage, by building on the history of Indian philosophy, which was inevitably connected with Hindu or Buddhist religious movements. Unfortunately, there are signs of ossification there too, in the form of a scholasticism based on the ideas of the past. Whatever was the case in that past, Indian philosophy is today no exception to the rule that connects its practice with the universities, but so far it has not achieved results that are remarkable.

7 CONCLUSION

1 For some elucidation of this see my *Metaphysics* (Cambridge, Cambridge University Press, 1984).
2 I myself was for five years Vice-Master of Birkbeck College and thus heavily involved in its affairs during that time. I hope that I contributed something to the conduct of those affairs *because I was a philosopher*, but I must leave that for others to judge. I do not think, however, that my philosophical colleagues entirely approved of my undertaking that role. I believe, if I am right about their attitudes, that they were wrong.
3 It is so maintained, for example, by Alasdair MacIntyre in his contribution to *Education and Values: the Richard Peters Lectures*, edited by Graham Haydon (London, Institute of Education, University of London, 1987).
4 It has to be said that a recent memorial meeting for A.J. Ayer was quite well attended by a company the majority of whom, probably, were non-philosophers. Nevertheless, that probably represents a special case.

INDEX

Abelard, Peter 37–9, 42, 43, 47, 52, 167
academies 62, 63, 64, 74, 76; dissenting 177
Academy, the 18–23, 24, 26, 29, 31; Middle Academy 31
administration 168
Adorno, Theodor 155
aesthetics 90, 155
Albertus Magnus 44
Albinus 31, 32
Alcibiades 16
Alembert, Jean D' 60, 68, 75
Alexander the Great 23, 24
Alexandria 32
Althusser, Louis 160
American Philosophical Association 136, 146
analytical philosophy 135, 136
Anaxagoras 7, 8, 9, 10–11, 12, 15
Anaximander 7
Anaximenes 7
Anscombe, Elizabeth 143, 144, 179
Antiochus 31
Aquinas, St Thomas 42, 43–6, 49, 65, 175
Arabs 35, 36, 43, 52
Arcesilaus 31
Archimedes 34
aretē 12, 14, 17
argument 135–6, 169
Aristophanes 2, 15, 17
Aristotelian Society 99, 100–1, 136, 142, 146, 148

Aristotle 5, 7, 19, 20, 21, 23–8, 29, 30, 31, 35, 41, 42, 43–4, 45, 46, 49, 51, 53, 100, 120, 141, 164, 166, 167, 171, 172, 174, 175
Aristoxenus 20
Arnauld, Antoine 57, 59, 62, 64
Athens 1, 2, 5, 9, 10, 11, 12, 13, 14, 15, 16, 17ff., 22, 23, 24, 26, 32, 33, 59, 171, 174
atomism 8, 11, 26, 51, 53, 54
Augustine, St 32, 35–6, 57, 59
Australia 150, 151
Averroes 43, 52
Avicenna 52
Ayer, A.J. 159, 177, 179, 180

baccalauréat 101, 122, 128
Bacon, Francis 51, 53, 176
Bain, Alexander 93, 98–9, 178
Barber, William 177
Bauer, Bruno 112
Bayle, Pierre 59
behaviourism 159
Bentham, Jeremy 93, 95, 172
Bentley, Richard 76
Bergson, Henri 122, 124, 125, 156–7
Berkeley, George 37, 76–9, 82, 83, 97, 177
Bernard, St of Clairvaux 38
Biran, Maine de 75, 122
Birkbeck College London x, 162, 174, 180
Boethius 35, 37, 42

INDEX

Boltzmann, Ludwig 120
books 9, 11, 12, 25, 42, 163
Bosanquet, Bernard 93, 107
Boumann, Ludwig 104
Boyle, Robert 68, 76
Bradley, F.H. 93, 107
Brentano, Franz 119, 120, 152
Britain 1, 3, 46, 53, 76, 83, 98, 107, 121, 130, 131, 137ff., 146, 148, 149, 151, 160, 161, 162
Britton, Karl 179
Brockliss, L.W.B. 177
Brown, Thomas 86
Bruno, Giordano 50
Buckle, H.T. 177-8
Burleigh, Walter 43
Burnyeat, Myles 175
Butler, Joseph 84, 177
Byzantium 36, 43

Camus, Albert 157-8
Carlyle, Thomas 87, 93, 97
Carnap, Rudolf 142, 150, 159
Carneades 31
Cartesianism 55, 56, 57, 65, 67, 68, 72, 73, 74, 164; *see also* Descartes
Caven, Brian 174
Charlemagne, palace school of 37
Charlemont, Lord 81, 177
Charles II 54
Cherniss, Harold 19, 20, 175
children, philosophy for 149
Christianity 30, 32, 33, 35, 44, 52, 116, 119
Chrysippus 30
Church, the 6, 37, 50, 51, 52, 53, 55, 56, 58, 68, 71, 75, 121, 164
Cicero 23, 26, 28, 36, 52
Clarke, Samuel 62
cognitive science 133, 168
Collège de France 122, 156, 157, 160, 162
Collingwood, R.G. 154
Comte, Auguste 122
Condillac, Étienne de 68, 75
conferences 136, 146, 163
consequentiae 43
Copernicus, Nicholas 50

Copleston, F.C. 174
Cousin, Victor 122-3
Croce, Benedetto 154
Cross, R.C. 178
Crusius, Christian A. 89
Cudworth, Ralph 176
Cynics 22, 29, 30
Cyrenaics 22, 29
Czechoslovakia 156

Damascius 33
Darwin, Charles 96
Davie, George 177, 178
Democritus 8
departments 130-2, 134-5, 136, 147, 149; extra-mural 149
Derrida, Jacques 160
Descartes, René 50, 51, 53, 54, 55-60, 61, 62, 64, 65, 67, 68, 69, 70, 71, 77, 144, 167, 176; *see also* Cartesianism
determinatio 41, 45
Dewey, John 125
dialectic 21, 27, 28, 33, 106, 107
dialectical materialism 156
dialogues, Platonic 14, 18, 19, 20, 22, 25
Diderot, Denis 60, 68, 75
Dilthey, Wilhelm 155
Diodorus Cronus 29
Diogenes the Cynic 29
Diogenes Laertius 5, 9, 19, 23, 25, 28, 29, 174
Dion 19, 175
Dionysius 19, 175
disputation 41, 42, 46, 49, 70, 88, 128
doctorate 88, 102, 125, 155
Dominicans 40, 44, 46
Duhem, Pierre 123
Duns Scotus, John 40, 41, 46-50, 176

educated public 85, 87, 171
Edwards, Jonathan 124
Eliot, T.S. 4
Emerson, Ralph Waldo 124
Empedocles 8, 10

182

INDEX

empiricism 47, 65, 75, 77, 82, 83, 87, 98, 110, 121, 139, 159
Engels, Friedrich 112, 113
England 2, 53, 54, 65ff., 72, 74, 76, 84, 92ff., 129, 161, 177
Enlightenment, the 73–6; French 60, 68, 73, 75–6; German 73; Scottish 76, 83–7, 177
Epictetus 33
Epicurus/Epicureanism 26, 29, 30, 53, 82, 112
epistemology 30–1, 53, 58, 75, 86, 90, 119, 138, 166
Eriugina, John Scotus 36–7
ethics *see* moral philosophy
Eucleides of Megara 19, 29
Euripides 11, 118
existentialism 115, 116, 119, 158, 159

fascism 154
Fechner, G.T. 120
Ferrier, James 97
Feuerbach, Ludwig 107, 108, 112, 113
Fichte, Johann G. 89, 102–3, 105, 109, 111
Filmer, Sir Robert 69
Findlay, J.N. 178
Foucault, Michel 160
France 55, 56, 64, 72, 74–6, 101–2, 121–3, 128, 148, 156–60, 172
Franciscans 40, 41, 46, 47, 48, 49
Frauenstädt, Julius 110
freedom 94, 157, 158, 159
Frege, Gottlob 120, 139, 141, 179
Freud, Sigmund 111, 120

Gadamer, Hans-Georg 155
Galileo Galilei 50, 53, 54
Gassendi, Pierre 51, 53, 57, 66
Gentile, Giovanni 154
geometry 58, 60, 61, 70
George I 63
Germany 64, 72, 73–4, 76, 84, 87, 101ff., 114, 119–21, 128, 148, 151–6, 171

Geulincx, Arnold 59
Gibbon, Edward 176
Goethe, Johann W. von 108
grandes écoles 102, 122, 123, 157, 162
Grayeff, Felix 24, 175
Green, T.H. 93, 107
Gregory of Nyssa 36
Guthrie, W.K.C. 13, 29, 175

Habermas, Jürgen 155
Hamilton, Sir William 86, 87, 97
Hamlyn, D.W. 174, 175, 178, 180
Hamlyn, Eileen Carlyle 178
Hegel, Georg W.F./Hegelianism 75, 93, 97, 102, 103–8, 109, 110, 111, 112, 113, 116, 117, 118, 119, 121, 122, 124, 158, 159, 178
Heidegger, Martin 152–4, 155, 158, 159, 160, 179
Helmholtz, Hermann von 120
Helvétius, Claude Adrien 75
Heraclitus 4, 5, 7, 9
Herbart, Johann F. 119, 120
Herbert, Thomas, Earl of Pembroke 177
Herder, Johann 178
hermeneutics 160
Hippias 12, 14
Hobbes, Thomas 51, 53–5, 57, 59, 71
Hodgson, Shadworth 100
Holland *see* Netherlands
Humboldt, Wilhelm von 88, 89, 102
Hume, David 68, 70, 76, 79–83, 84, 85, 86, 89, 177
Husserl, Edmund 119, 121, 152–3, 155, 158, 159
Hutcheson, Francis 79, 80, 81, 83, 84, 94
Huygens, Christian 60

Iamblichus 32
idealism 37, 77, 89, 93, 97, 100, 102, 103, 105, 107, 120, 121, 153, 154

INDEX

Index, the 56, 57, 71
India 180
industry 151, 154, 161
intellectuals 157, 158, 160, 161, 163
intentionality 121
Ireland 76, 77
Isocrates 21, 22
Italy 123, 154, 155

James, William 120, 122, 124–6, 133
Jansen, Cornelius 57, 59
Jesuits 52, 55, 56, 60, 80
journals 98–101, 127, 146, 163

Kant, Immanuel 6, 68, 73, 74, 83, 86, 87–91, 95, 101, 105, 106, 109, 110, 111, 116, 117, 118, 119, 120, 122
Kerferd, G.B. 174
Keynes, J.M. 139, 141
Kierkegaard, Søren 16, 110, 115–17, 118, 119
Kings College London 95
Knutzen, Martin 73, 89
Kuklick, Bruce 100, 124, 150, 178, 179

Laon 37, 38
lectures 25, 42, 45, 84, 102–3, 104, 105, 128, 130, 138, 139, 142, 143, 145, 146, 156, 157, 170
Leibniz, Gottfried 59, 60, 61–4, 65, 67, 68, 69, 70, 71, 73, 74, 138
Leucippus 8
Lewis, C.I. 150
libraries 9, 24, 26
Literae Humaniores 76, 80, 92, 129
Locke, John 62, 65–9, 70, 71, 72, 75, 76, 77, 78, 79, 82, 83, 87, 176, 177
logic 27, 30, 39, 42, 43, 47, 49, 64, 68, 114, 120, 126, 138, 141, 150, 151, 169
Lotze, R. H. 119, 120
lycées 157, 158, 159
Lyceum, the 23–8, 29, 33, 164

Lyco 26, 33

McClelland, C.E. 178, 180
Mach, Ernst 120, 142
MacIntyre Alasdair 180
McTaggart, J.M.E. 93, 107
Malcolm, Norman 143, 179
Malebranche, Nicholas 59, 77
Marcus Aurelius 14, 26, 32, 34
Marsilio Ficino 51
Marsilius of Padua 47
Marx, Karl 107, 108, 112–14, 117, 155, 160
Marxism 137, 154, 155, 156, 158, 160
materialism 75, 112, 135, 150
mathematics 20, 22, 23, 27, 56, 68, 77, 114, 120, 138, 139, 141, 152
medical ethics 151
Megarians 19, 29, 30
Meinong, Alexius von 119, 121, 152
Mendelssohn, Moses 89, 90
Merleau-Ponty, Maurice 153, 159–60
Mersenne, Abbé Marin 53, 54, 55, 56, 71
Metaphysical Club 100, 124
metaphysics 43, 53, 58, 64, 68, 77, 87, 89–90, 118, 119, 120, 126, 138, 154, 159, 166
Mettrie, Julian O. de la 75
Michael of Cesena 47
Middle Ages 5–6, 25, 35–50, 52, 59, 88, 128, 135, 164
Miletus 8
Mill, James 87, 93–4, 95, 97, 108
Mill, John Stuart 86, 87, 93–8, 107, 108, 110, 122, 126, 140
Mind 98–100, 142, 178, 179
Mind Association 99, 136, 142, 146
Montaigne, Michel de 51
Montesquieu, Charles de 69
Moore, G.E. 93, 99, 107, 138, 141, 142, 143
moral philosophy 82, 83, 86, 90, 166, 167
More, Henry 176

184

INDEX

Murray, Gilbert 29, 175

National Committee for Philosophy 146, 147, 148, 149
Nazism 137, 151, 152, 153
Neoplatonism 32, 33, 35, 36, 43, 51, 176
Netherlands/Holland 56, 123
Newton, Isaac 55, 62, 63, 64, 68, 74, 76, 77, 82, 108
Nicholas of Cusa 50
Nidditch, Peter N. 67, 176
Nietzsche, Friedrich 115, 117–19, 124, 154
Numenius 31, 32

Ockham *see* William of Ockham
Oldenburg, Henry 60
ordinatio 41, 49

Panaetius 31
Paris 11, 15, 158
Parmenides 7, 8, 9–10
Pascal, Blaise 57
Passmore, J.A. 178
Peirce, C.S. 125–6
Pericles 8, 10, 11, 12
Peter of Spain 42
phenomenology 119, 153, 155, 156, 160
Philoponus, John 33
philosophical faculty 89, 102, 103, 104, 165
Philosophy 100, 147, 148
philosophy, point of 165ff.
Piaget, Jean 133
Plato 5, 9, 12, 13, 14, 15, 16, 17–23, 24, 25, 28, 31, 37, 46, 50, 51, 84, 109, 129, 139, 140, 141, 158, 167, 172, 175, 176
Plotinus 32, 33
Poland 156
political/social philosophy 46, 48, 68–9, 75, 106, 113
polytechnics 1, 130, 147
Popper, K. 27, 150
Porphyry 32, 35
Posidonius 31
postgraduates 125, 128, 134, 147

PPE 129
pragmatism 125
Presocratics 7–11
Price, Richard 84, 86
Privatdozents 88, 105, 107, 108
Proclus 32
Prodicus 13, 14
professionalism 12, 79, 91, 97, 98, 100, 114, 117, 123, 126, 127–8, 131, 150, 162, 163, 169
professors 84, 88, 102, 137, 143, 160
Protagoras 12, 13, 25
Protestantism 56, 58, 64, 65, 115
Proust, Marcel 157
psychology 114, 120, 125, 132–3, 134
Pyrrho 31
Pythagoras 7, 9, 31

Quine, W.V. 150
Quinton, Anthony 148, 178
quodlibet 41, 49

rationalism 65, 68
Ravel, Maurice 140
Rée, Jonathan 58, 176
Reformation 51, 53
regents 40, 41, 49, 84, 87
Reid, Thomas 83, 84, 86, 97
religion 36, 45, 60, 75, 82, 85, 92, 103, 104, 106, 107, 110, 115, 116, 117, 124
Renaissance 6, 43, 46, 50–1, 52–5, 164, 176
reportatio 41, 45
research 134–5, 165
Rhees, Rush 144, 179
rhetoric 12, 21, 34
Robertson, G. Croom 99, 178
Romans, the 30, 31
romanticism 114–19, 154
Roscelin of Compiègne 38, 39
Rousseau, Jean-Jacques 75
Royal Institute of Philosophy 100, 101, 147–8, 167
Royal Society 60, 62, 64, 177
Royce, Josiah 107, 126
Russell, Bertrand 1, 3, 62, 63, 93,

98, 120, 137–40, 141, 142, 144, 145, 150, 152, 176, 179
Ryle, Gilbert 18, 144, 147, 175

Sartre, Jean-Paul 153, 157–9
scepticism 51, 59, 82, 109, 166, 172
Sceptics, the Greek 15, 31, 33, 109, 153
Scharfstein, Ben-Ami 176
Schelling, Friedrich W.J. von 103, 105
Schleiermacher, Friedrich E.D. 102
Schlick, Moritz 2, 142
Schmidt, Franz 141
scholarship 145, 160, 161, 163, 171
scholasticism 45, 50, 51, 53, 55, 67, 73, 74, 123, 176
schools 37, 121, 148–9, 179; of philosophy 22, 23, 24, 25, 29ff., 33, 34, 52
Schopenhauer, Arthur 105, 108–12, 114, 117, 118, 141, 143
Schulze, G.E. 109
science 2, 27, 31, 34, 55, 60, 68, 70, 106, 120, 123, 126, 150, 151, 154, 155, 164, 168, 170, 173
Scotland 72, 76, 79, 80, 81, 82–7, 161, 171, 178
seminars 102, 123, 128, 134, 147, 170
Sentences of Peter Lombard 38–9, 41, 47, 48
Sextus Empiricus 33, 51
Shaw, Bernard 119
Sidgwick, Henry 93, 99
Smith, Adam 81, 82, 83, 86
Smith, Norman Kemp 176
Socrates 1, 2, 5, 12, 13, 14, 15–17, 18, 19, 23, 24, 27, 28, 31, 59, 84, 85, 117, 118, 135, 162, 168, 174
Sophists 11–15, 16, 17, 34, 117
Sorabji, Richard 175
Sorbonne 40, 57, 159
Soviet Union 156
specialism/specialization 131, 132
Spencer, Herbert 96, 99
Speusippus 9, 21, 23

Spinoza, Benedict de 59, 60–1, 62, 63, 64, 65, 69, 71
Sprigge, Timothy 178
Stewart, Dugald 86, 87
Stilpo 29
Stirner, Max 107, 112, 113
Stoics 26, 29, 30, 31
Stout, G.F. 99
Strato of Lampsacus 26
Suarez 50
summer schools 124, 149
supposition 42
Svevo, Italo 157

teaching 57, 71, 84, 128ff., 135, 140, 165, 169, 170, 171
technicality 114, 126, 150, 162, 172
Thales 7, 8
theology 37, 38, 39, 41, 42, 45, 46, 49, 56, 57, 107, 124, 170, 176, 178; Presbyterian 85
Theophrastus 24, 25, 26, 28, 171, 174
theses 88, 128
Tomin, Julius 156
tutorials 84, 128–30, 131, 170

undergraduates 131, 134, 147, 167
universals 35, 38, 39
universities 1, 6, 37, 39–43, 53, 55, 60, 62, 63, 65, 66, 69–72, 73, 76, 77, 78, 87, 92, 98, 114, 118, 119, 120, 128, 130–7, 140, 146ff., 154, 156, 157, 161, 163, 165, 167, 168, 169, 171, 173, 180; Aberdeen 79, 80, 86, 87, 98; Berlin 89, 101–3, 104, 109, 112; Bologna 37, 39, 46; Cambridge 40, 65, 72, 74, 76, 88, 92, 93, 95, 96, 98, 99, 107, 129, 130, 137, 140, 141, 142, 143, 144, 146, 147, 161–2; Edinburgh 79, 80, 85, 87; English 76, 84, 87, 96, 97, 141; French 74, 75, 101, 121, 123, 159, 160; German 75, 87–91, 107, 109, 112, 114, 120, 128, 152, 153, 155; Glasgow

INDEX

79, 80, 81, 86, 87; Halle 73, 74; Harvard 100, 124–5, 150; Imperial Napoleonic 101, 122; London 96, 130, 146, 147, 172; Open 149; Oxford 37, 40, 46, 47, 48, 54, 65, 66, 67, 68, 69, 70, 71, 72, 76, 79, 80, 84, 88, 92, 93, 95, 96, 97, 98, 99, 107, 129, 130, 131, 136, 142, 144, 146, 147, 151, 161–2; Paris 37, 39, 40, 43–4, 45, 47; St Andrews 87, 97; Scottish 79–80, 83–7, 88, 91, 92, 97, 130; USA/American 100, 124, 126, 129, 131, 138, 143, 149–51
University College London 92, 95, 99
USA 123–6, 133, 136, 138, 145, 149–51, 162
utilitarianism 93ff.

Venn, John 99
Vico, Giambattista, 178
Vienna 120, 141, 142, 143, 152
Voltaire, François 64, 75

Wagner, Richard 109, 111, 118, 119
Waismann, Friedrich 142, 150
Wales 2
Ward, James 93
Weil, Simone 122, 157, 178, 179
Whewell, William 96
Whichcote, Benjamin 176
Whitehead, A.N. 138
William of Champeaux 38
William of Moerbeke 43
William of Ockham 35, 39, 42, 46–50, 52
William of Shyreswood 43
Wisdom, John 99, 143, 144
Wissenschaft 102, 103, 124, 155
Wittgenstein, Ludwig 1, 61, 111, 117, 137, 139, 140–5, 146, 150, 153, 179
Wittgenstein, Paul 140
Wolff, Christian 73–4, 88, 89
Wright, Georg von 143, 144, 179
Wundt, W. 120

Xenocrates 23

Zabarella, Jacobus 176
Zedlitz, Freiherr von 74
Zeno of Citium, the Stoic 26, 29
Zeno of Elea 10